John Macquarrie

ON BEING A THEOLOGIAN

Reflections at Eighty

Edited by John H. Morgan

with Georgina Morley and Eamonn Conway

SCM PRESS

0 334 02771 3

First published 1999
by SCM Press
9–17 St Albans Place, London N1 0NX

SCM Press is a division of
SCM-Canterbury Press Ltd

Typeset by Regent Typesetting, London
Printed in Great Britain by
Biddles Ltd, Guildford and King's Lynn

Contents

Author's Preface

When I retired from Oxford University in 1986, some of my former students and other friends, in conjunction with the SCM Press, were so kind as to present me with a *Festschrift*, a volume of essays touching on themes which had been of interest to me during my years of teaching and writing. A dozen years have passed since then, and now another group of friends have put together what may be considered as a second *Festschrift*, in celebration of my approaching eightieth birthday. I am deeply grateful for this totally gratuitous act of kindness, and especially to Dr John Morgan, President of the Theological Graduate Foundation in the United States, who initiated the project. I am especially pleased that any proceeds from the present book will be used to provide scholarship aid for young students in the theological field. Sixty years ago, I was enjoying the privilege of a scholarship myself, and perhaps would never have become a theologian without it.

This second *Festschrift* is very different from the first one. As I have mentioned, that first one, entitled *Being and Truth*, edited by Alistair Kee and Eugene Long, consisted of essays by various friends, and I did not even know who these contributors were until the finished volume was presented to me at a dinner in King's College, London. In this new volume, edited by John Morgan, and with contributions by Georgina Morley and Eamonn Conway, I have supplied most of the material myself. Dr Morgan's idea was to produce a book which would give a picture of what it is like to live and work as a theologian. So I was taken to a remote but beautiful corner of Ireland between the mountains and the sea in County Kerry, and for five days was engaged in conversation with a group of people who were interested in one aspect or another of my life and work. The material from that conference has been skilfully organized by Dr Morgan and his associates. Again I express my thanks to them, though I feel that they have been over indulgent towards me.

John Macquarrie

Editor's Preface

Already in his eightieth year, John Macquarrie has now offered the theological community a little gem of autobiographical reflections. Not intended to be a fully developed autobiography, these reflections are personal, specific, and demonstrative of both his genuine humility and passion for his life's work.

One of the few leading theological voices of international acclaim still working at the end of the twentieth century, Macquarrie recently spent time with a few individuals on the Irish shores of County Kerry reflecting upon his life and his work. At the Ireland Theological Conference in the spring of 1998, Macquarrie spoke for five days – in the morning on the topic of 'The Making of a Theologian', and in the afternoon, 'Theology in the Making'. The result is this book of reflections with supplementary materials for elaboration and clarification. These reflections are telling, stimulating, and full of insight into his private life and his very carefully constructed craft.

The book, however, is more than just his personal reflections upon theology and life as a theologian. Georgina Morley of the University of Nottingham, a promising young Macquarrie scholar herself, has added significantly to the value of this book by offering a substantial outline for each of his major books. These summaries are included in the book both for those who may not be fully acquainted with his work and for those who will value a fresh review of the major texts in his career. Also, the book includes two significant inaugural addresses given during his academic career – the inaugural address upon his taking the professorship in theology at the Union Theological Seminary in New York and the inaugural address given upon the occasion of his assuming the Lady Margaret Professorship in Divinity at Christ Church in the University of Oxford.

Additionally, major addresses given before the Russian Academy of Social Sciences in Moscow and the Chinese Academy of the Social Sciences in Beijing have been reproduced here. His address on the occasion of the celebration of Karl Rahner's eightieth birthday is also included owing to its historic significance.

Also, due to the growing interest in his latest theological development in the postconciliar Church, we have reproduced his major article on the papacy and have included a critical response by Father Eamonn Conway, DD, one of Ireland's leading young theologians, late of All Hallows College, Dublin, and a Teaching Fellow at the Graduate Theological Foundation in the United States.

Finally, the book includes a comprehensive bibliography of all of his writings from his first published article in 1955 to his most recent book published by SCM Press of London, *Christology Revisited* (1998).

For all those who studied with Macquarrie as a university peer in Scotland, or studied at his feet as a student in New York or Oxford, or taught with him as a colleague, or, more generally, for all those who have been influenced by the brilliance of his mind in the form of his many theological works, this book has been produced.

John H. Morgan

I

My Scottish Background

Today the Celtic peoples occupy only a few inhospitable areas on the Atlantic seaboard of Europe, and their ancient languages and distinctive culture are in serious danger of being swept away altogether. It is hard to believe that in the so-called 'Dark Age' preceding the end of the first millennium, the Celtic realms preserved not only a considerable level of culture and learning, but maintained also a strong tradition of Christian piety when much of Europe was still pagan. Ireland and likewise Scotland and Wales deserved at that time the description of being a land of saints and scholars. But that time is now long past.

It is still harder to believe that at an even earlier period, for roughly five hundred years before the birth of Christ, Celtic tribes were in possession of large tracts of the European continent. Now all that remains of that time of maximal Celtic expansion are the place-names of the former Celtic lands. The Greeks called these people Keltoi, the Romans called them Gauls. Many of us have, at one time or another, read or been forced to read parts of Julius Caesar's history of the Gallic Wars, and in his time much of France was Gaulish or Celtic country. Very far to the east, in what is nowadays part of Turkey, there was a region called Galatia, where another group of Celts or Gauls had been settled since the third century BC. It was to these Galatians that St Paul wrote one of his epistles, but this particular concentration of Celts was eventually swallowed up in the Hellenistic culture by which it was surrounded. On the borders of what are now Poland and the Ukraine, was the province of Galicia, another Gaulish area. At a later time, the Gauls or Celts were penetrating north-western Europe.

There is another Galicia in Spain, in the extreme north-west corner; at the same time, waves of Celtic immigrants were coming into the British Isles, and they too have left their name on the land which they called Wales, once again the same word Gaul that we see in Galicia and Galatia. But the difference in the case of Wales – which the French call Pays de Galles – is that the Celts left more than their name, for this is one of the few areas where the Celts have survived as a distinct people, and, in spite of being so close to England, have been remarkably successful in keeping alive their ancient language.

How do we know about the history of the Celts? Admittedly, our knowledge is only fragmentary. The Celts never formed an empire or even any strong kingdom, but were divided among many tribes, so they had no historians to record a Celtic history. The Greeks and Romans regarded them as barbarian peoples. But occasionally we find these barbarians breaking into the normal life of the civilized Mediterranean peoples. In 390 BC, Celts from the north actually captured and then plundered the city of Rome itself. The violent events of that time are recorded by Livy, and for a long time the Romans regarded the Celtic invasion as one of the blackest days in their history. About a century later, in 279 BC, another horde of Celts, presumably from the Balkans, descended into Greece and raided the sacred precincts of Delphi. Thus from classical authors, we are able to glean a few details of what the Celts were doing in the days when they were one of the dominant ethnic groups in all Europe.

The earliest reference to them is probably one found in the Greek historian, Herodotus. Writing about the middle of the fifth century BC, he informs his readers that the River Danube rises in the land of the Celts. This would seem to be good evidence that already at that time the Celts were established in central Europe. Very different but perhaps equally true is a remark made about a hundred years later by Plato in his dialogue, *The Laws*, where he mentions as a characteristic of the Celts or Keltoi that they were much given to intoxication. It would seem that this is still a distinguishing mark! But it must be admitted that the earlier history of the Celts is almost totally hidden from us. What we can deduce with a fair degree of certainty is that, caught between the pressure of the Roman state on the south and the pressure of migrating Germanic tribes on the north, the Celts were gradually squeezed out of the heart of Europe and driven westward into those fringe areas where they still precariously survive – western Scotland and western Ireland, Wales, the Isle of Man, Cornwall, and, across the Channel, Brittany. Even in these areas, however, the ancient languages have largely died out, in spite of attempts to revive them. After all, who writes textbooks of physics or computer science in Gaelic or Welsh?

Perhaps we learn more about the history of the Celts from archaeology than from the writings of historians. Monuments and artifacts of various kinds have survived and can tell us quite a lot. For instance, in the extreme north-west of Scotland on the Isle of Lewis, at a place called Callanish, is a circle of standing stones, so impressive that, if it were not so remote, it might be a rival attraction to Stonehenge. Some archaeologists believe that it is older than Stonehenge. It is possible that Callanish has had its stones for 3000 or even 4000 years. But these stones are so ancient that it seems quite probable that they were there before the Celts had appeared in the British Isles and belong to some still earlier and unknown people. Actually, it does not seem to have been the custom of the Celts to erect buildings to serve as temples or places of worship. Caesar, who spent ten years of his life in Gaul, tells us that the Celts there had no temples but set aside 'holy places' (*loci consecrati*), usually in the form of groves of oak trees. But though they did not build temples, the Celts did construct tombs for the departed, and many of these have been discovered and explored, in Ireland and in eastern Europe and elsewhere. Some of them have been found to contain artifacts of very high artistic quality, showing that these Celts were not quite the barbarians that the Greeks and Romans supposed them to be.

Language itself is a kind of museum, preserving information about ancient times and still deducible from the words which people use. This is very true of the Celtic languages which offer a fascinating field for study. These languages are still spoken by perhaps as many as half a million people in the western regions of the British Isles and in Brittany. Perhaps one should mention also a small Gaelic-speaking group in Nova Scotia, only about 3000, I believe. They emigrated from Scotland to Canada in the eighteenth and nineteenth centuries, and have preserved the language in their new home. They even manage to produce a Gaelic newspaper. I have been twice in Nova Scotia and it was quite an experience to find oneself in such a thoroughly Scottish and Gaelic environment. When I first arrived there, I was to be met by a Professor Mackinnon. He was unable to come, so he sent instead a Miss MacGillivray. How highland can you get! When I had a look around the town next morning, I found inscribed on the wall of the local church the words Tigh Dhe, 'House of God', in Gaelic. I don't think you could find a similar inscription in Glasgow nowadays.

The Celtic languages are, of course, part of the Indo-European group of languages, and their nearest neighbour is Latin. Those Celtic languages still spoken in western Europe fall into two groups. A northern group includes Scottish Gaelic, Irish and Manx. Manx has been extinct since the eighteenth century. Scottish and Irish Gaelic are both derived from old Irish and used to be virtually a single language, but they have diverged in the last few centuries. What distinguishes this northern group of Celtic tongues is that they have lost the letter 'p'. At least, they have lost it in a great many words. So the word for 'father', which in Latin is *pater*, appears in Scottish Gaelic as *athair*. The initial 'p' has been lost, and even the 't' in the middle of the word has been aspirated and is reduced in contemporary speech to a glottal stop. Another good example of the loss of the letter 'p' is the words *iasg*, which means 'fish' and is the cognate of the Latin *piscis*. Incidentally, that word is preserved in all those rivers throughout Britain that are called the River Esk, which means simply 'Fish River'. In the southern group of Celtic languages, Welsh, Cornish, Breton, the letter 'p' was retained.

Let me give a few examples of words showing the resemblances between Scottish Gaelic and Latin. The Gaelic word for 'king' is *righ*, which is very similar to the Latin *rex*; *bo* is Gaelic for 'cow' and shows the same root as the Latin *bos*, 'ox'; *cu* is Gaelic for 'dog', and is from the same root as Latin *canis*, though it resembles even more closely the Greek *kuon*. The examples I have given are of words in Gaelic and Latin which have arisen from common roots in the distant Indo-European past. There are many other words in Gaelic which were later borrowings from Latin, such as *eaglais*, 'church', from Latin/Greek *ecclesia*; *aiffrion*, the 'mass' or 'eucharist', from Latin *offerendum*, an 'offering' or 'sacrifice'; Taggart is quite a common surname in Scotland and represents the Gaelic, *an t-saggart*, 'the priest', from Latin *sacerdos*.

Like many other languages, the Celtic languages have tended to be simplified as time has gone on. For instance, in Scottish Gaelic the verb does not change its form with person or number. 'Am', 'art', 'is', 'are', are all represented by the single word *tha*. The Gaelic noun is considerably more complicated than the verb, but I think that what makes Gaelic seem so difficult to those who come to it for the first time is the orthography or spelling, because in many words letters are written which are not pronounced, though they may have been pronounced at one time. Let me give you an example from Ireland rather than Scotland. If you have ever sailed from Holyhead, you probably landed at a harbour just outside Dublin, called Dun Laoghaire. The late Eric Mascall, who had a genius for composing comic verse, made up a limerick as follows:

There was a young priest of Dun Laoghaire
Who stood on his head at the Kaoghaire.
When someone asked why,
He made the reply,
It's the latest liturgical thaoghaire.

The Irish have in fact tried to simplify the spelling of the language, but the trouble about that is that it obscures many of the very interesting philological associations. The Scots have been more conservative in keeping the traditional spellings. For instance, I mentioned that 'king' in Scottish Gaelic is *righ*. The last two letters of this word are silent. So why not cut them off and write simply *ri*? No doubt one could do that, but you would also have cut off the word from its roots in the Indo-European heritage.

I have made two or three allusions to the religion of the Celts, from that impressive stone circle at Callanish which was perhaps associated with sun-worship down to the borrowing of Latin words in Christian times to express the notions of church, priesthood and so on. The Celts have always been a deeply religious people, and the evidence for this comes not only from historians and archaeologists but above all from the rich treasury of poems which have been passed on from earlier times. In the late nineteenth century, devoted students of Celtic culture travelled around the Highlands and Islands collecting from the older people especially poems that had been transmitted for generations, and sometimes tunes as well. One of the most distinguished of these collectors was Alexander Carmichael who published the Gaelic originals with English translations in his monumental *Carmina Gadelica* (1900). Though these poems are, of course, Christian, one can still discern in them traces of the pre-Christian Celtic religion, and indeed, as I shall mention, certain features of that ancient pagan faith still appear in Celtic Christianity.

The Celts were a rural people and their ancient religion was very much a religion of nature. Not only their oak groves but, it would seem, every spring and well, every mountain and river, was a holy place, so that, like many other early peoples, they dwelt in a sacral environment. This in turn meant that each action of daily life was invested with religious significance. Their gods were mostly local, but the names of some of the more important deities have survived. One of the principal gods was Lugh, said to have been the master of all skills. Julius Caesar mentions him, and believed him to be the counter-part of the Roman god Mercury. The name of Lugh is preserved in some place-names, most notably the French city of Lyon (Lugdunum). There were also goddesses, one of them Brigitta or Brigid. When Christianity came to the Celtic lands, there was no sharp break with the past. The old sanctuaries continued to be frequented, though their numinous properties were now ascribed to local Christian saints, rather than to pagan divinities. Among the christianized Celts, there was widespread veneration for St Brigid, and whatever the historical details may have been, it seems clear that this saint inherited the prestige that had once belonged to the goddess Brigitta. At the old church of Govan, now within the city limits of Glasgow, there are some evidences of the apparently smooth transition from the old paganism to the new Christianity. On one of the ancient stones at Govan, a cross has been carved on one side, but on the back you will find a representation of the sun's disc, from an older stage of religion. The church-yard at Govan is circular in shape, and it is believed that it preserves the shape of an ancient stone circle where the sun may once have been worshipped. The stones themselves have long since disappeared.

By this time the high tide of the Celtic peoples had passed and they were already largely reduced to being a fringe people, as they are today. But by this time also they were emerging out of the mists of pre-history into history, and definite historical figures appear and we know something of their activities. Chief among them are the early Celtic saints and apostles,[1] men like Ninian and Patrick who planted

Christianity in Scotland and Ireland, and then, at a later time, Columba who crossed from Ireland to the Scottish island of Iona, where he founded his famous monastery in 563. Another personality of that period was Kentigern, who divided his time between Scotland and Wales, and who became patron saint of Glasgow. So Celtic culture had a new flowering and in the stormy centuries between the years 500 and 1000 the Celts did much to keep alive both Christianity and ancient learning.

Perhaps the most important heritage that Celtic Christianity received from the old paganism was a profound and even vivid sense of the immanence or indwelling of God in the world. God was not a distant power in the heavens, but a presence that surrounded them. Even in modern theologians of Celtic background, such as John Baillie, we note this sense of presence, which is indeed very important for the modern world, in which the reckless exploitation and destruction of the environment needs to be checked by a renewed reverence for the natural world. Celtic spirituality was very much down-to-earth. For every activity of the day, from kindling the fire in the morning to lying down at night, you will find a prayer in their treasury of poems.

> This morning I will kindle the fire upon my hearth
> Before the holy angels who stand about my path.
> No envy, hatred, malice, no fear upon my face,
> But the holy Son of God, the guardian of the place.

Or in the evening:

> With God will I lie down this night,
> And God will be lying with me.
> With Christ will I lie down this night,
> And Christ will be lying with me.
> With Spirit I lie down this night,
> The Spirit will lie down with me;
> God and Christ and Spirit, Three,
> Be they all down-lying with me.

The intimacy with God expressed in these lines reflects the kind of society in which these people lived, a society in which warm and genuine human relations flourished. Even the High King of Ireland was not so very high – he had his home on the Hill of Tara, a very low hill that did not remove him very far from his people. Must not the High King of Heaven be likewise close at hand?

This also helps to explain why the saints played so large a part in Celtic Christianity. These saints had been men and women subject to all the passions and temptations that we ourselves know, yet somehow the Spirit of God had been in them. The Celtic Christian lived every day in the communion of saints. They even accompanied him when he went out in the fishing-boat.

> Who are these in my fishing-boat today?
> Peter and Paul and John Baptist are they;
> At my helm the Christ is sitting to steer,
> The wind from the south making our way.
> Who makes the voice of the wind to grow faint?
> And who makes calm the kyle and the sea?
> It is Jesus Christ, the Chief of each saint.[2]

A philosophical basis for this spirituality was provided by John Scotus Eriugena (810-877). He was the greatest thinker that the Celtic peoples have produced. Although I would like to claim him for Scotland, he was probably Irish and studied at the centre of learning called Clon-mac-noise, near the estuary of the River Shannon. He knew Greek, a very rare accomplishment in those days, and he went to France to teach in the university founded by Charles the Bald. There is an amusing story told about his relation to the king. Charles had invited him to dinner, and they sat facing one another across the table. The king asked Eriugena a question in Latin: '*Quid distat inter Scotum et sotum?*' ('What is the difference between a Scot and a sot?') Eriugena thought for a moment and replied, 'Only this table!' The king, probably mellowed by wine, took this answer in good part. Eriugena's major work was entitled *De Naturae Divisione*, and began from an inclusive concept of nature which he held to embrace both God and the creatures. God is in all things and is said to be the essence of all things. A favourite word with Eriugena is 'theophany', an appearance of God, and it would not be going too far to say that for him the whole world was a theophany. Long after his death his teaching was condemned because of alleged pantheistic tendencies, but modern scholars have rehabilitated him, and claimed that he was a forerunner of such philosophers of recent times as Hegel and Whitehead. In any case, I think it may be fairly claimed that he brought to intellectual expression something of the beauty and depth of the Celtic vision of the world.

2

Beginning in Theology

When I reflect on my life and how I have grown from childhood to manhood, I begin by taking cognizance of my ethnic background. Not just my own family or the people of my hometown but of the Celtic peoples as described in the preceding chapter. I am a Scot, and the product of hundreds of years of Scottish pride and Scottish culture. The clans of Scotland are the roots of all true Scots and for me the Macquarries of the Isle of Ulva constitute my most fundamental origins. They migrated from Ulva to many of the islands off the west coast of Scotland and then at a later time to various parts of the British Empire, especially Canada and Australia. My own great-grandfather, Donald Macquarrie, lived on the island of Islay, where in 1839 he married Catherine Martin. They were blessed with several sons, most of whom left Islay. My grandfather, John Macquarrie, came to Clydeside, where in 1873 he married in Govan another emigrant from the Highlands, Mary MacGregor. My father, also John Macquarrie, was born in Renfrew in 1886 and married Robina McInnes in 1914, just before the outbreak of the Great War. He worked in the shipyards as a pattern-maker, and since this was a reserved (exempt) occupation, he was not called up for military service. My parents' first child did not survive, and I was born on 27 June 1919, one day before the signing of the Versailles Treaty, which ended the war.

I spent my childhood years growing up in the ancient if somewhat drab town of Renfrew, and had my schooling there, then later in the larger neighbouring town of Paisley.

The possibility of an academic career was foreshadowed when I was awarded the Gold Medal of Renfrew High School, an honour which came also four years later to the person whom I would one day marry, Jenny Welsh.

My life seems to have been largely a series of fortunate accidents, for I had no ambitious plans about a career or where I would eventually end up. One thing seemed to follow naturally on another in the process of living. Only gradually and without any dramatic moment of decision did I come to the realization that the Christian ministry would be my life's work. I certainly thought of myself as a Christian and was a faithful attender at worship in the Church of Scotland (Presbyterian) in which my father was an elder, though I was already feeling the attraction of the Episcopal Church.

For me, 1936 was an important year. In June, the University of Glasgow held its annual Bursary (scholarship) Competition and, with many other youngsters from the high schools of Scotland, I presented myself for the examinations. I was successful beyond my wildest hopes, and was given a substantial award that would sustain me for degree courses in both Arts and Divinity for a period of seven years. This opened to me the world of higher education, without placing any financial burden on my hardworking parents, who encouraged me in every way. I was in the midst of these studies when the Second World War broke out. Like many other students, I had come under the influence of such brilliant speakers as George MacLeod of Govan Parish Church, Dick Sheppard of St Paul's Cathedral, Charles Raven of Cambridge University. These were all veterans of the Great War, but they had embraced and now passionately proclaimed the cause of pacifism. As the British government had exempted theological students from military service, I was not myself liable to be conscripted. But as the war developed, I came to the conclusion that pacifism was not the right response in the face of such evil as Hitler's régime embodied.

In the meantime, my final examinations in Arts were

coming up, and in 1940 I had my reward by gaining a first-class honours degree in mental philosophy, together with the Caird Scholarship. But now I struck a very difficult period. I found the theology courses boring, and much less satisfying than philosophy. I began to doubt my vocation to the Christian ministry. Fortunately, a new light came into my life at this time. I have mentioned earlier Jenny Welsh. Like me, she had completed her high school work, entered university, and was studying mathematics and physics with a view to teaching these subjects in school. I decided that this was the person with whom I wanted to spend the rest of my life. Her family situation was difficult, as she was an only child and had a widowed mother to support, so it was not possible to contemplate marriage in the near future. We decided that it would take about seven years before we could marry (in fact, it took eight). For people in love, that is difficult but not unacceptable. I compared myself to Jacob, who served seven years for the adorable Rachel, and, so we are told, 'they seemed to him but a few days, because of the love he had for her'.

Though I was not enthused by theology, I had no difficulty in getting high marks in examinations and essays, and at the end of the course, in 1943, gained various awards. Among them was the offer of a fellowship to do doctoral work at Cambridge University. But I declined this for two reasons – I was still disillusioned with theology and, having been exempted from military service for the earlier years of the war, I felt that now I ought to join the service. I already had pastoral experience, as a seminarian at Dumbarton Parish Church, and as an assistant in charge of a new housing area in Paisley. So I volunteered for a chaplaincy in the Royal Army Chaplains Department.

The war was still being stubbornly fought in Europe, and it was generally expected that the war against Japan would go on for several years. Actually I served for three years, but within six months the war suddenly came to an end with the advent of the atomic bomb. I was then given the task of organizing religious services for the large number of German prisoners of war being held in camps in the Middle East. My responsibility was to ensure that about thirty German clergy among these prisoners had facilities for discharging their pastoral functions. I was given this job because I already had some knowledge of the German language, and was now able to expand this even to the point of giving a few lectures and addresses in German. I learned much about what those men thought of Hitler and the Nazi ideology, and also learned quite a lot about Islam as I moved around Egypt, Libya and Palestine. So I have often thought that my military service was not an interruption of my studies, but a new dimension in which (so I hope) I learned more about human nature than one can learn in a classroom. I was released from military service at the end of 1947, and within three months was invited to become the minister of St Ninian's Church in Brechin.

Brechin is an ancient city, with a mediaeval cathedral and a round tower going back to the days of the Vikings. Jenny and I were married in January 1949, and our first child was born in December of the same year. For most of the five years that we spent in that quiet and beautiful part of the country, life was largely uneventful and I went about my pastoral duties. But an unexpected event occurred which brought me back to serious theology, and ensured that theology would be at the centre of my work from then on. When I was a student, the Professor of Divinity at Glasgow University was Dr J. G. Riddell. He happened to be on vacation not far from Brechin, and called in one day to visit his former student. In the course of conversation, he recalled that when I had finished my theology course in 1943, I had declined the opportunity to go on to further studies. He suggested that perhaps I should consider that possibility now, for he thought that my parish duties in Brechin were not so onerous that I could not find time for study. I could enrol for a PhD at Glasgow, do my work at home and come down to Glasgow once a month or so to consult with my supervisor. He told me he had a new colleague, Professor Ian Henderson, who had made a special study of Rudolf Bultmann and the latter's theory of demythologizing. I was very much attracted by the idea. I went to see Professor Henderson, the pioneer of Bultmann studies in the UK, and was deeply impressed by him. So it was arranged that I would work on the relation between Bultmann's theology and the philosophy of Martin Heidegger. This combination of philosophical and theological interests suited me very well, and since the major works of both these German scholars had not yet been translated into English, it was obvious that my familiarity with the German language would be a great asset. So I commenced my doctoral studies in the context of my parish duties and the growing responsibilities of family life. In the midst of this, a new lectureship in theology was established at Glasgow University. I was encouraged to apply, and although my doctoral thesis was not yet completed, I was appointed to the new post, so we found ourselves packing up and going off to Glasgow.

We spent nine years in Glasgow. During that time, I was kept busy, preparing lectures and, in the early part of my time there, finishing my thesis. It was accepted, and became the basis for my first book, which I called *An Existentialist Theology*, with the explanatory subtitle, 'A Comparison of Heidegger and Bultmann'. I concentrated on Bultmann's exposition of Paul, which in turn focusses on Paul's anthropology. Three main topics had to be considered and brought into relation: Paul's own teaching, Bultmann's interpretation (including his demythologizing,) and the influence of Heidegger on this interpretation. So one had to show the correspondence between Paul's conceptuality and that of Heidegger, with Bultmann as intermediary. This meant comparing and contrasting, for instance, Paul on sin and Heidegger on fallenness, Paul on faith and Heidegger on resoluteness, both of these thinkers on their understanding of conscience. The plan of the book turns on Heidegger's distinction between authentic and inauthentic existence, roughly correlated with Paul's distinction between life in Christ and life after the flesh. The first part describes the actual human condition, sin as fallenness into the world of things and into what Paul calls the *kosmos*, by which he means not so much the physical world as a flawed social reality, comparable to Heidegger's *das Man*. The second half deals with the life of faith, compared with Heidegger's resolute authenticity. In his New Testament theology, Bultmann confined himself mainly to the existential element and avoided any objective or speculative thought. Heidegger, however, always denied that he was an existentialist. *Being and Time* was intended to lead into a study of Being as such, and was not just an analysis of human existence.

So I had to be critical of Bultmann at certain points. What about God? Is God only a subjective idea? What about Christ? What is his relation to God? What does Bultmann mean by saying that the word of Christ is the word of God? Bultmann claims that the death of Christ is a repeatable possibility for men and women, but he is strongly against any Pelagian doctrine of human self-sufficiency, and it is not clear that these positions are consistent. Also I criticized his individualism, indicated by his use of the expression *pro me* ('for me'). He asks, 'Does Jesus save me because he is the Son of God, or is he the Son of God because he saves me?' The question is worth considering, but it is too individualistically stated. Again, does Bultmann treat history as irrelevant to theology? Certainly, he is sceptical and argues against the quest for the historical Jesus. He claims that we can now know nothing of Jesus' life and personality. This remark is often quoted, but it has got to be put into context. It is not a total denial, for he believes that we know the core facts, that Jesus did exist and died on the cross. Bultmann clearly has been deeply influenced by Ritschl's teaching that faith in Christ depends on existential evaluation, rather than know-ledge of facts. But Donald Baillie (one of the examiners of my thesis) held that we need to know more than these core facts. We need to know more about this person who died. Many thousands must have been crucified in Roman times, but why single out Jesus, unless we have some further information that makes his death special? I criticized also Bultmann's view of 'modern man' and his claim that if such a person makes use of science, technology, contemporary medicine etc., he cannot believe in miracles. I pointed out that many modern persons go to Lourdes in search of cures. Bultmann's reply was dismissive: 'These are not modern men!' Perhaps one has to concede this point. They are persons still untouched by the Enlightenment. But can the Enlightenment be set up as the absolute standard of what is permissible in thought?

I sent a copy of the book to Professor Bultmann, who graciously replied in a lengthy letter in which he discussed some of the points raised. He also sent me, unsolicited, a testimonial *(Gutachten)* which I might use to further my career. I never needed to use it for that purpose, but, on the suggestion of the publishers, it was included as a Foreword to later printings of *An Existentialist Theology*. It read:

The author gives a picture of an 'existentialist theology' by showing how the hermeneutic principle which underlies my interpretation of the New Testament arises out of the existential analysis of man's Being given by Martin Heidegger in his work, *Being and Time*. In addition, the author pursues the question of whether and to what extent there is justification for such an 'ontological' method in the interpretation of the New Testament. The book is distinguished by great clarity in the unfolding of the problem and in the sequence of thought; also by great care and objectivity, and by independent judgment. The author rightly maintains that the existentialist philosophy, as represented by Heidegger's *Being and Time*, is not a speculative philosophy, but an analysis of the understanding of existence that is given with existence itself. He also affirms – and rightly so, I am convinced – that the understanding of man developed in existentialist philosophy possesses a certain kinship with the understanding that is contained implicitly in the New Testament. Thus he acknowledges my interpretation of the New Testament to be one that is valid in principle. He then makes a careful examination of my interpretation and comes to the conclusion that, on the one hand, I make relevant and intelligible many important ideas, especially in the Pauline and Johannine writings; but that, on the other hand, I sometimes overstep the limits that are set to an existentialist interpretation, and that justice is not done to the transcendent reality to which faith is directed in the New Testament. I cannot agree with the author's criticism at all points. But I must concede that the criticism is not only fair and perceptive, but also touches upon points that are really problematic and must be cleared up in future discussion. The author's criticism is not dogmatically introduced from outside, but arises from the inner understanding of the existential interpretation as the author takes part in it, and through his participation seeks to recognize its justification and its limits. Thus the criticism is a fruitful one. I have seldom found so unprejudiced and penetrating an understanding of my intentions and my work as in this book. It also evidences a penetrating and, as I believe, an essentially correct understanding of Heidegger, as well as a rare capacity for unfolding simply and clearly this philosopher's ideas, which are often hard to understand. So I must give my opinion that the author's book is a distinguished performance. He shows himself to be a thinker of high rank, with outstanding power of exposition. I am happy that the theological discussion at the present time has been enriched by this contribution which both clarifies it and carries it further, and I set great hope on the future work of the author.

My book, *An Existentialist Theology*, was well received in both the UK and the USA, and was probably the main reason for the next major event in my life, again something

unplanned and unforeseen. One morning in 1957 there
arrived a letter, out of the blue as it were, inviting me to give
some lectures at Union Theological Seminary, New York,
and mentioning that if they liked me and I liked them, I might
possibly be invited to go there as Professor of the Philosophy
of Religion. Union at that time enjoyed the highest reputation, and many would have said that it was foremost among
the theological schools of America. I had never been in the
United States, and it was quite a thrill to go there, which I did
during the Easter vacation. I flew from Glasgow, and landed
in New York at Idlewild Airport, only being built at that
time but later to become the famous John F. Kennedy
International Airport. I spent two weeks in New York City,
staying in the home of Dr and Mrs Van Dusen. Dr Van
Dusen was President of Union at that time. I gave several
lectures on Bultmann, met various groups at the Seminary,
saw the sights of New York, and was most attracted by it all.
I was very well received, and on the day before I left,
President Van Dusen invited me to accompany him on a visit
to Princeton and during the course of the day told me that the
committee charged with nominating a person for the vacant
chair in the philosophy of religion was unanimous in asking
me to come, and that he would be writing to me soon.

I should explain that (in those days at least) Union relied
on the Holy Spirit to make the right appointments. The
President told me that if anyone 'applied' for a position on
the Union faculty, he/she was automatically disqualified. It
had to be by invitation, by a call from the institution. Being
myself of a somewhat sceptical disposition, I took the view
that appointments through the agency of the Holy Spirit were
more likely to operate through the old-boy network. I did
indeed learn later that Professor John Baillie of Edinburgh
University, who had formerly served at Union and had
returned there for a year in 1956 as a visiting professor, had
suggested my name to the Seminary authorities. But in fact
the expected invitation was delayed for quite a long time, as
I shall explain very shortly.

In 1960 I published the lectures I had given at Union as my second book, with the title *The Scope of Demythologizing*. Bultmann's main works had now been translated into English and there was heated debate on his proposals for demythologizing. This new book of mine dealt with Bultmann and his critics. These fell into two camps, suggesting a simple plan for the book. The first half dealt with conservative critics who thought that Bultmann had conceded too much to the 'modern' point of view, while the other camp comprised a rather diverse group who thought that Bultmann had not been radical enough. Among the first group of critics was the great Karl Barth who had published a short book with the ironical title, *Rudolf Bultmann: An Attempt to Understand Him*. One of Barth's chief objections was that Bultmann made too much of the human decision in his analysis of faith, as against the Reformation principle that it is all God's doing, by grace alone – *sola gratia*. I argued that (at least, as Barth expounded the matter in this particular writing of his) human beings had been reduced to mere puppets. There must be a place for human decision and this need not and does not deny the initiative to God. More generally, Barth objected to Bultmann's heavy indebtedness to a secular philosophy, but it has always seemed to me that if Christianity is to be intelligible in modern times, it must use a modern language. On the radical side, Karl Jaspers, as a true philosopher, rejected the idea of a special revelation in Christ, though he did himself advocate a philosophical faith which seemed clearly to be close to a kind of radical Protestantism. Also among the radicals was the Swiss theologian, Fritz Buri, who urged that we should go on from demythologizing to what he called 'dekerygmatizing'. The kerygma must be cleared out with the mythology. This seemed to me to be going too far and to be incompatible with basic Christianity. But Buri had a point, namely that vestiges of mythology remain even in Bultmann, and perhaps can never be totally removed.

While I was still teaching at Glasgow, other writing projects began to take shape, though some of them were only completed after I had moved to the United States.

One of them, however, was completed in Glasgow, and occupied much of my time there. It was a kind of spin-off from my doctoral thesis, but a spin-off which was no less onerous than the thesis itself. In the course of my work on Bultmann and Heidegger, I had made a fairly detailed synopsis in English of *Being and Time*. My publisher suggested that, on the basis of this synopsis, I should go on to make a complete translation. Heidegger's book had been published in 1927, but had never been translated into English, though some attempts had been made. Some people declared the book was untranslatable, because it relies so much on the idiosyncrasies of the German language. I hesitated to take on this work, but my publisher meanwhile obtained the translation rights from the German publisher. We also discovered that an American philosopher, Professor Edward Robinson of the University of Kansas, was working on a translation, and it was suggested that the two of us might co-operate, to lessen the burden. Since we had to compare, criticize and harmonize each other's work, it is possible that the co-operation lengthened the time required. Robinson and I became very good friends, and we spent several summers together on the translation, which was published in 1962

The reviews were mainly favourable and Heidegger himself sent a letter of thanks to the translators. In it he confessed that his own knowledge of English was very imperfect, but that he had consulted 'competent judges' who had assured him of the accuracy of the translation. Unfortunately Robinson was killed in an automobile accident a few years after the translation appeared. If he had lived longer, we would undoubtedly have revised it, but I never felt like doing this on my own. I believe that there is at least one new English translation in the field, but the Macquarrie-Robinson version seems to be holding its own.

I come now to other works that were begun in Glasgow. I had become increasingly aware of the importance of language, and believed that one of the responsibilities of the modern theologian is to give an account of his language and the logic which informs it. This awareness arose not only out of my involvement in the demythologizing controversy but also from the aggressively anti-religious tone of much Anglo-Saxon linguistic philosophy. To what does religious language refer? To God? To human aspirations? To both of these? How does it refer? Is it coherent? Can it be supported by argument, or is it a free-floating language, needing no other justification than that people use it? An invitation to give the Hastie Lectures at Glasgow University allowed me to make a beginning with these problems and to write the early chapters of my book *God-Talk*, of which more later.

Another project arose out of a conversation I had with some of the editorial staff of Harper and Row during my New York visit. They told me there was great need for a book discussing the major developments in philosophy and religion during the twentieth century. This too would be a large undertaking requiring several years, so I shall come back to it when I write about our time in America.

But the most daunting obligation that I took upon myself before leaving Glasgow arose out of a letter received in 1961 from the New York publishing house of Charles Scribner's Sons. This was one of the most respected publishing houses in the United States, and was still at that time a family business, though it has since lost its identity in a whole series of mergers. The letter inquired whether I would undertake to write a one-volume systematic theology. This, it was hoped, would replace a work written by a former Union Professor, William Adams Brown. His book was entitled *Christian Theology in Outline*. The excellence of this book may be judged from the fact that it had been published in 1906 and was still going strong in 1961! But even the best of books may go out of date, and Scribner's believed that there would be a good market for a successor volume. I was at first doubtful about this invitation, thinking it had perhaps come too early in my theological career. I was forty-two at the time, and one of my heroes of those days, Paul Tillich, was sixty-seven when he published the first volume of his systematic work. However, a chance like this might never come again so I signed a contract and decided I would call the still unwritten book *Principles of Christian Theology*. So my order-book was full and I had committed myself to several years of hard work!

Just at this time the promised invitation to teach at Union came alive again. In early 1962, Dr Van Dusen wrote to me in the following terms: 'It gives me the greatest possible pleasure to inform you that the Seminary's Senior Faculty at their meeting yesterday voted unanimously and enthusiastically to nominate you to the Board of Directors, subject only to your readiness to accept, for appointment to the Seminary faculty as Professor of Systematic Theology. The appointment would be to a full professorship. In addition to the cash salary, your compensation would include a faculty apartment. A welcome of utmost warmth awaits you and your family.' He enclosed a plan of the apartment which was on the top (twelfth floor) of a new building, overlooking the Hudson River and with splendid views of the George Washington Bridge and the Palisades

The delay of five years from 1957 to 1962 was due to a change in the Seminary since my first visit. In those days, Barthianism was a powerful influence, and a good Barthian does not approve of philosophy of religion or of any kind of natural theology. Barth himself had been a Gifford Lecturer in Scotland, but he made it clear that he did not recognize that there is any valid natural theology. So Union had, since my first visit, suppressed the chair of philosophy of religion (it was later revived) and when they actually did invite me to go there, it was as Professor of Systematic Theology. There were at that time three full professors of the subject, Daniel Day Williams, Paul Lehmann and myself, representing three different types of theology. I much admired this comprehensiveness in Union's making available several options from the theological spectrum. However, that is possible only in a large and wealthy institution. So in 1962 my wife, my three children and myself packed our bags and set out for the United States of America.

Appendix: Some Reviews

Editor's Note

With characteristic diffidence, Macquarrie called attention to his first book and the one which established him beyond doubt as a leader among a new generation of promising young theologians. More than any other single event, the publication in the summer of 1955 of his An Existentialist Theology *set the stage for his impending notoriety in the United Kingdom and Europe and, most especially, in the United States. Scores of reviews of this magnificent book were published, but we have chosen only two. The very first one, brief, author unknown, appeared in the* British Weekly *on 29 September 1955, and another major one appeared under the name of H. G. Wood (of Birmingham University) in* The Expository Times *in February 1956. Both are included here for their historic merit.*

The third extract is from a Times Literary Supplement *article in 1996, in which Jonathan Reed, a Professor in Middlesex University, commented on the Macquarrie/ Robinson translation of Heidegger's* Being and Time.

From *The British Weekly*

The adjective that is appropriate to Dr Macquarrie's book is 'masterly'. The signs are that the phase in theological development associated with the names of Barth and Brunner is drawing to a close and that from now on we shall have to reckon with existentialist philosophy and Bultmann's inter- pretation of the New Testament. This book is the first in English to show the relation between the two in a manner at once sympathetic and critical, and anyone who wishes to catch a glimpse of the shape of things to come should read it. The two territories explored in this book abound in pitfalls, and no other investigator known to me has avoided these quite so well as Dr Macquarrie has done. He has based his study principally on two books, Heidegger's *Sein und Zeit*, and Bultmann's *Theologie das Neuen Testaments*. The former is one of the most difficult books ever written, and one of our professors of philosophy confesses that he attended Heidegger's lectures for a semester without understanding more than an occasional sentence! But Heidegger has given us an analysis of the human situation in which such terms as conscience, guilt, and death come into their place again, and Bultmann would use this as a means by which the New Testament message can be commended to our time. We may agree with him or not, but we must reckon with the fact that here we have a position that is neither orthodox nor liberal but that takes up into a higher synthesis what was of value in both. I would myself hold that we can find more to help us in Jaspers and Marcel than in Heidegger. Bultmann's purpose is still largely misunderstood, even by theologians of the acumen and eminence of Karl Barth. Dr Macquarrie deals admirably with what is undoubtedly the crux of the matter, the historical element in the New Testament as Bultmann understands this. He is by no means uncritical of Bultmann and points out how his existentialist bias at times leads him astray, as also how unnecessarily sceptical he is in his treatment of the ministry of Jesus. But he sees that if we care to probe what history really is, it may well be that 'Bultmann is so far from destroying the historical element in the New Testament that it might rather be claimed that he is making clear for us what the genuine historical element in the New Testament really is'.

From *The Expository Times*

What is the nature of human existence? What does it mean to be a human being? According to the Existentialists the primary task of philosophy is to analyse and describe what is involved in our awareness of ourselves as existing. That we exist requires no proof, but the nature of our existence needs to be explored. We are aware of ourselves as persons. We know that we are not things, nor are we just like other animals. What is the nature of these differences? Self-consciousness is that which sets us apart from the rest of creation. Along with it, and part of it goes our sense of freedom and of responsibility for our lives. Each one of us may have and should have a life of one's own. Yet the possibilities of human existence are not unlimited. We are aware of ourselves as existing in an external world which both helps and hinders us in realizing our possibilities. Like our own existence as persons, the reality of the external world is a datum, which needs no proof. Kant, indeed, thought it a scandal to philosophy that there was lacking a cogent proof for the reality of a world outside ourselves. Heidegger, the Existentialist, whose philosophy is the subject of Dr John Macquarrie's admirable study – *An Existentialist Theology* (SCM Press, 18s. net) – replies 'that the true scandal of philosophy is not that such a proof is lacking but that it was ever looked for'. A similar criticism would apply to Descartes. The famous 'Cogito ergo sum' may or may not be logically cogent. It is certainly a superfluity. Our awareness of ourselves as persons does not need any such proof and is not strengthened by it. As an introduction to the main features of Heidegger's analysis of human existence and existential knowledge Dr Macquarrie's book can hardly be bettered. And Heidegger deserves closer attention than his work has yet received in this country. His existential analysis may prove to be more fruitful for philosophic understanding of our human situation than the logical analysis whose vogue among British philosophers is not yet exhausted. In any case, Dr Macquarrie follows Rudolph Bultmann in recognizing the affinity between Existentialism and biblical theology. The knowledge of God offered to us in the Bible is existential knowledge, the kind of knowledge that friends have of one another. The Bible offers no philosophic proofs of the existence of God. It is concerned with ourselves as existing in some relation or other to God, either as alienated from God or as reconciled to Him. Bultmann's exposition of New Testament theology is directed and inspired in no small degree by Heidegger's Existentialism. Dr Macquarrie traces the influence of Heidegger on Bultmann in detail, and concludes that particularly for the understanding of St Paul, Bultmann's reliance on the analysis of Heidegger has proved illuminating. According to Heidegger, human existence may be authentic or inauthentic. Existence is authentic when we effectively shape our own lives. Wordsworth's Happy Warrior

> The generous Spirit, who, when brought
> Among the tasks of real life, hath wrought
> Upon the plan that pleased his boyish thought

had an authentic existence. Our existence becomes inauthentic when we surrender to what H. G. Wells called 'Everydayishness', or when with Emerson we find that

> Things are in the saddle,
> And ride mankind.

This distinction sets the theme for the two main parts of Dr Macquarrie's combined exposition of Heidegger's philosophy and Bultmann's theology. Part one deals with existence as inauthentic and fallen, and part two with the Christian life as authentic existence. Heidegger dominates part one and Bultmann part two, but throughout his sympathetic though critical appreciation of the philosophy of the former and the theology of the latter, Dr Macquarrie outlines his own conception of an existentialist theology. The book may be warmly commended to all who are seriously concerned with the relations of philosophy and Christian theology at the present time.

From *The Times Literary Supplement*

Of all the recent translations of philosophical texts, the most magnificent of all . . . is John Macquarrie and Edward Robinson's translation of Heidegger's *Being and Time*, whose publication in 1962 marked an epoch in English-language philosophy. The bonding of hieratic and demotic styles in Heidegger's prose must have made them quail; but Macquarrie and Robinson, as well as achieving exemplary word-by-word exactitude, somehow managed to make phrases like 'being-in-the-world', 'being-towards-death', or 'readiness-to-hand' sound almost like colloquial English.

3

The American Years

The making of theology is closely related to the making of a theologian, and eventually the actual writing of theology. As I have already said, my progression into this field was not something that I consciously planned. It was a chance visit by a former professor of mine and a chance remark of his that sent me back to theology after I had become largely disillusioned with it. It was an accident of my military service that forced me to cultivate the German language. I was certainly not intending at the time to use my German for the study of theology, though I was of course aware that the most important modern theology has been written in German. Looking back, it seems that my life has been shaped as much or even more by events that just seemed to happen than by deliberate choices. Many of the most important events in my life were, shall I say, 'serendipitous', which means, according to my dictionary, that they were not sought out, but when they happened, I found them valuable. I prefer this word to 'providential', which can easily be too egotistical. What seems providential from one person's point of view may seem quite the reverse to another person. Growing up in Renfrew and receiving a sound Scottish education, going to university, learning German, being called to New York, coming back to Oxford – these things were not planned by me, though some people in my hometown believed that they were!

If one emigrates to a new country with one's family, as I did in 1962, then one is indeed beginning a new life. Actually, the transition to the US was fairly painless. We found ourselves at once in a community, Union Seminary, and that community was, as Dr Van Dusen had promised, warmly welcoming. At that time, Union was also quite a happy community. There was a student body of about six hundred, mostly Americans, but with considerable numbers from Europe, Asia, Africa and elsewhere, making it a truly international institution. The faculty was composed of scholars of international eminence. Tillich had recently retired, and Niebuhr was in poor health, but both were still around and held seminars in their apartments. These were the two best-known members of the faculty but it included also such fine scholars as John Knox and W. D. Davies in New Testament, James Muilenburg and Samuel Terrien in Old Testament, Cyril Richardson, Robert Handy and Wilhelm Pauck in Church History, John Bennett (who succeeded Van Dusen as President in 1963) and Roger Shinn in Christian Ethics. I have already mentioned my colleagues in Systematic Theology, and there were other very able professors in Christian education, homiletics, liturgy, psychology, pastoral ministry, and even in the art of religious broadcasting, by radio or television. There were about forty full-time members of faculty, and a similar number of part-timers, specializing in various forms of ministry. Nor should I forget the splendid school of church music, though this has now moved to become part of Yale University. So Union is more than just another seminary, it is in fact a kind of theological university. At that time, it was probably about the height of its influence. I felt liberated in this environment, for at Glasgow I think there were fewer than a dozen of us teaching theology. Now I found myself a full professor with tenure in this great institution, and I suppose if anyone had asked me at the time, I would have said that I would probably stay on at Union for the rest of my working life. Indeed, my wife and I have often thought that our years there were among the most satisfying of our lives.

It may be interesting to the reader if I give here a very brief account of the history and character of Union Theological Seminary. The Seminary was founded in 1836 as the project

of a group of ministers and laypeople of Presbyterian background. The United States was already undergoing a process
of urbanization and the founders of the Seminary believed
that the training for Christian ministry could be best carried
out in a great city, the obvious choice being New York. The
aims which they set for the Seminary were academic excellence conjoined with an 'enlightened piety' that could be
developed in the urban environment. From the beginning, the
seminary was open to students of any Protestant denomination and was free from 'ecclesiastical domination'. On the
academic side, a magnificent library was built up over the
years, and is still the finest theological library in the United
States, perhaps in the entire English-speaking world. On the
practical side, 'enlightened piety' has taken the form of
involvement in the social problems of New York. In 1870 the
Seminary formalized its association with the Presbyterian
Church, giving to that denomination the right to veto professorial appointments. This was the time when biblical
criticism was striving to establish itself in the face of ultra-
conservative elements in the churches. A crisis arose when
Professor Charles Briggs, who taught the Old Testament at
Union, fell foul of the Presbyterian Church over his teaching.
True to its intention to remain free of 'ecclesiastical domination', Union refused to dismiss Dr Briggs and ended its
concordat with the Presbyterian Church, becoming again an
independent institution. Professor Briggs continued in office
and transferred his ecclesiastical allegiance to the Episcopal
Church.

The Seminary was originally located in downtown New
York but in 1910 moved to handsome new buildings in the
Morningside Heights area. Here it is in close proximity to
several other academic institutions, including Columbia
University, with which the Seminary has close ties.[1]

As I mentioned at the end of chapter 2, Robinson and I
had completed the Heidegger translation by the time I was
moving from Glasgow to New York, so that left me with
more time to attend to other projects. But the first thing I had

to do was to give an inaugural lecture at Union. The topic I chose was 'How is Theology Possible?' which seemed to me to be the basic question that any theologian has to answer in a secular age.

I had already done quite a lot of work in Glasgow on the book *Twentieth-Century Religious Thought*, which I had promised to Harper's. It appeared in 1963. It was over 400 pages in length, and I think I spent more care over its structure and organization than I have on any other book. How does one get acquainted in any significant way with such a vast area of thought? The answer is, only through many hours of hard and exacting reading, much of it well worthwhile but some of it boring and unprofitable! I subtitled the book 'The Frontiers of Philosophy and Theology' and included not only theologians and philosophers with an affirmative attitude to religion but also thinkers who were atheistic or negative in their evaluation of religious beliefs. A further problem was how to classify all this material, how to discern relationships and oppositions and to identify thinkers held together by similar ideas and procedures. Yet another problem was how to allocate the available space. Here one had to make somewhat controversial judgments on whether one person's thought was more important or more influential than another's. I did not want to present a blank statement of who said what, such as one might find in a series of encyclopaedia articles, but I wanted also to evaluate and to show how one line of development led into another. So I had to classify authors in terms of their importance, allotting perhaps 1500 words to some of the more outstanding, while others could be afforded only 400 words, about the least that can identify a distinct position. I think that authors, once they have finalized a book and let it go into print, are often dissatisfied with what they have written. I have always felt a vague dissatisfaction with *Twentieth-Century Religious Thought*, and I think the reason is that I tried to cover too much ground and to include too many thinkers. The book has in fact sold very well, has been updated at least four times, and has stayed continuously in print for 36 years. But if I were to undertake the task now, I would drastically reduce the number of persons discussed, and treat the survivors in more detail than was possible in the original plan. However, the book was never intended to do more than introduce readers to the enormous range of possibilities in modern religious thought, and then leave them to go on to a fuller study of those areas that seemed most promising.

In 1965 I collected together a number of lectures and articles I had written during the previous ten years, calling the collection *Studies in Christian Existentialism*. The title shows that I was still committed to existentialist philosophy at this time, but in fact I was already seeking to get beyond a pure existentialism to a more comprehensive kind of thought which would be less narrowly humanistic and would see human experience not as the 'measure of all things' but as itself embraced in a wider context of Being or Reality. The collection included my inaugural lecture, 'How is Theology Possible?' and this basic question was in my mind during most of my years at Union, especially after the theological world was thrown into confusion by the appearance in 1963 of John Robinson's famous paperback, *Honest to God*.[2]

But before we come to the controversies over the 'death of God', let me finish my account of the projects that were begun in Glasgow and finished in New York. I was still working on my *Principles of Christian Theology* for Scribner's. My teaching schedule at Union at that time was such that most mornings I had a period of free time when I could sit at my desk before a broad picture window looking out on the Hudson River, the George Washington Bridge and the Palisades (the lofty cliffs on the New Jersey bank). It was an ideal situation for writing theology! When I got tired, I would light a cigarette and contemplate the scene, until I felt ready to get on with the next paragraph. Like a great many other people, I gave up smoking more than thirty years ago, but I can't help thinking that it was a civilized habit, which caused us to pause from time to time in the headlong rush of activity.

Well, what is a systematic theology? It is an attempt to think Christianity as a whole. When you begin to do so, you are at once astonished by the coherence and consistency of this vision. One doctrine flows into another, each supports the other and strengthens the other, and the whole is a vision of incredible strength and beauty. One never, of course, entirely comprehends this, and so there can never be a final systematic theology – the work needs to be done again and again, as new insights and new problems arise. On the other hand, no theology should be anything less than systematic, seeking to show Christianity as not just a collection of doctrines, but a living organism in which the whole influences the parts and the parts contribute to the whole. I don't think I had ever been a thorough-going existentialist, for I feared that one might end up in a kind of subjectivism if one followed that path to the end. But now I was consciously moving on from existential(ist) theology to what I called an existential-ontological theology, which would make it clear that religion is not a purely human fabrication, and God is not just an ideal in the human mind, but that God is the ultimate reality and human life depends on God. Nevertheless, faith and religion always have two poles. God on the one hand, the human being on the other. I made two important decisions about this book of systematic theology. As far as the order is concerned, I would begin not with God or arguments for the existence of God, but with the human situation and man's search for a being beyond his own. The second decision was to use Heidegger's philosophy as a conceptual framework that could hold theology together in an intellectually expressed whole. In Bultmann, Heidegger does appear as a philosopher who can help the theologians by providing an analysis of human existence, showing the structures that are important for such theological ideas as sin, faith, salvation, conscience, and so on. But Heidegger went far beyond this existential philosophy to show how it demands for its completion no less than a philosophy of Being, in all its manifestations.

Here Heidegger is close to the classic tradition in Christian
theology. St Thomas, recalling the biblical story that God, in
reply to Moses' request for his name, responded, 'I am who
I am. Say to the Children of Israel, "I am" has sent me,'
claimed that the essence of God is simply Being, and the most
appropriate name for God is 'He Who Is'. In more recent
times, the theme was taken up by Tillich, who teaches that
the most basic truth we can enunciate about God is that he is
identical with Being. So the form of *Principles of Christian
Theology* eventually turned out to be threefold.

First, there is a 'new style natural theology' which traces a
path from our ordinary human existence to the question of
ultimate Being or God. Then follows what is called 'symbolic
theology', the description of this ultimate or divine Being by
various symbols or analogues. We learn that Being is itself
threefold, or a Trinity – Being in itself, or self-subsistent
Being; the phrase I used in *Principles* was 'primordial Being',
what in Christian Trinitarian language we call the Father; but
the Father goes out from himself to share the gift of existence
with a creation and this expressive activity of God I call
'expressive being', in traditional language the Son, or Word,
or Logos, the second person of the Trinity. But there is a third
movement or activity in God. Being does not, so to speak,
break into two, for at the same time the creation is being
held fast, in union with the creative Being from which it is
come, and this third mode of Being I call 'unitive Being', and
identify it with the Holy Spirit, the third person of the
Trinity. So the second part of the *Principles* discusses the
Triune God, Jesus Christ as the Incarnate Word, and
the Holy Spirit and the Christian hope of a final redemption.
The third part is 'Applied Theology', which turns to the
Church, the Sacraments, prayer and ends with ethics, the task
confronting believers in the present.

Scribner's did a very good job in advertising the *Principles*
before publication and the book proved to be the most
successful I have ever written. It was adopted in many
seminaries as the basic text in systematic theology, not

only Anglican seminaries, but across a very wide spread of churches and denominations, including Roman Catholic institutions. It was a good few years ago when the sales passed the 100,000 mark. I made some revisions in 1977 but have not attempted anything further, since within its limits, it states the basic truths of Christianity as clearly as it is possible for me to achieve.

I mentioned earlier that soon after my coming to Union Seminary the problem of God and of language concerning God had moved to the centre of theological concern. Robinson's *Honest to God* had started the debate, but soon it was carried further by more radical thinkers, such as Thomas J. J. Altizer, who denied that there is a God, and published *The Gospel of Christian Atheism*[3] as the manifesto of what became known as the 'death of God' theology. I need hardly say that I strongly opposed this new move, which seemed to me a complete surrender to secularization and the destruction of Christian faith.

I was not, of course, alone in this, and found myself standing alongside such defenders of belief in God as Schubert Ogden and Langdon Gilkey. In 1967 I published *God-Talk*, another work which I had begun in Glasgow, and which challenged the presuppositions of positivism. In this I argued that there is a perfectly defensible language for the expression of Christian theology. This book turned out to be quite influential in the controversy, and was translated into several foreign languages – German, Spanish, Italian, and even, eventually, Chinese!

The following year, 1968, saw a further book, *God and Secularity*, in which I took issue with various forms of what was called 'secular Christianity', a view founded on what has generally come to be regarded as a misinterpretation of Bonhoeffer. Among its proponents were the American Harvey Cox and my former Glasgow colleague, Ronald Gregor Smith. These writers did not deny the existence of God, as the 'death of God' theologians had done, but their teaching so exalted the 'horizontal' in Christianity that the 'vertical' was put very much in second place. They did not, however, agree among themselves. Gregor Smith severely criticized the optimism of such Americans as Harvey Cox and also the latter's glorification of technology. But many of these tendencies were short lived as new and impressive figures appeared on the theological scene, such as Moltmann and Pannenberg with their stress on eschatology, and the new breed of important Roman Catholic theologians who emerged at and after Vatican II, such as Karl Rahner and Hans Küng.

Two more short books were published while I was still teaching in the United States. In *Three Issues in Ethics*, I criticized what was called at that time the 'new morality' and especially 'situation ethics'. I called instead for a reassessment of natural law, and an openness on the part of Christians to non-Christian ethics so far as they are founded on natural law and conscience. The other book was *Martin Heidegger*, and was a brief introduction to his thought and to its significance for theology.

But let me not give the impression that life at Union was only or even primarily a writing of books. At this time I became deeply involved in the Episcopal Church, and was also affected by radical changes in Union Seminary itself.

I have mentioned that for a long time I had felt the attraction of the Episcopal Church. Back in Scotland, for family reasons, it was difficult for me to break away from the prevailing Presbyterianism and I had been a Presbyterian minister since 1944. But now, in my new situation, I felt that I must take the decisive step of identifying with the Episcopal Church. It was not so much that I was renouncing something, for my upbringing itself had brought me to this point, but I believed, as I still do, that at the Reformation the Episcopal Church had preserved some things of great value that had been lost by the majority of Protestant churches; namely, a liturgy that was continuous with the worship of the early church, and a ministry of bishops, priests, and deacons which stood in historic succession to the ministry of the apostles who had been appointed by Christ himself.

Union itself is not tied to any denomination and just about the time I went there, one of its most outstanding professors, John Knox, was heading for the Episcopal Church. John had been a lifelong Methodist and the son of a Methodist minister. But now, at the age of sixty-two, he had resolved to make a new beginning in the Episcopal Church, and I was present at his ordination to the priesthood by the Bishop of New York.

We began attending a small Episcopal Church at 126th Street, on the edge of Harlem, where the Sunday congregation was a good racial mix, partly from the neighbourhood and partly from Columbia University and Union Seminary, both nearby. In 1965, I was ordained first to the diaconate, then to the priesthood, and at that time felt a real sense of spiritual renewal. This was slightly dampened in 1968 when at the invitation of the Archbishop of Canterbury, I served as a consultant at the decennial Lambeth Conference, and felt that 500 bishops, many of them rather mediocre, when gathered in one place are just too much for comfort!

I had a busy life at Union, teaching, writing, travelling all over the US to lecture in colleges and seminaries. But, as the decade of the 1960s wore on, a change was coming over Union. The first thing I noticed was the loss of a sense of humour. Everyone seemed to become very defensive. With the coming of the Vietnam War, there was much discontent among the students. Some of them said frankly they had no interest in theology and had come to Union only to avoid the draft. The faculty became divided. John Bennett, though an admirable person, was too weak in the face of student demands. The whole authority structure was breaking down, and, of course, some of the faculty took sides with the more radical factions among the students. A crisis was reached in the summer of 1969. John Bennett was retiring and there was much contention about what kind of person was needed to succeed him as President. Things reached such a pitch that the summer examinations had to be cancelled, and radical students occupied the faculty offices. Anything in the way of academic activity became virtually impossible. Union was entering on a state of unrest, close to anarchy.

In the midst of all this, I received one morning a letter from England, or rather two letters, one official and one personal. To my surprise, the official letter contained the offer of a professorial chair of theology at Oxford University. It was the Lady Margaret Professorship of Divinity, the oldest chair of divinity in the English-speaking world. I had not applied for this position or had any thought of it. So once again the direction of my life was shifting in a way I had neither planned nor anticipated. The personal letter was from Dr Henry Chadwick, at that time Regius Professor of Divinity at Oxford, and shortly to become Dean of Christ Church, in succession to Dr Cuthbert Simpson. Professor Chadwick's letter was a very cordial encouragement to accept the University's invitation and gave me some of the reasons that had led the electors to make it. For a long time the teaching of theology at Oxford had been governed by historical considerations, and the faculty there had a worldwide reputation for scholarship in historical and especially patristic theology. Systematic theology had certainly never been without some representation, but there was a general belief in the divinity faculty that it now deserved more prominence. Furthermore, a new Honour School in Philosophy and Theology had been instituted. The electors had come to the conclusion that they would invite me to come.

It was only a few days before receiving these letters that I had met Cyril Richardson in the quadrangle at Union, and we were exchanging a few words on the sad state of the Seminary. 'Why do you stay on here, John?' he asked me. I remember the exact words I used in reply: 'Come hell or high water, Cyril, I will stay here,' and gave him my reason, namely, that my oldest boy had, in spite of severe disability, gained a place in Manhattan College. But now this offer threw the whole situation open. I got the family together and asked them how they felt. Somewhat to my surprise, the children (all teenagers by this time) were unanimous in wanting to go back to Britain. My wife, who was teaching mathematics at St Hilda's and St Hugh's Episcopal School in New York would have been happy to stay on, but she was not utterly resolved to do so. Although we had lived long enough in the United States and had enjoyed the experience, so that we qualified for citizenship, I had never taken that step, chiefly because, as a good royalist, I would not renounce allegiance to the Queen. However, we had time to consider matters. It was already the early summer of 1969 and I had announced my teaching programme for 1969–70, so I felt it would be impossible to leave Union before the middle of 1970. The Oxford people were prepared to keep the position vacant for a year. But in fairness both to them and to ourselves, we felt that we should come to a decision as soon as possible.

So Jenny and I decided in the summer of 1969 that we would make a trip over to Oxford and see the situation for ourselves. We did so, and now follows the story of an amusing incident which I have often described to people, and which in some ways illustrates a difference between British and American temperaments. As already mentioned, Union was in a state of crisis, with many people uptight and committed to some political agenda or other. When we arrived at Oxford, we were invited to visit Christ Church at, I think, eleven o'clock on a particular morning, when the treasurer of the college would show us round. We would be shown the house where we would stay, and then we would meet various people who would explain the teaching and other duties related to the appointment. But just before eleven o'clock a message was delivered to us to the effect that the official who was to show us round was delayed. There was a crisis in the college, and he was closeted with the solicitors (lawyers) trying to work out how to deal with it. It seemed an all-too-familiar situation, and I said to Jenny, 'Are we jumping from the frying pan into the fire?' It was suggested that until the official could come, we might take a walk round Christ Church. In due course, the treasurer of the college appeared and apologized profusely for the delay. He told us that a crisis had arisen in the college. 'You see', he said, 'we own a pack of beagles' (dogs used for hunting). 'The beagles have kennels in Garsington' (a residential area not far from Oxford) 'and the people of Garsington are complaining that the baying of the beagles during the night is keeping them from their sleep, and, moreover, their properties are losing value. So they have clapped a lawsuit on the college to get the beagles out of Garsington, and we have been considering what to do about this.'

Remembering the state of affairs back at Union, I whispered to Jenny, 'I think I could live with this kind of crisis!' We went on our tour of inspection, including the medieval Priory House, the residence assigned to the Lady Margaret Professor, containing about sixteen rooms, some of them beautifully panelled, but with very few modern amenities. The college representatives hastened to assure us that central heating would be installed, as we must have become accustomed to it in New York. Before we left, I signed a paper accepting the appointment and promising to come in 1970. I had also been able to make satisfactory arrangements for my son to continue his studies in England.

Appendix: Lecture in New York

How is Theology Possible?[1]

Soon after I first became a teacher of theology, I was invited to take part in an interesting university teachers' conference. Its aim was to do something towards combating the unfortunate results of the increasing specialization of studies, whereby a theologian, let us say, is in the dark about science, while an engineer finds philosophy unintelligible. The plan was to get a representative from each major field to explain as clearly as possible to scholars from other fields just what was the nature of his own studies. Knowing that I would have scientists, classicists, lawyers, medical men and, indeed, all sorts and conditions of scholars in my audience, I took great care to prepare a paper which, I fondly hoped, might transmit the theological theme on a wave-length that could be picked up by all present. The hope was speedily shattered in the discussion that followed the paper. A physicist said something like this: 'The speaker was quite intelligible until he introduced the word "God" into his talk. This word does not stand for anything within my range of concepts or experience, and so every sentence in which it was used was to me meaningless, and the whole paper became unintelligible. Will the speaker kindly tell us what the word "God" signifies?'

These remarks were, of course, somewhat disconcerting to me at the time. But it soon became clear to me that my scientific colleague had rendered me a valuable service. He had taught me a first principle of hermeneutics, namely, that there must be at least some basis of common ground between an interpreter and his audience if the interpretation is to get under way. He had shown me further that in a secular age one may not assume that language about God affords a universally intelligible starting point for an interpretation of the Christian faith. Above all, he had raised for me very acutely

the question: 'How is theology possible?' For if theology is
the interpretation of our Christian faith in God, and if this
interpretation is not merely an academic exercise within an
esoteric Christian community but has become, in the words
of the founders of Union Theological Seminary, 'impressed
with the claims of the world', so that it must address the
world, then where is a beginning to be made?

Whether we are Christians or secularists, we share our
humanity. Is this then the common ground from which a
theological interpretation can begin today? Christianity is a
doctrine of man as well as of God. John Calvin, as is well
known, having remarked that true and solid wisdom consists
almost entirely of two parts, the knowledge of God and the
knowledge of ourselves, went on to say that 'as these are
connected together by many ties, it is not easy to determine
which of the two precedes and gives birth to the other'.[2]
Calvin himself began with the doctrine of God, and this is
probably the logical place to begin, and was also an intelligible beginning in an age when most people took religion
very seriously and could discourse in a theological idiom. But
in a secular age, we have to consider the alternative.

Someone, of course, may object here that Calvin began
with the doctrine of God for quite another reason, namely,
that man can be properly understood only in the light of
God. Every Christian would agree that this is true, but it is a
truth which by no means rules out the possibility of taking
man as the starting point for an interpretation of the
Christian faith. If man is, as Christianity asserts, a creature of
God and dependent on him, then this should show itself in a
study of man. It should be possible to see man as fragmentary
and incomplete in himself, so that we are pointed to God;
and if we can see man in this way, then we can go on to a
fuller understanding of him in his relation to God. The
advantage of such a procedure is that it would help us to
answer the question put by people like my scientific colleague
at the conference. If we can begin from the humanity which
we all share, and if we find that this humanity points beyond

itself for its completion, then we have, so to speak, indicated the place of the word 'God' on the map of meaningful discourse. Union Theological Seminary's President, Henry P. Van Dusen, has written some time ago: 'It is an accepted premise of Christian thought that all the major beliefs of its faith are mutually involved and interdependent. It should be possible and legitimate to make one's start from any one of them, and approach all the others through it.'³ Let us then accept his statement, and see how far it is possible to travel along the road that begins from man himself.

Our question then is, 'What is man?' or, to put it more concretely, 'Who are you?' Obviously this question admits of many answers, according to the context in which it is asked. It could be answered, 'I am a British subject', or 'I am a Protestant', or 'I am a graduate'; and each of these answers might be quite adequate and appropriate within a particular context. To elicit the Christian answer, and to see how it makes sense, we must first understand the kind of question to which it claims to give the appropriate response. A German writer, Hans Zehrer, tells us about 'the man from the hut'. This man was a refugee from the East, now living in an overcrowded hut in what had once been a military camp. Once he had had a wife and two children as well as numerous friends, once he had had a home and a well stocked farm, once he had had what we call the comforts of life and a secure place in society. Now all these have been stripped from him and he is thrown back on himself. For the first time, the question 'Who are you?' has thrust itself on this man in a radical way. As Zehrer formulates it: 'Well, tell me, who am I, then, and what am I living for, and what is the sense of it all?'⁴ We are likely to ask the question about ourselves in this radical way only very rarely. It may even be the case, as some philosophers tell us, that we shrink from the question and screen ourselves from it. Yet perhaps everyone faces it at least once in his life. To this question, 'Who are you *at bottom?*' the partial and superficial answers that normally suffice for the question 'Who are you?' are no longer adequate.

Perhaps our secularist friend will cut in at this point with the brusque observation that this radical question about ourselves just is *unanswerable*. In a sense, he would undoubtedly speak correctly. For if we are to answer so radical a question about ourselves, would it not be necessary for us, so to speak, to detach ourselves from ourselves, and to stand back so as to view all time and all existence, and thus learn where we fit into the scheme of things? Manifestly it is impossible to do this. So if the question 'Who are you?' has disturbed us, would we not do well to put it out of our minds as an insoluble enigma?

We might gladly do this, and perhaps for a large part of our time we might succeed in doing it. But surely we are deceiving ourselves if we believe that we can get rid of the question altogether. If it is true in one sense that *we cannot answer the question*, it is paradoxically true in another sense that *we cannot help answering it*. For this is no speculative question, such that we could take it up or lay it aside at pleasure. It is the question of ourselves, and because we have to live and make ourselves, the question is demanding an answer all the time. In every policy that we adopt and in every unrepeatable action that we perform, we are giving an answer and taking upon ourselves an identity. Always and already, we have decided to understand ourselves in one way or another, though such self-understanding may not be explicit in every case.

These reflections introduce us to the basic polarity of our human existence. We are on the one hand *limited*. We find ourselves thrown into an existence, and we cannot by any means step out of this existence in order to get a detached objective view of it. Thus we can never know with certitude its why and wherefore. On the other hand, we are *responsible* for this existence. Every day we have to take the risk of deciding to understand our existence in one way or another. It is little wonder if to some this polarity seems to be just an insoluble contradiction, so that human existence is essentially an absurdity and foredoomed to failure. 'Man,'

Jean-Paul Sartre tells us, 'is a useless passion. To get drunk by yourself in a bar or to be a leader of the nations is equally pointless.'⁵ But before yielding to such pessimistic conclusions, let us ask if it is possible to understand our existence in a more hopeful way. If we are willing to entertain such a possibility, then we are ready to consider what Christianity tells us concerning ourselves.

The Christian answer to the question 'Who are you?' frankly acknowledges the polarity or tension that lies at the core of all human existence. The finitude and precariousness of man's life is a familiar theme in the Bible – his origin from the dust, the limitation of his power and knowledge, the brevity of his life and the inevitability of his death. At the same time, there is the theme of man's freedom and distinctive place in the world – he has dominion over nature, he aspires after ideals and realizes values, he is under judgment as one who is accountable for what he makes of his life and his world. There is here no flight from the human condition, no comforting concealment of its dilemma. Man has to walk the razor edge between his finitude and his responsibility.

A further element in the Christian understanding of man seems to heighten the difficulty of making sense of human existence, and to carry us just as far as Sartre in the direction of hopelessness. This further element is the doctrine of sin. There is a pathological disorder in human life, a radical alienation deep within our existence, and on account of it we fall down on one side or the other from that narrow precipitous path along which we have to walk. Sometimes, perhaps in protest against optimistic humanism, theologians have exaggerated the doctrine of sin, especially in some of their formulations of the ideas of 'original sin' and 'total depravity', but all of them agree with the New Testament in maintaining the universality of sin and its gravity.

Some theologians, such as Reinhold Niebuhr, have seen the essence of sin in pride, so that sin is interpreted as man's attempt to be rid of the finite pole of his existence and to exercise an unlimited freedom. Niebuhr, however, has been criticized for his alleged neglect of the sins of indulgence, which would seem to arise rather from an attempt to be rid of the pole of freedom and responsibility, in seeking to descend to the level of a merely animal existence. But in either case, man becomes untrue to the being that is his. He refuses to accept himself as at once free and finite. Of course, although he may not accept his destiny, he cannot escape it either, and hence comes the language of 'alienation' in regard to sin. Sinful man is estranged from himself by his refusal to take upon himself an identity which on the other hand he cannot completely discard, an identity which includes both the poles of his freedom and his finitude.

This Christian understanding of man, as so far expounded, is just as desperate and radical as Sartre's. But of course, Christian theology does not remain at the point of despair. It must bring us to this point, to make clear its conviction that *there is no human solution to the human problem.* If man is abandoned to his own resources in the world, then Sartre seems to be right; our life is a useless passion and its in- eluctable outcome is failure. But must we halt here? Already the analysis of the situation points to another possibility, though only as a possibility. This is the possibility of *grace* – a power from beyond man which can heal his estrangement and enable him to live as the being which he is, the being in whom are conjoined the polarities of finitude and responsi- bility. This possibility of grace seems to be the only alterna- tive to despair if we are to take as honest a view of the human condition as Sartre does, and not conceal from ourselves how insoluble is the enigma of man in human terms.

But where are we to look for grace? Clearly, we cannot look to the world of things. That world knows nothing of our predicament. Sartre indeed feels nausea for its solid plenitude of senseless being, which throws into poignant relief the isolated lot of man as the fragile existent that is 'condemned to be free'.[6] We may not share Sartre's disgust, but clearly a lower order of being cannot *of itself* provide grace, even though it might become a vehicle of grace. Are we then to look to other persons? Sartre is inclined to see other persons chiefly as obstacles to the ambitions projected in one's own existence. We would hope that we did not share such an ego-centric understanding of life, and would acknowledge that a man can be helped and strengthened by his fellows. But is even this the source of grace we are looking for? Clearly not, for without depreciating the help that one may receive from another, we must not lose sight of the fact that all men are in the human situation together and that sin and its divisiveness are universal.

If grace is to be found anywhere, it must come from beyond the world of things and the society of human beings, though it may indeed come through these. We are directed towards a transcendent source of grace. This is neither a senseless nor a speculative idea, but rather a question of life and death that arises directly out of the structure of our own existence. It is the question of God, for 'God' is the word which the religious man uses for the transcendent source of grace. When people like my sophisticated colleague ask what the word 'God' signifies, we can only invite them to ask themselves in a radical way 'Who am I?', for this question of man already implies the question of God or is even, as Bultmann says, identical with it.[7] The quest for grace allows the word 'God' to find its place on the map of meaningful discourse; and with it, other theological words find their places – 'finitude' may be equivalent to 'creatureliness', and 'sin' may acquire its full signification as 'separation from God'.

So far this is a meagre result. We have raised only the *question* of God. Nothing has been said about his reality, and the very word 'God' remains as a formal expression with a bare minimum of content. It is of course important that we have found this question to be one that is raised by the very structure of our existence, for this provides the orientation that enables us to see the possibility of theology as a mean-ingful and important area of discourse. But can we now go further?

In asking the question of God, man must already have some idea of God, for every question has its direction, and it is impossible to seek anything without having some understanding of what is sought, however vague and minimal that understanding may be. The next step towards grappling with our problem is simply a phenomenological exploration of the question of God itself. What is the structure of this question? How should it properly be formulated? What is already implicit in the question? What conditions would have to be fulfilled for it to receive an affirmative answer?

We must remember that our question is the *religious* question of God, and that it has an *existential* structure. That is to say, it is not a theoretical or speculative question, raised by the intellect alone and asked in a general, disinterested way, but a *practical question* posed by the whole being of man, who has to exist in the world and decide about his existence. Perhaps the question of God can be raised in a purely theoretical way, but this would not be a question of any direct interest to theology, and perhaps it would not even be a manageable question. We could think, for instance, of the question of God as a *cosmological* question, in which 'God' would stand for an explanatory hypothesis, put forward to account either for the world as a whole or for certain events in the world. For a long time men did try to account for many happenings in terms of supernatural agencies. With the rise of science, however, we have learned to look for our explanations in terms of factors immanent in the natural process itself. The famous remark of Laplace to Napoleon, 'I have no need of that hypothesis,' simply expresses our modern attitude to the world as a self-regulating entity. Science, of course, stops short of the ultimate question of why there is a world at all, but this is simply an acknowledgment that for the finite human intellect which is within the world, such a question is unanswerable. The religious question of God, as existentially structured, is different from any theoretical question about an explanatory hypothesis. We are not looking for some invisible intangible entity to the existence of which we might infer. Perhaps we are not looking for an entity at all, or for anything that could be conceived as a possible object among others.

These remarks at once suggest that we must be highly suspicious of the traditional formulation of the question of God – a formulation which runs, 'Does God exist?' For this question already contains implicitly the idea of God as a possible existent entity. The question is parallel to such a question as, 'Does there exist another planet beyond Pluto?' This is not at all like the religious, existentially structured question of God. This later would need to be formulated in some such way as, 'Can we regard Being as gracious?' It is a question about the character of Being. Either Being may have the character of indifference towards man, in which case he is thrown back on himself and must understand himself in a secular way; or else Being has the character of grace, so that human life can be lived in the strength of a power from beyond man himself, and ceases to be the tragic contradiction, the useless passion, which it would be in the absence of grace.

'God' is the religious word for Being, understood as gracious. The words 'God' and 'Being' are not synonyms, for Being may have the character of indifference, and in that case it could not be called 'God' nor would any religious attitude towards it be appropriate. 'Being' can be equated with 'God' only if Being has the character of grace and is responsive to man's existential predicament. Now Being cannot itself be regarded as an entity, for it is manifestly absurd to say 'Being exists' or 'Being is'. Being does not itself belong within the category of particular beings – or 'entities', as they may be called to avoid confusion – of which one can assert that they either exist or do not exist. In Heidegger's language, Being stands to entities as the wholly other, the *transcendens*, the non-entity which is yet 'more beingful' (*seiender*) than any possible entity. But if God is equated with Being as gracious, then the question, 'Does God exist?' involves what British analytical philosophers have taught us to call a 'category mistake'. The question is not whether some entity or other exists, but whether Being has such a character as would fulfil man's quest for grace.

Can we see more clearly what conditions must be fulfilled if Being can be recognized as God? We have seen that the question of God arises from man's estrangement from himself, and from his inability to bring into unity the poles of finitude and freedom which together constitute his being. These two poles must remain in perpetual and frustrating conflict if there is no positive relation between the Being out of which man has emerged as a finite centre of existence, and the values and aspirations towards which, in his freedom, he aims at as the goal of his being. If Being has the character of grace and can be identified with God, the condition to be satisfied is that the Being out of which man arises coincides with the end of his freedom, thus bringing into unity the polarities of his existence and healing his estrangement. Among modern theologians, this idea comes out most clearly in Paul Tillich, who has two typical ways of talking about God, namely, as 'ground of being' and as 'ultimate concern'. But precisely the same structure is discernible in the more traditional accounts of God. For instance, Oliver Quick writes: 'God is the alpha and omega of all things, the source from which they proceed, the end toward which they move, the unity in which they cohere.'[8] The language here is perhaps cosmological rather than existential, but this description of God has precisely the same structure as the one at which we arrived by an existential and ontological route.

This must suffice for the phenomenological description of the question of God. The question has, so it is hoped, been clarified, and we see better its meaning and requirements. But the matter cannot be left here. If it were, I might be accused of showing that theology is a possible study of the possible, rather than showing that theology is possible as a study of the most concrete reality. But what kind of evidence can we now seek, to bring content into the hitherto formal structures of the analysis?

It is clear that even if in what has been said I have been

engaged in some kind of philosophical or natural theology, I have cut myself off from the rational or deductive style of natural theology, by which so many theologians of the past sought to ground their subject and to establish the reality of its matter. Apart from the fact that their arguments have been largely discredited by modern criticism, I have tried to show that their speculative approach was a mistaken one and that their leading question about the existence of God involved a logical defect in its formulation. In any case, their speculative approach, if we may call it such, was an artificial one, for all those who tried to prove the existence of God already believed in him, and must have had a more primordial source for their conviction than their own arguments. Where then are we to look?

At the risk of lapsing into theological incomprehensibility, I must now boldly introduce the word 'revelation'. Yet this is not a word that need frighten us. Clearly, nothing whatever can be known unless in some way it reveals or manifests itself. Of course, something more than this obvious commonplace is implied in the theological idea of revelation. When it is said that the knowledge of God is revealed, the word is used to point to a kind of knowledge distinct from that which we attain through our own effort of thought. The knowledge of God, it is claimed, comes to us as a gift, and to indicate its distinctiveness by the word 'revelation' is simply to remain true to the phenomenological analysis of belief in God, for such belief testifies that it arises through God's making himself known to us, rather than through our attaining to the knowledge of him. The Bible never suggests that man has to strain his mind to figure out a shadowy Something behind the phenomena. There is indeed recognition of man's innate quest for God, but it is maintained that God himself meets and satisfies the quest. Man does not search out God, but rather the reverse is true. One of the greatest of the Psalms begins: 'O Lord, thou hast searched me and known me!'[9] and goes on to describe the ubiquity and inevitability of the encounter with God.

What kind of language is this? Of what kind is this knowledge of God, where that which is known towers above us, as
it were, and it is as if we ourselves were known and brought
into subjection? Perhaps we glimpse an answer to these
questions if we consider three possible ways in which we may
be related to that which presents itself to us in such a way
that it becomes known to us. The first case is our everyday
relation to things, as objects of which we make use or have
knowledge. They are at our disposal, and even by knowing
them, we acquire a certain mastery over them; for instance,
we can predict natural phenomena and be prepared for them.
The second case is our relation to other persons. This 'I-thou'
relation, as Martin Buber has taught us to call it, is of a
different order, for the other person is not my object and is
not at my disposal. I know him in a different manner. The
relation here is one between subjects. It is a mutual or reciprocal relation, founded on the same kind of being – personal
being – on both sides. Now it is possible also to envisage a
third kind of relation, we do not have the other term of the
relation at our disposal, nor do we stand to it in a relation of
equality, but rather we are grasped by it, our eyes are opened
to it, and we are brought into subjection to it, but in such a
way that something of its character is disclosed to us, so that
to some extent it becomes known to us.

Correspondingly, we may say that there are three modes of
thinking. We think of things in objective terms, and this presumably is the commonest type of thinking. We think of our
friends differently, as those with whom all kinds of relations
are possible that are impossible with things. And it is possible
to think too of Being which, though it towers above us, does
not annihilate us but rather communicates itself and gives
itself in the experience of grace. To talk of revelation does not
mean an abrogation of thinking, but only that all our thinking is not of the same pattern. Tillich talks of the ecstatic
reason which still does not cease to be reason.[10] Heidegger
speaks perhaps more soberly of the thinking that is sub-
missive (*hörig*) to Being.[11] Whatever expression we may

prefer, this is the kind of thinking that makes theology possible. Theology is the task of sifting and explicating and interpreting God's encounter with man, as this is recollected in tranquility.

If someone is still asking, 'What does all this prove?' then the answer must be in line with what has already been said – it *proves* precisely nothing, for the kind of philosophical (or natural) theology that has been sketched out here is not demonstrative but descriptive. Perhaps what we take to be the encounter with God is an illusion; perhaps it is all explicable in terms of a naturalistic psychology; perhaps all our talk of sin and grace and existence and Being is only mystification. These are possibilities that cannot entirely be excluded, even when within the community of faith the experience of grace has begun to produce the fruits of wholeness and serenity in place of estrangement and anxiety. The impossibility of demonstration in these matters is simply a consequence of what we have learned from the analysis of man himself – that he is finite, that his is not the godlike but rather the worm's-eye view, that so long as he is *homo viator* he lacks the unclouded clarity of vision, and must go forward in the attitude of faith, and in the risk of faith.

But on the other hand, if nothing has been proved, at least something has been described. The way has been described that leads from man's confrontation with himself to his confrontation with God and, with the aid of concepts drawn from contemporary philosophy and theology, this way has been shown to possess a coherent pattern, an intelligible structure, and its own inner logic. When challenged to produce the credentials of his subject, the theologian cannot in the nature of the case offer a proof, but he can describe this area of experience in which his discourse about God is meaningful, he can ask his questioner whether he recognizes his own existence in the Christian doctrine of man as finite, responsible and sinful, whether he finds hidden in himself the question of God. The theologian can also show that faith is not just an arbitrary matter, and he can make clear what is the alternative to faith. Beyond this, perhaps, he cannot go, but is not this sufficient? For it brings us to the point where we see that this discourse about God has to do with the most radical and concrete matters in life, the point where, exercising our freedom in finitude in all the light that we can get, we decide to take either the risk of faith or the risk of unfaith.

4

Life at Christ Church

In September, 1970, we moved back to the United Kingdom and took up residence in Oxford. This was a major change in almost every respect. From a great metropolis of 8,000,000 people, with extensive suburbs beyond, we had moved to a city of about 100,000 inhabitants, situated in open and still unspoiled countryside. From a twentieth-century environment of high-rise buildings and broad avenues, we had come to a compact town with many ancient buildings and narrow streets unable to cope with the volume of traffic that they now have to bear. Yet Oxford remains one of the world's greatest centres of learning, with experts on everything from ancient languages and cultures to the most up-to-date developments in science and medicine.

The beginnings of the university go back to the twelfth century, and during the nine hundred years of its existence it has passed through many phases of Western culture and collected many traditions and even anomalies. Visitors to Oxford sometimes ask me about the arcane workings of the institution, but I usually have to confess that I have never properly understood them myself. The university consists of more than thirty colleges, each of which is a kind of mini-university with fellows or tutors in all or most of the subjects studied in a university. But when one asks how the university is related to these colleges, it is hard to give an answer.

One could say that the university is nothing apart from the colleges. The university's professors and other teachers and its major officials are members of colleges; but the colleges are not just a collection of educational institutions but constitute a unity as the university. On arriving in Oxford, visitors often ask, 'Where is the university?' or 'Where is the campus?' These questions are unanswerable. The university is the colleges scattered through the central part of Oxford. There are a few buildings which do not belong to any particular college but are used by all; the administrative offices in Wellington Square, the examination schools, the faculty centres, the Bodleian Library, etc., but these are not the university, though they are university buildings

The university controls some matters, the colleges others. The university awards degrees and sets examinations, thus maintaining a common academic standard. But the colleges control admission. There is a certain amount of duplication. The university provides a library, the famous Bodleian Library, which may be used by all the colleges; there are also libraries for the various faculties, arts, law, science, theology and so on; but each college has its own library, and some of them are very good. The university also provides laboratories for the different sciences, but these are not normally duplicated in the colleges. There is a university church, St Mary's in the High Street, but each college has its chapel and chaplain. In trying to explain these matters to American visitors, I often use the very imperfect analogy of federal and state government in the USA. The federal government was created by the states in the eighteenth century, but has become so powerful that now from time to time we hear of states asserting their rights, and in the same way Oxford colleges have created the university in the course of centuries but are now sometimes jealous of their rights in face of encroachments by the university. Needless to say, problems and anomalies often arise.

Teaching appointments at Oxford are normally made through the agency of electoral boards or committees on which both university and college representatives sit, and each professor or fellow is both a teacher in the university and a fellow of one of the colleges.

As has already been mentioned, my own appointment was to the Lady Margaret Chair of Divinity, and this professorship is attached to the college of Christ Church. Lady Margaret Beaufort[1] (1443–1509) was an English noblewoman in the time of the Wars of the Roses. She eventually married Edmund Tudor, Earl of Richmond, to whom she bore a son who became King Henry VII after the Battle of Bosworth. She was a woman of great piety and founded a readership (professorship) in theology at Oxford in 1502. So there have been Lady Margaret Professors at Oxford for almost five hundred years.

The Lady Margaret Professor of Divinity is also a Canon of Christ Church (*Aedes Christi*) and I should say something about that institution. Probably Christ Church is unique in the world because, although a single corporation, it is both a cathedral and a college. It is often called simply 'The House', though it is not by any means the oldest of the Oxford colleges – that honour belongs to University College (*Aula Universitatis*). Christ Church dates only from 1526 when it was founded as Cardinal College, so-called because the founder was Cardinal Wolsey. He began by building the kitchen and the great dining hall, one of the most magnificent halls in the world, and soon was added the spacious quadrangle (Tom Quad). In 1546 Wolsey died, having in the meantime fallen from the royal favour, and the college was refounded by King Henry VIII and was renamed Christ Church. The college incorporated an old religious house going back to Anglo-Saxon times, and to the Princess Frideswide, its foundress. These old religious buildings included a splendid church, and this church became and continues to be not only the college chapel but the cathedral of the diocese of Oxford. Previously Oxford had been within the diocese of Lincoln but became a separate see in 1542. Part of the west end of the church had been cut off in Wolsey's time to make way for his quadrangle, so the cathedral is relatively small. Another act of destruction from those days was the demolition of the shrine of St Frideswide by some over zealous Reformers, though currently there are plans for its restoration. The cathedral is famous for its music and has a school for the choir boys – a school in which my wife soon resumed her teaching of mathematics, having been called in to restore order in a class of boys which the young maths master had been unable to control.

As one of the canons, I had regular duties in the cathedral as well as my teaching duties. There are services in the cathedral every day of the year – matins at 7.15 am, followed by a eucharist, then at 6 pm evensong is sung by the choir. On Sundays matins and the eucharist are also sung. In describing my life at Union in the preceding chapter, I spoke of an 'ideal situation for writing theology', but my new situation at Christ Church, though very different, was equally ideal! There are usually six canons at Christ Church, four of them being professors in the theology faculty, so the liturgical duties are not too heavy.

My arrival at Oxford coincided with that of Professor Maurice Wiles. He had been appointed to succeed Henry Chadwick (who had become Dean of Christ Church) in the Regius Chair of Divinity. Maurice Wiles and I were colleagues and worked closely together during all of my time at Oxford. We helped each other come to terms with the strange new world of Oxford. Though we had different approaches to theology, I think the students profited from this diversity, and between us we taught a goodly number of students, many of whom are now themselves teaching in various parts of the world.

Within the precincts of Christ Church are living accommodations for the canons and undergraduates, teaching rooms, and a splendid eighteenth-century library. Needless to say, Christ Church attracts an unending flow of tourists, from America, Japan, the European continent and elsewhere. The number of visitors was so great that it was beginning to affect the teaching and other activities of the college, and to cut down the number of visitors, the authorities decided some years ago to impose a charge for admission. We ourselves lived in the mediaeval Priory House, away from the main quadrangle and the stream of tourists. We were immediately adjacent to the cathedral, and our front door was in the cloister. Behind the house was an extensive garden, sloping down to the Christ Church Meadow, a large park-like area in the land just above the confluence of the Thames and Cherwell rivers.

In the surroundings of Christ Church, it was impossible not to have a sense of the history of the place. How many great figures had spent their student years here! John Locke, the philosopher; William Gladstone, the statesman – and I think about a dozen other Christ Church men were Prime Ministers; Edward Bouverie Pusey the churchman, who must have set a record by living at Christ Church as a canon-professor for fifty-four years; Henry Liddell, the Dean and Greek lexicographer, perhaps less famous than his daughter Alice, of Wonderland fame, her story having been written by Charles Lutwidge Dodgson (Lewis Carroll), Christ Church's tutor in mathematics.

Oxford – and Christ Church too – have their own special customs and anomalies, as I mentioned. For instance, at Christ Church, the fellows are known as 'Students', and I don't think this is out of modesty on their part. The students, in the ordinary sense of the word, are always called 'undergraduates'. Another odd custom, reflecting, I suppose, the several centuries when Oxford and Cambridge were the only two universities in the whole of England, is the reluctance to acknowledge that degrees granted by other universities could have any real value. Oxford does recognize degrees from Cambridge and from Trinity College, Dublin (founded by Queen Elizabeth I) and 'incorporates' them by recognizing the holders as having the equivalent Oxford degree. But of course these courtesies are not extended to such an outlandish place as the University of Glasgow, though in fact it was founded by the Renaissance pope and educator, Nicholas V, in 1451, roughly a century before Christ Church. It happened, therefore, that soon after I had arrived in Oxford, I received a note from the university office informing me that if no objection had been received, I would, with effect from 12 noon on such and such a date, be deemed to be an MA of the University of Oxford. (I am told that in America's Harvard University there is a similar custom for dealing with 'lesser breeds without the law' who are elected to the faculty.) I always felt that my Oxford MA was somewhat phony. The word 'deemed' does convey a slight suggestion of 'as if'. So a few years later I took an Oxford DD, which is an earned degree for published work, and about the same time I was elected a Fellow of the British Academy, and so attained to intellectual respectability.

Another distinctive feature of life at Oxford is the 'high table' in each college dining room. Here the professors and fellows dine every evening in quite a sumptuous style. After the meal, they adjourn to another room where conversation, often very witty but sometimes quite boring, takes place over port or Madeira wine.

While I lectured perhaps three times a week to undergraduates, most of my time was spent in supervising graduate students who were working towards a doctorate. Many of them came from overseas, from the United States, Canada and Australia, but also from Europe and Asia. Also in each year I would give lectures in other countries, often back in the US, but now in countries of the eastern hemisphere too: in Rome, where I met Pope Paul VI; in Basel, where I caught up with two former acquaintances, Fritz Buri and Heinrich Ott, but was unable to meet Hans Urs von Balthasar because there had been some disagreement between him and my host in Basel; in Louvain (or Leuven) which, like Basel, was founded about the same time as Glasgow; in Copenhagen, with its memories of Kierkegaard. Other trips took me further afield, to India and Australia, and in 1977, when the Japan Society invited me to that country, Jenny and I decided this was the time to go round the world. By this time I had been teaching long enough to have former students in many places along the route – a Union student in Japan, another in Singapore, a whole group of Indian students who had been with me in Oxford.

I have spoken about England and the United States, but I should mention visits to Scotland and Ireland. In 1979 I went back to Glasgow to preach at the jubilee of the university chapel and had the privilege of sharing the service with Archie Craig, a retired chaplain of the university. By now he was over ninety years old, and it was he who had welcomed me when I went up to the university in 1936. In 1983 I had a very pleasant stay at Scotland's oldest university, St Andrews, founded in 1411. The occasion was to give the Gifford Lectures, a subject to which I shall come back. One day in Oxford I was visited by the Primus (Presiding Bishop) of the Scottish Episcopal Church and one of his fellow bishops, with the proposition that I should allow myself to be nominated to the vacant bishopric of Argyll and the Isles. Emotionally, I felt a very strong inclination to accept this invitation. It would have meant going back to my roots. I agreed to think about it, but rational consideration proved stronger than romantic impulse, and I respectfully declined. I thought there must be experienced pastors back in Scotland far better suited to the position than I was, and also that I was probably doing a more useful job teaching in Oxford than I could do in that extensive, sparsely populated, but supremely beautiful diocese. In 1972 I spent two weeks lecturing on christology at St Patrick's College, Maynooth. This is the principal Roman Catholic seminary in Ireland, and has the status of a Pontifical University. This visit to Maynooth was only one of many which I paid to Ireland, sometimes under Catholic and sometimes under Protestant auspices. I was warmly received by both groups and believe that there are many fine people of goodwill on both sides who would gladly welcome an end to strife and a true peace.

Not only was I teaching and writing during these years at Christ Church. I found myself more involved in the affairs of the Church of England than perhaps I had been when I was serving in the American Episcopal Church. Thus I was again a consultant at the Lambeth Conference of 1978 when Archbishop Coggan laid on me the delicate task of introducing the 'hearing', as it was called, on the question of admitting women to the priesthood. Soon I found myself also on the Commission on Doctrine and on two church commissions dealing with ecumenical problems. On the whole, I enjoyed my work on these bodies, but they seemed to achieve very little. At the time when I served on it (it may have changed since then) the members of the Doctrine Commission were far too individualistic. One had the feeling that they came to the meetings with readymade speeches, and there was very little genuine discussion or meeting of ideas. As far as ecumenism is concerned, I was, like many people of my generation, at one time an enthusiast. But in fact, as one looks back over what has happened in the twentieth century, the ecumenical movement seems to have run out of steam. The World Council of Churches, which seemed so important when it was founded in 1948, has been a disappointment. In the first place, it was never entitled to call itself a 'world council' for the largest of all the Christian churches and the only one which might be called a worldwide church, namely, the Roman Catholic Church, has never belonged to the WCC. In the second place, in its earlier years the WCC was very deeply under the influence of Barthian theology, which among other things meant that there could be no dialogue with non-Christian religions. Fortunately, that particular phase passed, but it was succeeded by one in which the WCC became intensely political and seemed to be more influenced by ideology than by theology.

From an Anglican point of view, a new era of ecumenism opened with the launching of ARCIC (the Anglican-Roman Catholic International Commission) in the early 1970s. I was not myself a member of ARCIC, but had many contacts. Two of the leading participants on the Anglican side were people with whom I had very friendly relations, Henry Chadwick, Dean of Christ Church, and Arthur Vogel, Bishop of Western Missouri. I had also a good relation with Dr Edward Yarnold, SJ, on the Roman Catholic side. He was a near neighbour at Campion Hall, and the two of us used to go out together to address meetings designed to encourage interest in ARCIC. Valuable statements of agreement on such controversial issues as eucharist, ministry and authority were produced by ARCIC, and it should be remembered that these agreements were not drawn up by an unofficial group of like-minded persons, but by duly appointed representatives of the two communions and therefore have a certain ecclesiastical standing. But once again very little has come of it, at least so far. The lack of progress cannot be blamed on one side or the other, for both sides have contributed to it.

Nevertheless, since Vatican II and the new interest which Rome has showed since that time in improving relations with the churches which emerged at the Reformation, there is, I think, the possibility of some ecumenical advance in the future. I have mentioned ARCIC and will come back to the question of relations with the Roman Catholic Church later, but here I shall briefly recall a conference of so-called 'church leaders' which took place at Birmingham in 1972[2] while I was still settling in to the new situation at Oxford. This was a very interesting occasion, when Roman Catholics, including Cardinal Heenan, took part along with Anglicans and Free Church representatives in a very wide-ranging discussion of theological and practical questions confronting the churches of the British Isles. My task was to chair a section on the very central question of 'God and Prayer'. A member of the section was Bishop Christopher Butler, one of the auxiliary bishops of the Roman Catholic archdiocese of Westminster. I was profoundly impressed by Bishop Butler and had valuable discussion and correspondence with him, which I shall mention later.

One of my early duties after coming to Oxford was to give an inaugural lecture. As was explained in the last chapter, I had been called to Oxford in the hope that I would bring a higher profile to systematic theology, for the tradition had been one which emphasized historical theology, especially patristics. That tradition was a very fine one, especially as the Church of England has usually claimed that it has no doctrine of its own but continues the doctrine of what it likes to call the 'undivided church', that is to say, the church of the early centuries. An excellent example of that way of teaching theology can be seen in the book called simply *Christian Theology* by A.C. Headlam,[3] based on his lectures when he was Regius Professor of Divinity at Oxford in the years following the Great War. The book covers the main Christian doctrines, beginning from the Bible and tracing their development through the Fathers. He states plainly his reason for the scheme – he is training candidates for the ministry of the Church of England and this church has always assumed that its doctrine is that of the ancient church. Modern theology, especially the great theologians of Germany, gets a very scanty mention.

I have often wished that I myself had received that thorough grounding in the Fathers that Headlam had imparted to his students, but our tradition in Scotland was very different and (at the time when I was a student in Glasgow) definitely deficient in patristics. The subject was included in church history rather than theology, for church history was taken to include not only the history of events but also of thought, but the thought was merely summarized by the professors and there was very little in the way of engagement with patristic texts. So I gave my inaugural lecture on what was at the time a very up-to-date issue – the relation of theology and especially the doctrine of creation to the environmental crisis. This was already a hotly-debated topic in the United States, where it had been sparked off in 1968, largely by Rachel Carson's warning book, *Silent Spring*, and then stirred up by the California historian Lynn White, who argued that the Christian doctrine of creation had been one of the major influences leading to a reckless exploitation of earth's resources. Some months before my lecture, Hugh Montefiore, later Bishop of Birmingham, had introduced the environmental question into English theology in his book, *Can Man Survive?*[4] Since then, much has been written on the subject on both sides of the Atlantic, and the question still remains an important one on the theological agenda.

In these early years at Oxford, I worked toward the completion of three books which I had earlier begun in the United States. All three of them were published in 1972. One of them was *The Faith of the People of God*. I had been asked to write this book by Mr Scribner, who suggested a more popular version of my *Principles of Christian Theology*, such as might appeal to laypeople. In a weak moment, I said I would do this, but soon realized that I had taken on a much more difficult task than was at first apparent. Theology, like any other serious study, demands its own technical terms and also a knowledge of its past development. But one could not produce a theology for the laity simply by avoiding technical terms or leaving out explanations of how people came to believe as they did. That would be called nowadays 'dumbing down', and would be an insult to laypeople. Something much more radical than a mere simplification was needed, a different approach. *Principles* has at its centre the philosophical notion of Being, and this is what unifies the book and ties it in with the classical tradition in Christian theology. The book of lay theology needed a different centre. The laity is the people of God, from the Greek word *laos*, 'people'. So a lay theology would be one which makes the people of God its central *motif*, and organizes all the Christian doctrines around this centre. The book was enthusiastically received by Scribner's and had some success, but less than I had hoped.

The second book published in 1972 was *Paths in Spirituality*. It remains one of my own favourites, because it expresses not just my ideas but some of my feelings about things I considered important. I should say that feelings are not just blind emotions, but have a cognitive dimension and can be a mode of perception. I see a close connection between religious experience and aesthetic experience. In aesthetic experience we perceive the beautiful. The beautiful is not just subjective (not just 'in the eye of the beholder') and it is not just emotional, but a complex experience with several dimensions. In religious experience we perceive the holy or numinous. This, I believe, is the root of all religion. It comes before theology, which is our imperfect attempt to give an intellectual (or perhaps better expressed, a thoughtful) explication of the experience. The book was my attempt to describe an alternative to the religionless or secular Christianity being canvassed in the 1960s. It was a recall to the experience of the holy, as it encounters us in various forms. Founded firmly on eucharistic worship, it was written in terms of things which had been meaningful in my own experience, most of them quite traditional. At a time of theological and liturgical confusion, I felt compelled to take a stand for these things, though I made it clear in the book that I was not for a moment denying other forms of spirituality, and their effectualness.

The third book from 1972 was called simply *Existentialism*. This too had been begun in America where I had used some of the chapters as lectures at Union. It was written for a Washington firm which planned to publish a whole series of book-length treatments of themes connected with catholic theology, the whole series adding up to a gigantic theological encyclopaedia. When I mention that I was allowed 100,000 words for my piece on existentialism, the reader will get an idea of the colossal scale of the projected encyclopaedia. It will be no surprise when he or she hears that the enterprise collapsed and the publishing firm went out of business. However, individual items were salvaged, including my own book, which was a critical survey of the main themes of existentialism. After a hardback edition, it was taken up by Penguin and still has a flourishing life.

Another book from this period was *The Concept of Peace*. I had been invited to give a course of lectures at the University of Nottingham, and though I had moved far beyond my youthful flirtations with pacifism, I was still deeply interested in the question of peace. We were still in the period of the 'cold war'. The book, which was quite short, tried to explore the meaning of peace once we get beyond the negative idea that it is simply the absence of armed conflict. A reward of writing the book was to learn that it had been studied by peace-seeking groups in both Northern Ireland and South Africa. It was reissued with a new preface when the cold war came to an end in 1989, but subsequent events have shown that we are still a long way from comprehending what peace requires.

I have mentioned my involvement in ecumenical discussions. In 1975 I decided to set down some of my thoughts on the subject, and the result was a book which I called *Christian Unity and Christian Diversity*. I had by this time come to the conclusion that much of the ecumenical discussion in the earlier part of the century had been a waste of time. First of all, it was wrong to use words like 'ecumenical' if the largest of all the Christian communions, Rome, was not included. Pan-Protestant unions, as they have sometimes been called, simply re-arrange the denominations, and leave untouched the really serious breaches in the Christian church. Second, the older ecumenism aimed at uniting the churches within a given country or region, for example, a 'united church' of Canada, say, or of South India. The idea of a 'national church' is one of the less happy legacies of the Reformation. The Christian church is supposed to transcend national boundaries. But during all the modern period, we have been confronted with the sad spectacle of the national church – not least, the Church of England – lining up behind the political authority and giving its blessing to the nation's warlike activities. Third, the union of churches was conceived in terms of a fairly tight uniformity, more like a merger of institutions than a spiritual coming together that would leave room for legitimate diversity. All three of these disadvantages were overcome in the new situation created by Rome's entry into the ecumenical field. That explains why I had much more positive feelings about ARCIC than about any of the earlier Anglican movements towards fuller church unity. The documents of Vatican II do in fact mention Anglicanism alone among the churches of the Reformation as having retained some catholic characteristics, so that there were good hopes for progress. But obviously there were also formidable obstacles, of which the chief would probably be the papacy. I included a chapter on the papacy in my book of 1975 in which I did acknowledge the seriousness of the obstacle which it might present to many Anglicans. But subsequent discussion with Roman Catholics, perhaps especially with Bishop Butler, led me to be more optimistic. I revised the chapter in the form of a lecture, 'The Papacy in a Unified Church', but this lecture was not given until 1989 in Australia, and it is included in chapter 6 in this book, with a reply by Dr Eamonn Conway.

In my book on *Christian Unity and Christian Diversity*, I went so far as to say that diversity is just as important as unity in the church. Though diversity has become division in church history, this need not be so. A wealth of expression is needed to accommodate the needs of different kinds of people, but if they can agree on the essentials of Christian faith, they can recognize one another and be in communion with one another. There can be 'unity without absorption', to use an expression employed in the Malines conversations between Anglicans and Belgian Catholics in the 1920s. When I lived in America, I was impressed with the fact that, while there is an almost embarrassing pluralism among Christians in that country (there are said to be about 430 denominations!) there is far more support for religion than in most European countries, in most of which one single church or at most a few denominations have a dominant position. The aim should not be to create a monolithic church – and I think this has become increasingly recognized – but a much looser kind of relationship in which there is communion and in which prejudices and hostilities are under control. I have long thought that Rome's relation to the uniate churches supplies a model. I am well aware that historically there have been many difficulties in the uniate relation, but the underlying idea of unity without absorption is a good one.

In 1975 I published another book besides the book on

ecumenism. *Thinking about God* was a collection of essays and lectures given over the previous ten years, including my inaugural lecture at Oxford, and tributes to two deceased colleagues whom I had greatly admired, Ian Henderson at Glasgow and Daniel Day Williams at Union. This book incidentally gained an award from the American Religious Publishers Association.

In 1977 the theological peace in England was disturbed by a controversial book with the deliberately provocative title of *The Myth of God Incarnate*.[5] It was edited by John Hick, a very able philosophical theologian, who had in recent years specialized in the study of world religions. The other contributors included some distinguished scholars, among whom was my colleague, Maurice Wiles. The book had no unified teaching, but was mainly an expression of dissatisfaction with the traditional doctrine of incarnation. To some of the authors, incarnation appeared to be a mythological idea, a point that was not unfamiliar to me, considering my earlier studies of Bultmann. But 'myth' is not really an appropriate term in this context. Apart from the common use of the word to denote something false or irrational, when used in a more technical sense, 'myth' is a story indefinite as to place and time, whereas the story of Jesus has a quite definite setting in first-century Palestine (admittedly with legendary and mythical embellishments); and myth uses highly symbolic narrative language, whereas the Christian doctrine of incarnation finds its normative expression in the philosophical or conceptual language of, say, the Chalcedonian formula or the Athanasian Creed. To other contributors, including Hick himself, the idea of a special incarnation in Jesus Christ seemed like a denial of any value to the non-Christian religions, though to this it could be replied that 'incarnation' (or a similar idea) is found in Indian religion, for instance, in the *Bhagavadgita*, and can be a point of contact rather than a cut-off between religions. In reviewing the book for one of the journals, I argued that incarnation need not be understood in crudely mythological ways, but that the term expresses at least three truths which appear to me to be indispensable to Christianity. 1. The initiative in salvation comes from God. 2. God is deeply immersed in his creation and its affairs. 3. Jesus Christ is the centre of this divine activity in and for the world. Hick's book provoked a good deal of debate. Moreover, it showed the vulnerability of Christian faith in the modern environment, and the need to rethink and re-express its doctrines, which too often are still being expressed in the language of a former age.

I began therefore increasingly to think of christology as the heart of Christian theology. In my student days, I do not think I ever really doubted the reality of God, perhaps because I thought that God (without trying to define 'God' too precisely) is the most rationally satisfying explanation of why there exists anything at all; but I was much more vague about the place of Jesus Christ. For a long time I rebelled against what I thought was the extravagant language of Pascal's famous declaration: 'Jesus Christ is the goal of everything, and the centre to which everything tends. He who knows him knows the reason of all things.' Even today, I can't help wondering if there may be some hint of fanaticism in such words. Yet I see also their supreme importance. They express the central Christian insight of incarnation, which revolutionized the understanding of God derived from natural theology. So far as that vaguely defined God has a character, it is power, and this idea of God lives on even among Christians. Where was Jesus Christ and where was the belief in incarnation in all those centuries when the God whom he called 'Father' was seen as a punishing God or a national God? If *The Myth of God Incarnate* did anything for me, it was to persuade me finally that we cannot speak of God apart from Jesus Christ. Even Kant's rational religion did not attempt to do this. Some such thoughts were in my mind even before the appearance of Hick's book, and found expression in a small book of mine published in 1978, *The Humility of God*. This book was perhaps more a spiritual than a theological writing, but it was based on the theological belief that our thinking about God, even in the mighty act of creation, must be informed by what we see in Jesus Christ.

Two other books from the later years of my time at Christ Church may be mentioned briefly. *Christian Hope* took up a theme that was popular at the time and drew me into discussion about the significance of Christian beliefs concerning the last things. I must confess, however, that such matters are so speculative that I have generally avoided them. Just before my retirement from Christ Church I published another collection of essays (these collections seem to come at ten-yearly intervals!) on *Theology, Church and Ministry*, which included my address on 'The Ordination of Women to the Priesthood', given at the Lambeth Conference of 1978.

But my thoughts kept coming back to christology as the central question on which Christianity stands or falls. I began to think of a writing project larger than any I had so far undertaken – a trilogy, of which the first volume would be a study of the human being in the light of modern knowledge (this too could be called the 'central problem' of theology, for Jesus Christ is certainly human, perhaps even *the* Human Being, the fulfilment of the essential human potentiality); the second volume would be a study of God or the divine; and since the Christian teaching about Jesus is that 'God was in Christ', the third volume would draw on the first two to show how (so far as one could hope to show it) one person, Jesus Christ, can embody humanity and divinity in the 'God-man', as he has been called.

The first volume was written over several years, and took shape bit by bit as I gave lectures in various places. In that volume, I tried to set out the main characteristics which belong to a human being. There were twenty chapters, each designated by a single word – becoming, freedom, embodiment and so on. The emphasis was on the human being as a dynamic self-creating entity whose nature is open to new developments. Looking back, I wonder whether I was too optimistic. I did include a chapter on alienation and sin, but I may have paid too little attention to what may be called the 'mean streak' that seems to be in everyone. This book was published in 1982 with the title *In Search of Humanity*.

In the meantime, I had been invited to give the Gifford Lectures at St Andrews University. These lectures, founded by the Scottish judge Lord Gifford in 1887 are, by the terms of the foundation, to be devoted to 'natural theology'. The interpretation of this expression has been fairly wide during the century, as is shown by the lectures which have been given. I was always myself an avid reader of Gifford Lectures, but now found myself faced with the task of preparing a series of lectures on this difficult subject. However, it fitted in well with my writing programme at that time, for I saw the opportunity to write volume two of my proposed trilogy, which I entitled *In Search of Deity*. I defended the possibility of natural theology, and then presented a series of studies of philosophical concepts of God, beginning with Plotinus, then the one great Celtic philosopher Eriugena, and coming up into modern times. Out of this I tried to distil a dynamic concept of God, just as I had sought a dynamic concept of man. When I look back critically, I doubt if I did justice to St Thomas Aquinas, whom I took as representative of traditional theism. I presented Thomas's conception of God as static, but now I would say that he can be understood in a much more dynamic way, and this has in fact been done by Gilson, by Mascall and by the transcendental Thomists.

I then turned to the third volume of my trilogy, but although I wrote parts of it while still at Christ Church, it was not completed until after I had retired. However, it seems appropriate to mention it here, in conjunction with the preceding volumes. To show the connection with these volumes, it ought perhaps to have been called *In Search of a Divine Humanity* or *In Search of the God-Man*, but these titles, I felt, were too abstract or too off-putting for the average reader, so I settled for *Jesus Christ in Modern Thought*. The book begins from the New Testament witnesses to Jesus Christ and briefly summarizes what I call the 'classical christology' of the creeds and the Fathers, the christology which lasted through the Middle Ages, survived the Reformation, and only began to falter with the Enlightenment. Then I deal in some detail with modern attempts to re-express the significance of Jesus Christ, ending with my own attempt at a reconstruction. Incidentally, this book was awarded the Collins Religious Book Prize of £5000, very useful to someone who by this time was on a retirement pension!

In 1984 Dr Karl Rahner, SJ, whom I had met on several occasions and to whose writings I owed much, celebrated his eightieth birthday. Among the events to mark this occasion was a visit to the Jesuit community in London. I was invited to give a lecture in the presence of this great but modest German scholar, and I chose as my subject 'The Anthropological Approach to Theology', of which Rahner is an outstanding exemplar. The text of the lecture is included in the Appendix to this chapter. Next day Rahner came up to Oxford and visited with us at the Priory House. He then flew back to Innsbruck, where he died very soon after.

My retirement was marked by the presentation to me of a *Festschrift*, entitled *Being and Truth*, edited by two former students, now professors, one in the UK and the other in the US, Alistair Kee and Eugene Long. The publishers were SCM Press, London, who have published most of my books since 1955. It gave me special pleasure that two well-known Japanese Buddhist scholars, Dr Abe and Dr Takeuchi, were among the contributors.

We had spent sixteen very interesting years at Christ Church. But the story does not end there for already I have enjoyed more than twelve years of retirement, and something will be said about these years in the next chapter.

Appendix: Lectures in the UK

Creation and Environment[1]

It has been fashionable in recent years among some theologians to make much of the claim that Western science and technology owe their origins to biblical influences, and especially to the biblical doctrine of creation. Among Protestant writers, Harvey Cox has been one of the best-known proponents of this view. The Hebrew understanding of creation, he claims, 'separates nature from God'. Nature thus becomes 'disenchanted' and can be seen in a 'matter-of-fact' way. 'This disenchantment of the natural world provides an absolute precondition for the development of natural science' and 'makes nature itself available for man's use'.[2] Among Catholic theologians, Johannes Metz has put forward similar views. He writes: 'We could say that where there is no faith in a transcendent Creator, there is also no genuine secularization of the world and no genuine availability of this world to men.' He contrasts the Greek view in which God is a kind of immanent principle of the world and in which the world therefore retains some kind of numinous quality with the Hebrew view in which the world is entirely external to the creator God and therefore itself 'godless', pure world available for man's 'active disposing'.[3]

That there is a measure of truth in the position advocated by the theologians mentioned need not be denied. But their presentation of it is oversimplified and one-sided. Furthermore, some disconcerting conclusions have been drawn from the claims which Cox, Metz and the others have been so anxious to press. It would not be unfair, perhaps, to suppose that at the time when these claims were being made the theologians concerned were hoping to re-establish the relevance to the contemporary world of the somewhat faded doctrine of creation and even to gain for it some reflection of the glamour that is popularly ascribed to science and technology. But in the meanwhile, serious questions have arisen about technology itself. Even in its peaceful applications it has revealed unsuspected ambiguities. In particular, it has already had such far-reaching effects on the environment that if present trends continue unchecked, man's very survival will be threatened through depletion of resources, overpopulation, pollution of various kinds, health hazards and so on. I do not propose to dwell on dismal matters with which we are all familiar, and I do not wish either to seem unduly pessimistic about the outcome, for man has surmounted many appalling difficulties in the past, and one may hope that he will continue to do the same in the future.

But one of the ironies of the new situation is that some secular writers have taken up the theological point that technology has its charter in the Bible, and, instead of reckoning this as a credit to the Bible and an illustration of its continuing relevance, have rather blamed biblical teaching and especially the doctrine of creation as major factors that have contributed to the misuse and consequent deterioration of the environment. Thus Lynn White, in an essay entitled 'The Historical Roots of Our Ecological Crisis' states that 'especially in its Western form, Christianity is the most anthropocentric religion the world has ever seen'. He points out that in the creation stories of the Bible, everything is planned explicitly for 'man's benefit and rule', and that 'it is God's will that man exploit nature'. As far as our ecological crisis is concerned, he thinks that 'Christianity bears a huge burden of guilt'.[4] It should be noted that White is not opposed to Christianity in a general way, and he calls for the renewal of the Franciscan elements in the Christian tradition to promote a better balance.

While Cox and Metz on the one hand and White on the other differ in their evaluation of the doctrine of creation, they are in agreement about its profound effects in shaping Western man's attitude towards nature – effects which continue to this day, even if an explicit acceptance of the doctrine

of creation has been abandoned by large numbers of people.
I believe they are correct in thinking that our practical everyday attitudes are influenced by deep-lying convictions of a
kind that may be called theological or metaphysical or ontological, and that these may continue to exert an influence in
a culture even after they have ceased to be explicit. From this
it would follow, however, that any lasting change in practical attitudes, such as might help us to cope better with the
problems of environment in a technological age, must be
correlated with a change in our deep convictions (perhaps
barely conscious) about man and his relation to the world,
for it is from these convictions that our motivations and
evaluations proceed.

In saying this, I am agreeing with Lynn White that the
problems arising from technology's impact on the environment cannot be solved *only* through the application of more
and better technology. Certainly improved technology must
be part of the answer, but to suppose that the problems of
technology can themselves be solved purely by technology
strikes me as not only superficial but illogical as well. Herbert
Marcuse seems to be much nearer the mark when he declares
that we need 'a new type of man, a different type of human
being, with new needs, capable of finding a qualitatively
different way of life, and of constructing a qualitatively
different environment'.[5] But this seems to me to be virtually
a religious demand, for a new type of man emerges only
where there are fundamentally new evaluations, and those in
turn spring from fundamental convictions of a theological or
metaphysical kind. It is at this point that the theologian may
make his contribution to the problem – a contribution no
more important but surely no less important than those
offered by the technologists in the various fields. The theologian will make his contribution by looking again at the
Christian tradition, by inquiring at what points in the
development of that tradition some elements in it came to be
distorted through an exaggerated emphasis while others got
lost, and by asking what latent resources remain in the tradi-

tion such as might respond to the needs of the present situation by introducing correctives and promoting the new attitudes required.

I have said that the doctrine found in Metz, Gogarten, Cox and other 'secular' theologians of recent times that the biblical doctrine of creation provided the charter for Western science and technology, though partially true, is over-simplified and onesided. This becomes apparent if we attend to a few facts which just do not fit the theory. The Hebrews themselves held to a doctrine of creation for several centuries, but they developed no science worth mentioning, and tech-nologically they were inferior to most of the neighbouring peoples in the arts both of peace and war. The science of the ancient world (though admittedly it was different in import-ant regards from modern science) arose among the Greeks for whom God was not a transcendent creator apart from the world, but rather he belonged to the cosmos or was an immanent world-soul. Again, although all Christians have accepted the doctrine of creation, science and technology have not developed equally among them. Early Christianity did not continue the rising science of Greece. Science and technology, as we know them today, are a relatively late development in Christendom, and even so they have arisen in Western rather than Eastern Christianity. So obviously some refinements and distinctions are needed if we are to dis-entangle the complicated influences that have been at work.

First of all, we may take note that the Hebrew tradition is itself a complex one. It is true that if we confine our attention to the creation stories, we read there of a divine *fiat* which brings into being a world quite external to God the creator. We read also that man is the primary end of the creation, and that he is commanded to subdue the earth. While man is at the centre of both creation stories, there is a remarkable difference between them. In the older story, the creation of man comes first, and he is then provided with a suitable environment. In the later and more sophisticated story, the environment seems to be accorded more importance, for it has to be prepared in successive stages over a period of time before man appears on the scene. As we go on through the Old Testament, however, we come upon other strains which, although never dominant, qualify both the transcendent and the anthropocentric emphases of the creation stories. A notable instance is the covenant which God makes with Noah after the flood. The covenant is made not only with Noah and his descendants, that is to say, with the human race; it is also made 'with every living creature . . . the birds, the cattle, and every beast of the earth' (Gen. 9.10). Again, while the Psalms typically celebrate the deeds of the Lord in the history of Israel, some of them frankly delight in the natural world and recognize God there. 'The heavens declare the glory of God . . . ' (Ps. 19.1). One commentator says about these words, almost in rebuke, that they 'come strangely from the pen of a Hebrew writer', and he claims that this psalm and others in similar vein have introduced non-Hebrew sources.[6] But surely we should be glad that these foreign elements (if they are foreign) have found a place in the Old Testament, thereby tempering the notes of transcendence and anthropocentricity that characterize the mainstream of Hebrew thought. Above all, there is the survival of priestly religion alongside the dominant prophetic religion of the Old Testament, and this priestly religion, though overshadowed, had its indispensable role. Prophetic religion stresses history against nature and upholds the transcendence and otherness of God. Priestly religion smacks rather of the earthy, the immanent, even the pagan. A contemporary Jewish scholar, Richard Rubenstein, writes: 'The priests of ancient Israel wisely never suffered Yahweh entirely to win his war with Baal, Astarte and Anath.'[7] Some elements of an earthy, immanent naturalism remained unexpunged in Hebrew religion, and perhaps they still survive at a deep unconscious level and we see a symptom of this in the incredible attachment of the Jews to the soil of Palestine after so many centuries of exile.

No doubt the dominant model for understanding the relation of God to the world in the Old Testament is what we may call the monarchical model. God is a self-sufficient and transcendent being who by an act of will creates the world external to himself. But, obscure and fragmentary though it may be, there are at least traces of an alternative model which we may call the organic model, a view in which God and the world are not so sharply separated.

With the rise of Christianity, the Hebrew heritage was speedily fused with contributions from Greek thought. The idea of God was profoundly affected by these new influences. Since Greek thought itself contained so many strains, it is difficult to say anything briefly without being guilty of serious oversimplification. We must remember too that its influence had already been felt in Jewish thought before the emergence of Christianity. It is certainly true that in some forms of Greek philosophy, especially the Platonist tradition, God was conceived as so utterly transcendent in his unchangeable perfection that he was beyond the bounds of speech or thought. In the Stoic tradition, on the other hand, God was an immanent world principle. But both views differed sharply from the monarchical model of the dominant Hebrew tradition. In the Greek conception, God, even in his transcendence, was a kind of cosmic absolute, and such a conception leans toward the organic rather than the monarchical model. The world itself might be conceived as eternal, and its relation to God understood in terms of emanation rather than making. Apparently the great Christian thinker Origen took over both of these ideas, though of course, his teaching was deemed to be heterodox. But even if most Christian thinkers did not go as far as Origen in these matters, the general result of the impact of Greek philosophy was to forge closer bonds between God and nature. An important role came to be assigned to natural theology and, even more significantly, to natural law. It was not indeed supposed that even God was subject to a natural law more ultimate than himself, but this law was nevertheless supposed to be inherent in the divine nature and not just a product of the divine will. As Paul Tillich has indicated, the impact of Greek rationalism on the early church forced it to raise the ontological questions hidden in the personalism of Hebrew religion.[8] As a result, there took place a qualification of the monarchical idea of God and its accompanying anthropo-centricity, and this meant in turn a higher estimate of nature and world. Perhaps it was the continuance of these ideas in Eastern Christianity which ensured the different attitude to nature that has prevailed there. And there are also affinities with the non-Christian religions of the east where, if there is an idea of God, he is usually conceived in terms of immanence and an organic relationship to the world.

However, our concern is with the attitudes that have arisen in the West. Long before the secular theologians of recent years had made their claim that science and technology have their origins in the biblical doctrine of creation and certainly long before there was any talk of an ecological crisis, philosopher Michael Foster had published an important article on 'The Christian Doctrine of Creation and the Rise of Modern Natural Science'.[9] Unlike Christian theologians who have tried to eliminate or minimize those elements in Christian teaching inherited from the Greeks in favour of what they would like to consider a purely biblical and revealed faith, Foster was quite clear that a balanced Christianity needs the contributions of the Greeks as well as that of the Hebrews. Concerning the Christian doctrine of creation, he wrote: 'The Christian doctrine on this, as on all other subjects, itself includes an element derived from Greek philosophy, and any doctrine from which all Greek elements are excluded is less than Christian.'[10] He was also clearer than some of the secularizing theologians that the rise of science required not only a doctrine of creation but, more importantly, a knowledge of mathematics. Obviously, we did not get that from the Bible, and perhaps the lack of it accounts for the absence of any science among the ancient Hebrews. But Foster's analysis also shows that from a very early time there was a drive within Christendom to rid Christian doctrine of Greek influence and to return to a pure biblicism, and especially the monarchical model of God. This drive, taking with it elements of Greek rationalism and combining them with an extreme Hebrew voluntarism, made possible, so it is claimed, the harnessing of science to technology and the transformation of the environment that has come about in the modern world. The ancient Greek science, by contrast, was pursued without much regard to its practical applications.

We see the attempt to expel Greek influences already at work in the late Middle Ages. Among the Scotists, natural law arising from the nature of God gave way to the conception of a law based purely on the will of God, while the Ockhamists rejected natural theology to rely on revelation alone. These tendencies reached their most extreme pitch in Calvinism. The sovereignty of God is the keystone of the Calvinist system and the monarchical model of God receives uncompromising expression. Everything happens by the divine will. The world itself is a product of the free act of God's will, and he might equally well have refrained from creating, so that in no sense is the world organic to God. There is a continuous line from Calvin to our time, to Barth, Gogarten, Brunner and finally the secular theologians who have pushed Barthianism to its conclusions. It was Brunner who gave one of the most extreme statements of that utter devaluation and profanation of the world which seems to follow from regarding it as a more or less arbitrary product of will. He put the statement in the form of two equations:

God minus the world = God
The world minus God = Zero

This may well be pure biblical theology, purged of all Greek influences. But it seems to me an acosmism, and possibly also expresses an unconscious will to power.

Concerning this doctrine that the world is the product of divine will and nothing in itself, Ludwig Feuerbach wrote: 'In the inmost depth of thy soul, thou wouldest rather there were no world, for where the world is, there is matter, and where there is matter, there is weight and resistance, space and time, limitation and necessity. Nevertheless, there *is* a world and there *is* matter. How dost thou escape from the dilemma of this contradiction? How dost thou expel the world from thy consciousness, that it may not disturb thee in the beatitude of the unlimited soul? Only by making the world itself a product of will, by giving it an arbitrary existence, always hovering between existence and non existence, always awaiting its annihilation.'[11] And if it is this acosmic or anti-cosmic attitude that has led us to exploit with recklessness and indifference the resources of the world and to subject science increasingly to the service of acquisitive ends, then White's accusation would stand – that Christianity, or at least one influential form of it, bears a huge burden of guilt for some of our present troubles.

The argument I have outlined might be compared at some points to the famous thesis of Weber connecting the rise of capitalism with Protestantism. Reinhold Niebuhr draws attention to a point of contact when he claims that 'the spirit of capitalism is the spirit of an irreverent exploitation of nature, conceived as a treasure house of riches which will guarantee everything which might be regarded as the good life'.[12] It might be added that in this particular regard, there seems to be no difference between capitalism and socialism.

Of course, it must be acknowledged that even in Western Christendom there have been other ways of understanding the meaning of the creation and these have conduced to better practical attitudes towards the natural world. I have mentioned already that White commends St Francis for his sense of affinity with the whole creation. A later example is Luther, who believed that because the world is God's creation, even the meanest objects in nature have some interest and dignity. To mention his own homely example, he says that God is present in a louse's belly. One might contrast this with the obvious contempt shown by Aristophanes for the alleged investigations by Socrates into such humble creatures as fleas and gnats: 'Thrice happy Socrates! It would not be difficult to succeed in a law suit, knowing so much about a gnat's guts!'[13] Karl Jaspers is a modern philosopher who has taken up the view that the Christian doctrine of creation has conferred upon everyday objects an interest which they did not have for the Greeks. But while there are some evidences to support this view, I fear that for the majority the doctrine of voluntary creation has led to depriving the world of intrinsic interest and to causing it to be seen primarily in a utilitarian way as an object for exploitation – a way in which the Greeks did not see it. Still another idea that has sometimes gained currency is that of stewardship. Belief in a creator, it is said, implies that the world is not placed at man's absolute disposal, for he is accountable to God. Unfortunately, however, the notion of a transcendent God who hands over the world to men can easily develop into a kind of deism in which this distant God who started things off has pretty well bowed himself out of the picture, and then there is not much validity left to the notion of stewardship. I think this has happened in some versions of secular theology which stress man's coming of age and his taking over the world – in Gogarten, for example.

Nevertheless, there are other possible ways of using the stewardship idea. Hugh Montefiore, one of the few Christian writers who has tried to face the theological issues raised by the ecological crisis, has rightly seen that 'what is needed is . . . a redirection of inward attitudes'[14] and he believes that this might be achieved through a better awareness of our responsibility as stewards of creation. I believe that the idea of responsibility is of the greatest importance in this connection, but I have some doubt whether it can be adequately supported by a doctrine of stewardship, for in such a doctrine, it seems to me, the world is still considered as a piece of property and primarily from an anthropocentric viewpoint. Perhaps a better model is to be found in Heidegger's idea of man as the shepherd of being.

Least hopeful of all is still another attitude which sometimes clothes itself with religious phraseology – a kind of nostalgic, romantic, sentimental conservationism. This attitude is frequently hypocritical as well, as when Americans and Europeans who enjoy the affluence of technological civilization urge upon Africans or Asians the duty of keeping their forest lands in the unspoiled state in which God has created them. If this means a continuing marginal existence for the peoples of these lands except for the occasional crumbs that might fall from the picnic tables of vacationing tourists from the West, then the plea is likely to go unheard, and deservedly so.

In all parts of the world, science and technology will – if no unforeseen calamities occur – continue to advance, and so will the industrialization and urbanization that accompany them. I do not think we would have it otherwise, and even if we did, I do not think we could reverse the process, for these things have acquired a certain momentum. But it becomes increasingly important to control the process, to set limits to the exploitation of nature, to become sensitive to those points at which, in damaging his environment, man is also damaging himself, not only physically but mentally and spiritually as well. With technology as with so much else, we have still to learn the truth of that ancient piece of moral wisdom, *meden agan*, nothing too much.

We have, however, seen reason to believe that we shall not learn this truth unless there takes place a very profound change in our basic beliefs, so far as these shape our attitude towards the physical environment. As far as Christian theology is concerned, my thesis is that we need to move away somewhat from the monarchical model of God towards the organic model. The monarchical model is deeply entrenched in much traditional Christian language, including the language of liturgy, it is widespread in popular theology, and it is encouraged by those forms of biblical theology which try to exclude all philosophical influences and to found themselves on revelation alone. On the other hand, as the crisis in theism during recent years has shown, the monarchical model of God has become increasingly less credible to many people today. The organic model, by contrast, has gained ground in philosophical theology, and I think most philosophical versions of theism today, even those that proceed from very different schools, tend to the organic type. They seek to recover what was of value in the non-Hebraic elements of the Christian tradition, and especially the affinity between God and the world in opposition to the sharp separation of them. Of course, there is no attempt to isolate these elements. Rather, they have to be integrated into the mainstream of Christian thought on God, but when this happens, they profoundly qualify the monarchical model of God in the direction of the organic model.

If we go back to Brunner's two equations, mentioned earlier, organic theism has no difficulty in accepting one of them, namely, that without God, without the creative Spirit, the world ceases to exist. But it denies the other equation, namely, that without the world God is still God, as if quite unaffected in his majesty and self-sufficiency. For if God is indeed loving and creative Spirit, his creation cannot be a mere arbitrary product of will, so that he might either have created or not have created, or so that he would be un-affected by the absence of a creation. This does not mean that he *needs* to create, but that it is his nature *as God* to create. There is an analogy with natural law, which does not *bind* God but *flows from* him.

But what chiefly concerns us here is that the organic model of theism and of creation allows to the world a dignity and mystery that it could hardly have on the monarchical model. This means in turn that the world cannot be conceived from a narrowly anthropocentric viewpoint, as if it were provided solely for man's exploitation. If, as Christian theologians rethink the meaning of theism, the organic model becomes more influential and is allowed to qualify the monarchical model, then I think this will promote better attitudes towards the physical environment and will perhaps in some measure atone for excesses which in the past may have been encour-aged by the exclusive dominance of the monarchical view.

We shall learn better to relate to the world not only in manipulation but in appreciation. Regarding these two ways, manipulation and appreciation, Abraham Heschel has said: 'In the first way, man sees in what surrounds him things to be handled, forces to be managed, objects to be put to use. In the second way, he sees in what surrounds him things to be acknowledged, understood, valued or admired.'[15] Clearly we have to relate in both ways, and we have to search for the right balance between them.

But a final question remains to trouble us. Is it not too late for this theological rethinking to take place? I do not mean too late in the sense that the environmental crisis is so pressing that there is no time left for the reshaping of our attitudes before the day of reckoning arrives, though that, unfortunately, may be true. I mean rather that it may be too late for any theological model to have an influence because of the decline of theology and the secularization of our outlook. Is either a monarchical or an organic model of God's relation to the world of any relevance when many people have come to think of God himself as a projection of man? Possibly two answers can be given to this question. The first is that the theological understanding of these matters has still a considerable influence, perhaps more than is commonly supposed, and that in any case the theologian does have a duty to address himself to the problems vexing our time and to make what contribution he can from his resources. The second answer is that the position of the humanist may not be so very different, and that he too has to choose between different models. I think it would be true to say that there is a monarchical type of humanism, and there is an organic type. The monarchical type makes man the measure of all things and sets the world over against him as his object. This is the type which would maintain that the problem of technology and environment must be seen as itself a purely technological problem, or a series of such problems. The organic type of humanism is much more aware of man's affinity with the world and recognizes that he is part of something much bigger than he has yet understood and to which he owes a responsibility as yet undefined.

Since the theist believes that man is made in the image of God, then an organic type of theism and an organic type of humanism have some kinship. On the basis of this kinship, adherents of these different beliefs can work together to build up a better and more responsible attitude towards the environment, and so play some part in enabling man to survive the dangers which threaten him.

The Anthropological Approach to Theology[16]

Christian theology is concerned with a single comprehensive truth – the truth of God in Jesus Christ. If we possessed the intellectual powers which Dionysius attributed to the higher celestial beings, we would be able to grasp that truth intuitively in all its fullness. We would receive its total illumination, without obscurities and without distortions. Incidentally, such a state of affairs would render at a stroke all theologians redundant, and their painstaking work, from the careful study of texts to the frustrating search for words in which to give a contemporary interpretation, would be unnecessary. So perhaps it is just as well that we are mere human beings, that our thought proceeds discursively from point to point, that our theology is broken down into manageable units – dogmas, propositions, arguments, opinions. It follows inevitably that any theology will have its blind spots as well as its illuminations and that it will get some things out of proportion. If these defects are to be avoided (so far as it is possible) then the theologian must constantly bear in mind the underlying unity of the truth he seeks, and make explicit the organic connection that links all the items which enter into his theological statement. This means in turn that there must be some unifying perspective, not imposed from outside but drawn from within the matter of theology itself.

Another consequence that follows from what has already been said is that within Christian theology it ought to be possible to take any single doctrine as a starting point, and from it to work through the whole corpus of truth. For if the whole has the organic character that I have claimed for it, then each item belonging to it must, like a Leibnizian monad, be a mirror of the whole. I do believe that any Christian doctrine could serve as a point from which one could reach out into the whole texture of theology, but I do not want to suggest that it is a matter of indifference where one begins. Clearly, the beginning establishes a perspective, and gives a certain character to the complete theological enterprise. Some doctrines are more central and have more ramifications than others. Such a doctrine would be more likely to lead us into an inclusive and balanced appreciation of the whole than a doctrine that is more peripheral and not so obviously inter-woven with the others. Again, there is always the danger that theology may turn into an abstruse intellectual exercise, so it is important to select a doctrine that has existential as well as logical connections with other doctrines and that will there-fore keep before us soteriological concerns, so reminding us that Christian theology has spiritual as well as scientific interests.

The purpose of this lecture is to state the claims for anthro-pology or the doctrine of man as an area of study which fulfils many of the requirements I have just outlined. I make these claims not only because I have myself been long convinced of their validity but because the distinguished theologian in whose honour this lecture is being given, Dr Rahner, has employed the anthropological approach in an extraordinarily fruitful way and the estimate we make of his contribution to theology must in large measure depend upon our opinion about the validity of this way into theological problems.

For obviously the matter is a controversial one. Many of the greatest theologians of the past have begun their investi-gations not from the human end but directly with God, and since theology is precisely discourse about God, it might seem that they were correct in this, and that to begin with anthropology can lead only to a humanism, tricked out perhaps with some Christian terminology but never really finding its way into a genuine theology. So we find St Thomas in his great work beginning with God, his existence, our knowledge of him, his knowledge, will and providence, his trinity and so on, before he turns to the created order, including the human race. The most systematic theologian of the Reformation, John Calvin, begins his exposition of Christian theology by acknowledging the close connection between the knowledge of God and the knowledge of ourselves. 'Our wisdom,' he claims, 'in so far as it ought to be deemed true and solid wisdom, consists almost entirely of two parts: the knowledge of God and of ourselves. But as these are connected together by many ties, it is not easy to determine which of the two precedes and gives birth to the other.'[17] But he goes on to say that a correct method requires us to begin with the knowledge of God, and only in the light of that can we hope to attain to a true self-knowledge. To these two classic exponents of Christianity we may add the greatest Protestant theologian of the present century, Karl Barth. His *Church Dogmatics* begins with the Word of God and he is uncompromising in denying that there is any way by which the human mind could rise from its finite and sinful condition to any genuine theological insight. Natural theology is dismissed as a sinful and arrogant attempt to turn God into an object at our disposal; religion is described as man's attempt to grasp God, and contrasted with the Christian revelation which moves in the opposite direction; there is declared to be no analogy of being (*analogia entis*) relating humanity and deity, and Barth does not conceal his belief that the doctrine of an *analogia entis* is little short of blasphemous. So the weight of opinion among the great theologians would not seem to favour the anthropological approach.

Yet even if the classical approach – and I suppose Barth can be regarded as a late flowering of classical theology, indeed, a conscious imitator of the Reformers – considered it right to place the doctrine of God at the forefront of theology, it does not follow that this approach remains valid for all time or that circumstances might not arise in which it had become simply inappropriate. I believe that in fact such circumstances have now overtaken us. For the first time in history, we find ourselves living in the age of the godless man. I do not mean that we are living in the midst of explicit atheism, though indeed there is a good deal of openly professed atheism, and it is even the officially supported creed of several large and powerful countries. I refer rather to implicit atheism, to the fact that the very concept of God has faded in large measure from the modern consciousness. There was a time when 'God' was a word of everyday use. God's commands were thought to determine what is right and what is wrong; God's providence was supposed to govern the course of this world's happenings, which might then be interpreted as evidences of divine favour or disapproval; in the face of suffering or privation, prayer to God was the natural response. But that whole manner of God-talk has virtually disappeared, together with the beliefs which underlay it. Not only physics and chemistry and astronomy, but ethics and history and human behaviour are discussed and investigated and even (by some rash spirits) 'explained' without reference to God. The word 'God' seems to have become superfluous. Even those who profess to believe in God find it difficult to say precisely what they mean. If there really is a God, we do not find him where people once thought they found him. For a long time, he has been retreating into hiddenness, and we are uncertain where to look. We seem able to get through the day very well without any thought of God. This is what I mean by saying that we live in a godless time. There need not be the conscious or deliberate denial of God. But it cannot be denied that for a great many people he has ceased to be a reality. Dr Rahner has familiarized us with the idea of the 'anonymous Christian', the person who may intellectually profess disbelief but who existentially is committed to those values which for the Christian are concretized in God. Perhaps we should also allow for the idea of the 'anonymous atheist', the person who does not deny God and who may even persist in the outward observances of religion, but for whom it has gone dead, so to speak, and God has become an indistinct blur, the total disappearance of which would make little difference.

If theology aims, as I think it should, at expounding Christian faith in as clear and intelligible a way as the subject matter will allow, then it must take account of the mentality of those to whom it is addressed. The theme of theology is and must remain God (for a theology in which 'God is dead' is a mere contradiction), but in a godless time such as I have described, one cannot put the doctrine of God at the beginning. The approach must be more indirect, or the result will be failure to communicate, misapprehension and incomprehension. Nor could one say that perhaps in apologetic theology, a different approach is permissible, but that in dogmatic theology, the traditional order that begins from God must be maintained. I would reply that the distinction between apologetics and dogmatics has now disappeared. The mood of godlessness (which is perhaps not culpable) has moved within the church, so that God is a problem to the believer as well as to the unbeliever. All dogmatic theology must therefore be at the same time an apologetic theology, though conversely the best apologetic theology is also dogmatic theology, letting the great Christian doctrines be clearly seen in their own light.

It was at the time when the Enlightenment was eroding the idea of a supernatural revelation and was even placing in question the God of natural religion that the anthropological approach to theology found its first powerful expression. This, of course, was in the work of Schleiermacher. Dogmas were declared to be, in the first instance, transcripts of human experience, having only an indirect reference to God. The new direction of theology, though apparent in all Schleiermacher's teaching, is especially clear in his treatment of christology. The traditional language of descent is virtually eliminated or radically reinterpreted, the Chalcedonian doctrine of two natures is acutely criticized, and the heart of the new christology is the affirmation that Christ is the completion of the creation of humanity.[18] It was not, of course, Schleiermacher's intention to make Christianity a purely subjective affair, but the danger that his anthropocentrism could lead to such results was heavily underscored two or three decades later when Feuerbach argued that God is nothing but a projection of the human consciousness, an idealized human nature which has been objectified and to which has been ascribed an independent existence. Surprisingly, Feuerbach's view has been taken up by Barth, who argues that any attempt to move from the side of the human to the divine can never arrive at any genuine knowledge of God but can end up only by putting in God's place the idolatrous projections of the human mind. But this is a dangerous game to play, for why should Barth's own thought of God be an exception? He indeed claims that it is based on a revelation coming to us from beyond ourselves and therefore possessing objectivity, but the projectionist would reply that this supposedly revealed God is, just as much as any other, a fabrication of the human mind, and his alleged objectivity is an illusion. The threat to Christian theology arising from Feuerbach and other advocates of a projection theory of religion is not confined to theologians who have employed an anthropological approach, though admittedly Feuerbach did think that Schleiermacher's teaching was a virtual admission that God has no existence beyond the subjectivity of the believer.

Barth, following Calvin, has another reason for believing that any move from the manward side towards God can lead only to an idol or false God. This is his understanding of sin. Even allowing that an understanding of the being and nature of God might be discernible in the created order, including the human being or even especially in the human being, it would be impossible for us to perceive this because our understanding is blinded and distorted by sin. Sin has infected not only the moral being of man, but his whole being, including his powers of understanding. The image of God is not to take sin seriously. But what would this mean – 'not to take sin seriously'? No doubt sin has been taken with varying degrees of seriousness at different epochs of history. At the time of the Reformation, sin weighed very heavily on people's consciences. In the nineteenth century, a time of optimism and supposedly of progress, the category of sin virtually disappeared from the writings of liberal theologians. Barth and Niebuhr and others did an undoubted service in bringing back the doctrine of sin in the early decades of this century. But as the century nears its close, the earlier emphasis on sin has been muted among theologians (perhaps especially Catholic theologians) and one hears instead talk of hope and human transcendence. I come back to the question, 'What does it mean to take sin seriously'? Anyone who denies the presence of sin in human life is simply unrealistic, but it does not follow that the alternative is to ascribe to sin that totally disabling character which we find in the tradition which runs from Calvin to Barth. The scepticism which it engenders is, like all scepticism, finally self-destroying, for if the human mind is so disabled that it cannot discern any traces of God in the created order, how could it possibly recognize the presence of God in Jesus Christ? The revelation is made impossible, and so is the very idea of incarnation as God's self-communication.

Incidentally, in replying to these objections to the anthropological approach in theology, I have at the same time denied that there is any sharp distinction between natural and revealed theology, just as I earlier called in question the distinction between apologetics and dogmatics. It is not possible to reject natural theology and cling to revealed theology alone. The two stand or fall together. All natural theology is revealed theology, in the sense that, as Newman claimed, there is no 'unaided' knowledge of God, though there is a genuine self-communication of God given in and through the created order, and this may properly be called 'revelation', though it is distinct from the specific revelations of Christian and biblical faith. On the other hand, all revealed theology is natural theology, in the sense that the specific revelations of faith are communicated through this-worldly realities. To say otherwise would, I have suggested, amount to an implicit denial of the possibility of incarnation and would drive one in the direction of some docetic or gnostic view.

But having, at least in a provisional way, defended the anthropological approach against some of the more obvious criticisms, what is to be said affirmatively in its favour? It is to stating the affirmative case that we must turn in the remaining sections of this lecture.

I think the first point to be made is that to begin the exposition of Christian truth from the consideration of human nature is, in a secular time, a sound educational method. If it is true that the very word 'God' has to a large extent fallen out of serious use and that even nominal believers have only the vaguest idea of what they mean by the word and, for practical purposes, live as if there were no God, so that, as I suggested, not, I hope, too unkindly, they are in fact 'anonymous atheists' – if all that is so, then it would seem very odd indeed to begin expounding Christianity, even within the church, by talking about the word of God or the revelation of God. These concepts will, and in any genuinely Christian theology, must be encountered, but only further down the road. Bernard Lonergan has declared that a presupposition for entering into the study of theology is what he called 'orientation to transcendental mystery'.[19] These words were well chosen. He did not insist on an explicit belief in God, but only openness toward transcendence. There has to be orientation and preparation before the mind that has been shaped in a godless age is able to hear in any meaningful way that word 'God', which can be both the fullest and the emptiest of all. As Martin Buber once said, the word 'God' has become the most misused and heavily burdened of all.[20] To rehabilitate this word and to let it be understood in something like its Christian sense, we have to go back to those situations where the everyday talking of the secular world has come to the end of its resources and is confronted with a mystery, the mystery which we name as 'God', though without supposing that by naming it we have also comprehended it. But to explore these situations where faith and theology have their origins is to explore the human condition. This is a low-key approach to theology, but it begins where people really are and by using the language that is current among them. And this is not just an educational or apologetic device, but can be seen as theological obedience to the incarnation, in which God came into the human condition and stood beside human beings in solidarity with them, even in their godlessness and sin. The way into theology which I have been describing may be compared with an important principle recognized by Newman and his collaborators in the Oxford Movement. This was called the 'principle of reserve'. Perhaps it reflects the divine incognito of the incarnation itself. The expression of revelation is indirect, and there is always more to be learned. The theologian who employs reserve tries not to be too explicit or exhaustive in his treatment of Christian doctrine, but holds something back in order that, having so to speak whetted the appetite of the learner, he may lead him into deeper truth and ultimately to the point where he recognizes that the deepest truth is ineffable. Only in some such way can the teacher be true to God and make sure that he does not profane the mystery. We find Newman himself writing: 'Religious men are very reserved, if only that they dare not betray, if we may so speak, God's confidence.'[21] A commentator has offered the following definition: 'Reserve is concerned with fostering the reverence due to sacred things by withholding them until men are ready to receive them.'[22] This is surely needed above all when one speaks of the final mystery of Holy Being which we name 'God'.

The connection of the foregoing remarks with the question of the appropriateness of taking anthropology as the vestibule to theology is, I think, obvious. Human nature is unquestionably a this-worldly phenomenon, and the question about the true nature and destiny of man has become for the contemporary secular person just as urgent and irresistible as the question of God appears to have become otiose and dispensable. But this question about the human being, while it begins within the horizons of the empirical, does not remain there. The empirical investigation of the human being comes up against limits where, to use the expression popularized by sociologist Peter Berger, we receive 'signals of transcendence'.[23] Human freedom, which, in practice, is assumed by everyone, is perhaps the fundamental human characteristic that breaks out beyond the empirical. Even so severe a critic of speculative metaphysics as Kant was prepared to admit that with the knowledge of my own freedom 'the fact that a being (I myself) belonging to the world of sense, belongs also to the supersensible world, this is also positively *known*, and thus the reality of the supersensible world is established, and in practical respects *definitely* given'.[24] There is hardly a modern philosophical anthropology that has not taken up the theme of human transcendence, so that if the transcendence of God has now become veiled to us, there has been a rediscovery of transcendence at the centre of human existence. This notion of transcendence plays a key role in the new expression of Thomism developed by Lonergan and others. Even neo-Marxists speak now of transcendence, and although I do not think that the actual word was used by Marx himself, something very close to the idea of transcendence was present in his philosophy. Atheistic existentialists also – Sartre is an example – have found it necessary to introduce the idea of transcendence into their analyses of human existence. All of these philosophical anthropologies have come to regard the human person as an unfinished and dynamic being, thrusting toward a fulfilment, both individual and social, that lies indefinitely ahead.

But has this human transcendence anything to do with what theologians have called the transcendence of God, or is this relocation of transcendence in the human being just one more evidence of the secularization of thought and the final erosion through the absorption of its most distinctive characteristic into the human? To this question, one may reply that the philosophers concerned have set no bounds to human transcendence. What is taking place here is not the finitization of transcendence, but the recognition of an openness in man reaching towards the infinite. Man is the finite being who nevertheless has the sense and taste for the infinite. What is the mystery constituting the goal of human transcendence if it is not God? Is not this transcendence which we find within ourselves that 'orientation to transcendental mystery' of which Lonergan has spoken and which he regards as the *sine qua non* of the theological quest?

Admittedly, the two kinds of transcendence, the human and the divine, do not precisely coincide. But here we may ask whether we should not revise our understanding of the divine transcendence in the light of the transcendence that we know directly in human experience. This human transcendence, as we have seen, is an intensely dynamic idea – it is the drive to go beyond. Has not our theological understanding of divine transcendence been, on the contrary, far too static? By the transcendence of God, we have understood primarily his otherness and distance from the created order. But what if the transcendence of God is also dynamic, the energy of the divine love thrusting out beyond, God's *exitus* into the world of the finite? Some such idea comes to expression in a striking passage in the writings of Dionysius. He says: 'And we must dare to affirm (for it is true) that the Creator of the universe himself, in his beautiful and good yearning towards the universe, is through the excessive yearning of his goodness transported out of himself in his providential activities towards all things that have being, and is touched by the sweet spell of goodness, love and yearning, and so is drawn from his transcendent throne above all things, to dwell in the heart of all things, through an ecstatic power that is above being and whereby he yet stays within himself.'[25] This is not the static transcendence of a lordly monarchical God, but the active transcendence of a God of love. It is therefore untouched by the objections of those philosophers who would say that a transcendent God is oppressive, and incompatible with the reality of human transcendence. On the contrary, the transcendence of God, understood in dynamic terms, is precisely his self-emptying (*kenosis*) and his coming to dwell at the heart of creation. Paradoxically therefore his transcendence coincides with his immanence, the supreme instance of the *coincidentia oppositorum*.

Another way in which the transcendence of the human being points to the mystery of God can be seen when we contemplate the natural world as a whole. As I have pointed out, the trend of thought for several centuries has been leading us in the direction of taking the world as something grounded in itself and needing no reality more ultimate than itself to account for it. If the natural world has this self-completeness, then there is no God and even human transcendence is a limited inner-worldly phenomenon. But if there is a reality more ultimate than nature and transcending nature, then perhaps there is something in the world that points to it. Surely it is the existence of humanity, the form of being that has made a breach in nature through its freedom, that does so point beyond the natural world. There may be other mysteries even at the level of physical reality that point beyond themselves, but we can never be sure whether these are not simply gaps in our knowledge that will eventually be filled in. Man alone seems to be the irreducible mystery, the place where finite and infinite meet and so the place where an orientation to transcendental mystery becomes possible.

Let me express the point in still a third way. From ancient times, the human being has been described as a microcosm. He is so because he sums up in himself all the levels of being that we can observe in the universe – the physico-chemical, the organic, the sentient, the rational, the personal and whatever intermediate levels one might want to add. The idea of the human being as a microcosm was taken just one step further by Leibniz. In his view, a human being mirrors not only the universe but, as gifted with mind and personality, God himself in his relation to the world. 'Minds', he declares, 'are also images of the deity or the author of nature himself, capable of knowing the system of the universe and, to some extent, of imitating it through their own inventions.'[26] So Leibniz can say that each human being or spirit is like a 'little god' in its own world. For this, of course, one may appeal to the Bible, with its teaching that the first human couple were made in 'the image and likeness of God' (Gen. 1.26).

So far, except for the very last sentence, I have been moving in the area of natural theology. The whole claim that man is the initial datum for theological reflection is enormously strengthened when we turn to the Christian revelation and specifically to the doctrine of incarnation. For according to this teaching, God has made himself known in and through a human person. We could on the one hand say that in Jesus Christ humanity was brought to that level of transcendence at which the image and likeness of God, obscured in our humanity through sin, has been brought to its full and explicit realization. I think this is what Dr Rahner had in mind when he stated, surely in a very strong form of words: 'Only someone who forgets that the essence of man . . . is to be unbounded . . . can suppose that it is impossible for there to be a man, who, precisely by being man in the fullest sense (which we never attain), is God's existence into the world.'[27] I think too that this is not far from Schleiermacher's description of Jesus Christ as the 'completion of the creation of man'.[28]

But something remains to be said. This is neither projection of the human image on an imaginary God nor is it a reduced and merely reductionist christology. Indeed, the antithesis between adoptionism and incarnationism is a false one. These two are complementary. A human being can manifest the being of God only because God himself has descended into the created order. There can be a divinity in man only because there is already a humanity in God. At this point we can pay Karl Barth his just due, but while he was right in affirming the ontological priority of God in this as in everything, and we would have no desire to differ from him on this point, it leaves unchanged our own contention that in the order of knowing, there is a legitimate and indeed compelling way that leads from the knowledge of the human to the knowledge of the divine.

5

Retirement

The retirement age at Oxford is sixty-seven, so I completed my duties as Lady Margaret Professor at the end of the academic year in 1986. Among other things, this meant that we had to move out of the Priory House. So where should we go? Jenny and I both felt the pull of Scotland quite strongly. We have a son in Glasgow and a daughter in Inverness. But we also have a son in Oxford. It was a long time since we had left Scotland and, apart from the son and daughter mentioned above, we have nowadays few personal ties remaining in that part of the world. I had seen several examples of people retiring back to their native areas, and then finding themselves rather isolated. On the other hand, we had made many good friends in the south. Oxford is in many ways an ideal place to live in, especially for an academic, and when compared with Scotland, the climate is just a little bit better.

So we decided to stay on in Oxford. We had in 1972 bought a house in the pleasant suburb of Headington. That was a time when house prices were rising rapidly, and we had bought the house not with a view to retirement but simply to have a piece of real estate before prices became impossibly high. But now we saw that it had considerable attractiveness as our retirement home. It is small and so is the garden, and so it does not demand too much attention. It was important to me to keep my library, for which of course there had been plenty of space in the Priory House, but there was a good loft in Headington, so I had it strengthened, shelved and provided with easy access, and we have lived here very comfortably.

Also, there are very good road and rail communications from Oxford and a regular coach service to the London airports, so I think our decision to stay here was a wise one.

We were obviously going to miss the cathedral and its splendid music, but there is much to be said for belonging to a parish church. Headington, for most of its long history, was a village outside the city limits of Oxford, and although it is now within the city, it preserves something of its earlier character. Its centre is St Andrew's Church, founded in the twelfth century and still graced by a fine Norman chancel arch. Our services at the cathedral had been solidly traditional, and I wondered how I would take to the modern liturgy in use at St Andrew's. However, the transition was less painful than I had expected, and it has been my privilege to have functioned there as an honorary curate, much as I had done at St Mary's, Manhattanville, near Union Theological Seminary in New York.

One of the great benefits of retirement is that it is no longer necessary to attend the endless meetings of committees, faculties, governing bodies of one kind or another, that are a feature of university life. I was never a great enthusiast for high table and senior common room, so I did not miss these very much. I still have the privileges of dining or lunching at Christ Church when I wish to do so, and (what is perhaps even more valuable) of parking my car in the college precincts in the very heart of Oxford.

If someone has been studying, teaching and writing for three or four decades, these activities have become so much a part of his/her life that the person concerned cannot give them up. I have noticed that when such a person has, for one reason or another, been compelled to give up these activities on retirement, very often there has followed a speedy decline.

As I mentioned, I made a special effort to retain my books on retirement, and have made constant use of them, for if one is seriously engaged in theology (or, I suppose, any other demanding subject), there is no end to that study. On the one hand, an effort must be made to keep up with new developments, at least in a general way. But one of the great advantages of retirement is that one has time to read very long books, or books outside one's immediate interests, which there was not time to read when actively engaged in the day-to-day duties of a university professor or lecturer. For instance, not long ago I read the four volumes (about 2000 pages) of Liddon's *Life of Edward Bouverie Pusey*. I would never have found time for this during my active teaching years, for it is only tangential to systematic theology, yet it is a wonderful panorama of Anglican life in the nineteenth century. Karl Barth's principal legacy, his *Church Dogmatics*, still unfinished at his death, but in the English edition occupying twelve large volumes clad in solemn black and containing (so I learned somewhere) 6,000,000 words, is something which I think I read very laboriously in bits during my teaching years, but now I can read it relaxed and at leisure, and find it very good spiritual reading even if I have theological disagreements. So one can say that in retirement it is still possible to be an active student, but free of the pressures that go with one's earlier studies.

But teaching too gets a grip on the person who teaches, and it is not easy just to give it up. So I have continued to lecture and even to give occasional tutorials. In the very first year of our retirement, my friend Professor William Green, whom I have known since the 1950s and who taught for many years in the Episcopal Seminary at Austin, Texas, was going on a sabbatical leave, and asked me to look after his students during his absence. This was a very good experience for both Jenny and myself. It meant that we had to continue something we enjoyed doing, yet without pressures, for a visiting professor is spared the harassments of administration. Moreover, we were able to escape the rigours of a British winter and it all helped to ease the transition from working life to retirement.

Writing also seems to be addictive. I mentioned in the last chapter that I had still not finished my trilogy on humanity – deity – christhood when I left Christ Church. I was able to do the research for this volume partly by lecturing on christology in Texas and partly in preparing a long article on the subject for the German *Theologische Realenzyclopedie*. I delivered the text to SCM Press in London in late 1989, and it was published in 1990 as *Jesus Christ in Modern Thought*. From then on, I have been publishing approximately one book each year.

In 1991, the book was *Mary for All Christians*. I had been for several years a member of the Ecumenical Society of the Blessed Virgin Mary and had given papers at some of its meetings. In this book I was again as a Catholic Anglican seeking to foster the relation to Rome, while at the same time showing that non-Romans have nothing to fear from a positive appreciation of Mary's place in the church and in the Christian scheme of salvation. The ecumenical society, to which I have referred, has not only Anglicans and Roman Catholics in its membership, but also Methodists and Presbyterians. I deliberately included in the book chapters on the Immaculate Conception and Assumption of Mary, and on the notion of Mary as Corredemptrix, knowing that these ideas are highly controversial, but believing that they contain truths which, if properly interpreted, are implicates of central Christain teachings, and so acceptable to all Christians. Whether I succeeded is not for me to say, but I was agreeably surprised by the friendly reviews which the book elicited from both Catholic and Protestant writers. I am sure that the reception of the book was greatly helped by the front cover, on which, with the permission of the National Gallery, there was reproduced Velazquez' great painting, 'The Immaculate Conception'.

No more books were published until 1994, which saw two. One was a short book intended for inquirers or for Christians who felt that they needed to rethink the basis of their faith. It began as a series of Lenten addresses given at the parish church of Headington, and was first of all issued in aid of a church extension plan by a local publisher, Harold Copeman, with the title, *Starting from Scratch*, but when the local demand had been satisfied, it was taken up a year later by SCM Press and given a wider circulation with the title *Invitation to Faith*. It is very much a 'back to basics' book, with chapters on faith, God, Christ and the church. The second book, based on a series of Hensley Henson Lectures at Oxford, was called *Heidegger and Christianity*. I had published a short book on Heidegger in 1968, while the philosopher was still alive, but he had died in 1976 and I thought that there was need for a somewhat fuller study of his thought and its relation to Christianity. This is a complex and controversial subject, mainly because Heidegger was a member of the Nazi party in the 1930s. After the war, however, he was exonerated from serious involvement and was allowed to continue to lecture at Freiburg. I shall not go into the question again, but I think I was justified in saying that his philosophy is 'highly compatible' with Christianity. How else could people like Bultmann, Tillich and Rahner have made such an extensive use of it? Heidegger was by no means the only famous German philosopher to have embraced nationalism in the past two hundred years, or the only one holding such views to have been taken up by theologians. Here of course another difficult question comes up – the relation of someone's personal opinions to that person's professional competence as a philosopher, politician or whatever it may be.

In 1995 my main publication was a book which I called *The Mediators* with the subtitle 'Nine Stars in the Human Sky'. This was a series of studies of nine major prophets or founders of religions, beginning chronologically with Moses and ending with Muhammad, and including Jesus Christ. In writing this, I was returning to a subject that had fascinated me since student days, namely, the non-Christian religions and their relation to Christianity. I think that my first published treatment of the subject was an article of 1964 appearing in the *Union Seminary Quarterly Review*, entitled 'Christianity and Other Faiths'. I deliberately used the word 'faith' in this title to indicate my disagreement with the

Barthian attempt to monopolize the word 'faith' for
Christianity and to denigrate non-Christian approaches to
God as 'religions', a word which Barth used in a bad sense to
denote human attempts to grasp at God, and which he
believed to be devoid of any self-revelation of God to his
creatures. The article was in the main a defence of the
religions against this Barthian dismissal, which at that time
was very influential, both among theologians and in the
World Council of Churches. I did not, however, advocate a
relativism, such as has seemed at a later time to have been
advocated by John Hick and others. Nevertheless, the article
was sufficiently controversial at that time to provoke some
responses in the next issue of the journal. In *The Mediators* I
do not think I was advocating a position very different from
that of the 1964 article, but I was able to go into more detail
and I hope that during the thirty years that had elapsed
between the two writings, I had made some advances with
the problem and was able to give a clearer statement of what
might be involved in maintaining the balance between an
openness to whatever is true in the non-Christian religions
and a commitment to Christian faith as the avenue by which
God had become a reality to me. Some reviewers question the
appropriateness of the term 'mediator'. I did in fact choose it
after a good deal of reflection. I do not say that it is entirely
adequate, but it was the most general term I could find. Some
of the great religious leaders could be called 'saviours', but
the title would not be suitable for others; all of them, I
suppose, were 'teachers', but they were more than teachers,
just as their messages had more than an intellectual content;
another possible title would be 'prophets', but perhaps this
word is too closely associated with the Jewish and Christian
traditions, and leaves out the mystics. I chose 'mediator'
because I think all or most of them had at some point a
visionary, revelatory or conversion experience which they felt
they had to transmit to their fellows. I quoted in the book
some lines from the poet Friedrich Hölderlin, who was
actually thinking of poets when he wrote:

Yet it behoves us, under the storms of God,
Ye poets, with uncovered head to stand,
With our own hand to grasp the Father's lightning-flash
And to pass on, clothed in words,
The divine gift to the people.[1]

It seems to me that the 'religious geniuses' discussed in the book had a vision of a spirituality which some of them called God, others by a different name, but it was something of highest importance that they felt impelled to pass on. In that sense, I called them mediators between God and his human creatures.

I did not publish any book in 1996, but I did give two sets of lectures on the Christian sacraments, and by the end of the year had organized this material in the form of a book which I entitled *A Guide to the Sacraments*. The word 'guide' in this title was chosen deliberately. The book was not meant to be either a detailed theological treatment of the sacraments or a historical study of their origin and development, though of course both theology and history and even a certain amount of philosophy are involved when we try to analyse and vindicate the sacramental principle in our understanding of human existence in the world. The book was meant to be rather an educational and even pastoral essay, intended to lead both clergy and laypeople into a deeper understanding and appreciation of the sacraments. Again, this was a book with which I could fully identify, for I was not just writing about an interesting subject, but expressing something of my own feelings and experience. The book was published in 1997.

In the meantime, I had been invited to give a series of lectures (The Albert Cardinal Meyer Memorial Lectures) at Mundelein Seminary, currently the largest Roman Catholic Seminary in the United States, situated not far from Chicago. I chose for the theme christology, and the book which resulted from it was entitled *Christology Revisited*. It was 'revisited' because I had already written at length on christology both in *Jesus Christ in Modern Thought* and in *Principles of Christian Theology*, and because the theme of christology is apparently an inexhaustible one, and every theologian keeps revisiting it as long as he theologizes. I don't think this book introduced any major changes from what I had written before, but I tried to make some things clearer and more explicit, for example, the complexity of factors that enter into our knowledge of Jesus Christ.

During the years of retirement, I have continued to travel around giving lectures or preaching sermons. Most of these travels have been in areas where I have been before – the British Isles, the United States, Canada, Australia, Italy, Scandinavia – but two of these journeys are worth mentioning, for they had thitherto been off limits to lecturing theologians. One was the Soviet Union, where Gorbachev came to power in the late 1980s, and *glasnost* or 'openness' became the slogan. I had long before resolved that I would never go to Russia even as a tourist while the country was still under the Soviet régime. I remember the thrill of hearing and seeing on British television that the Russian Patriarch had celebrated the eucharist in St Basil's Cathedral for the first time in about seventy years. It was in 1991 that I received an invitation to give a paper at a conference in Moscow, to be held at the Soviet Academy of the Social Sciences. The general subject of the conference was 'Religion and Culture'. I wondered what I would choose as the theme of my paper. To talk directly about God might be very difficult in a society that for so long had repressed Christianity. So once again I found myself drawn towards an anthropological approach, something that had long underlain my own theologizing, from my existentialist phase until my encounter with Rahner at his birthday celebrations. The title of my lecture was: 'The Human Being as the Central Problem for Theology'. After all, was it not a Russian, Nikolai Berdyaev, a one-time communist, who had said, 'The one and only reason for belief in God is the existence of the divine element in man' – a sentence which I had quoted in my book, *Twentieth-Century Religious*

Thought. The lecture, which is included in full in the Appendix to this chapter, argued for a spiritual dimension within humanity.

I was able to have some conversation with members of the conference who spoke English, and was impressed by their seriousness and also by their friendly attitude. I saw the sights of Moscow, including the carefully preserved churches (they are called 'cathedrals') within the walls of the Kremlin, and St Basil's Cathedral in the Red Square. This cathedral is a masterpiece of complex architecture, though there is no large interior space but rather a series of interconnected chapels. I was so impressed with it all that I decided I must take my wife to see it, so in the following year we went as tourists on a trip to Moscow and St Petersburg (which we had grown up calling Leningrad).

The second trip into a former 'no go' area was even more exciting. The reason for this visit was that back in 1980 I had been surprised to receive a letter from a Chinese graduate student who had written a thesis on my own work for his doctorate at the Chinese Academy of Social Sciences. He had in the meanwhile become a professor at the Academy and he persuaded his colleagues to invite me to go to Beijing to lecture and have conversations. Jenny accompanied me on this visit. There is a direct flight non-stop from London to Beijing, where we were met at the airport and taken to a western-style hotel. Professor He Guanghu has now translated three of my books into Chinese, including *Principles of Christian Theology*, which, written in Pinyin, the official romanized spelling of Chinese, is *Jí Dú Jiaò Shón Xúe Yuán Lî*. The book looks very impressive when printed in the traditional Chinese characters which, unfortunately, I cannot read, but I am enormously indebted to Professor He for his labours in translating these books into Chinese. He also acted as translator at my lectures in Beijing. Allowing for the extra time needed for Professor He to read paragraph by paragraph in Chinese after I had spoken them in English, and then to allow for similar duplication of questions and answers, a session took about three hours. Again I had to wonder what would be suitable topics. At the Academy, I spoke on 'Dialogue among the World Religions'. The Academy includes an Institute of World Religions, and although until recently the subject had to be treated in accordance with Marxist theory, this is no longer the case, and I was completely free to say what I wanted to say. The lecture forms part of the Appendix to this chapter.

My other major lecture was given at Peking University,[2] where I was the first British theologian to give a lecture on theology since the communist revolution of 1949. Here I chose as subject 'The Ebb and Flow of Hope: Christian Theology at the End of the Second Millennium'. The lecture sketched the changing moods of Western theologians from 1900 onwards. I was impressed by the questions asked, which showed that the audience, mostly students, were certainly not ignorant of the subject. This lecture too is included in the Appendix at the end of the present chapter.

Our stay in Beijing included a Sunday, and we were given the opportunity to attend church. The churches are restricted in many ways and there are few of them in Beijing which, with its suburbs, is a bustling city of eleven million people. Nevertheless, the experience was encouraging. We were taken to an old church which looked as if it had been there since imperial times. Inside there were a thousand people, with around two hundred sitting in a courtyard outside. There was an excellent public address system and a robed choir. Four clergy took part, the sermon being given by the Bishop of California. The most striking moment came when, after a reading of Acts chapter 10 – and almost like a re-enactment of it – fifty adults were presented for baptism. They appeared to cover all ages, and all sections of the population. On days when I had no teaching duties, a car would come to the hotel and take us off to see the Great Wall and other sights of the city, with one of the professors as guide. So we came back feeling that we had had a very friendly reception.

This brings the story up to date, since the only other book to mention is the one you are presently reading. Whether it will be the last, I do not know. There is, however, one more chapter to write. It did not quite fit in to the chronology and has its origins in several of the earlier chapters, but it deals with an important subject.

Appendix: Lectures in Moscow and China

The Human Being as the Central Problem
for Theology[1]

Ever since human beings became self-conscious, their own being has been a question for them. Many conflicting answers have been given, ranging from the materialist view that a human being is no more than an animal with a highly developed brain conjoined with a more than commonly aggressive temperament to the belief of Gnostics and others that human beings have somehow strayed into this earthly environment from an original homeland of pure spirit. Whatever answers have been given, they seem to contain elements of paradox or even of contradiction. Are we any further forward today, in spite of all the sophistication of the twentieth century? Or must we still join in the schizophrenic confession of that prototype of the modern Western man, Goethe's Faust:

> Two souls, alas! Reside within my breast,
> And each is eager for a separation.[2]

And if we do think in this way, are we resigned to a separation or do we hope that a reconciliation is still possible? Certainly, a great deal depends on how we resolve this question. For theories that try to answer the question about the nature of the human being become themselves a constitutive element in that being, having a profound influence on the goals which such a being chooses and on the relations established with other human beings.

Even in the two centuries that have elapsed since Goethe wrote the first part of his great work, our situation seems to have become more complicated. Are there only two souls that struggle within us, or are we like the Gadarene demoniac in the sense that a legion of different images and theories and ideologies compete for our allegiance? There are indeed many images or conceptions of the human being proliferating in the world today, but at the risk of over-simplification, I suggest that they could be arranged on a spectrum which would reveal a basic distinction between two types of anthropology, and that these might be called respectively 'naturalistic' and 'personalistic'. The naturalistic type will probably have departed far from the kind of materialism that was common in the eighteenth and nineteenth centuries, but would still think of a human being as a phenomenon, however complex, that is explicable in terms of the laws regulating the behaviour of the physical universe. The personalistic type may have departed equally far from any purely idealist or spiritualist conception of the human being, but continues to believe that there is a distinctive element in humanity, by which it is marked off from the merely natural forms of being.

At the present time, a naturalistic view of man is widely accepted in the societies of Europe and North America, especially perhaps among scientists. In the pre-scientific and pre-Enlightenment age, it was not difficult to believe that the human race has a privileged position in the universe, and so it was not difficult to believe that there is a sharp division between the human level of existence and what were regarded as lower levels, both animate and inanimate. A series of body-blows has been dealt to the presuppositions on which the belief on the privileged position of humanity rested. First, the earth was seen to be not the centre of the universe but a planet belonging to an undistinguished star located in one of a vast multitude of galaxies, so that even if the human race stood high in the terrestrial hierarchy, this might not count for much in the cosmos as a whole. Then the cosmic time scale had to be expanded, far beyond anything that had earlier been surmised or that the human mind can imagine, and it became apparent that the largest part by far of this cosmic history has taken place and indeed is still taking place without any human participation. Next, the theory of evolution showed that human beings are not a special creation introduced into this world from elsewhere, but have evolved out of a common stream of life. Biochemists in turn have shown that human life has its material basis in the same chemical affinities and responses that are found throughout the animal kingdom, so that, in the words of Sir Charles Sherrington, 'The body of a worm and the face of a man are alike chemical response.'[3] More recently still, the discovery of the genetic code has shown the fundamental role played by the substance we call DNA not only in human life but in the lives of animals, plants and even bacteria, to all of which we now seem to be firmly related. This discovery prompted Nobel prizewinner Jacques Monod to say (in obvious contradiction of Teilhard de Chardin): 'The universe was not pregnant with life, nor the biosphere with man; our number came up in the Monte Carlo game.'[4] Of course, this remark of Monod goes far beyond the evidence he cites, but it is typical of much contemporary thinking about our human constitution. Thus more and more, in the past two or three hundred years, the effort has been made to bring human life wholly within the sphere of nature, and to study that life in all its manifestations according to the methods of the natural sciences. We can see that there were good reasons for this, for if the empirical sciences have been so prodigiously successful in penetrating the workings of the physical world, might we not hope that the same methods would be equally successful when applied to the enigma of the human being? They already have had successes in this field, as progress has been made from the crude materialism of the eighteenth-century *philosophe* Cabanis who taught that the brain secretes thought in a manner analogous to that in which the liver secretes bile to the highly sophisticated 'naturalisms' of the present day. But the general direction of all these theories has been the same. They are reductionist, and the human being has been 'demystified' and is to be conceived as a natural phenomenon.

The consequences of this revolution in the understanding

of the human being are confused, and have led to new conflicts. The general direction is, as I have said, reductionist. The sciences seem to have demeaned man and robbed him of his ancient dignity, whether it was real or imagined. If this dignity was only imagined, then it must be a good thing that we should be disillusioned. There would be nothing 'sacred' about humanity. Man is revealed as the 'naked ape', to use the description devised by Desmond Morris. But then serious questions must arise about what consequences this view may have for the foundations of morality and of interpersonal relations. But at this point, we have to note the other and apparently contradictory side of our present confusion about who or what we ourselves are. If the sciences have in some respects cut down the human race to size and dissipated our grandiose pretensions, they have at the same time enhanced man's estimate of himself. In his famous essay of 1784, 'An Answer to the Question, "What is Enlightenment?"' Immanuel Kant had made the notion of autonomy the key to understanding the new human mentality.[5] So long as the human race had been dependent on powers beyond itself, whether natural, human or divine, it had made little advance. But let human beings now use their own powers of understanding and take their destiny into their own hands, and they would get on much better than they had done in the past. So, on this side of the balance sheet, the modern self-understanding has instilled a new confidence into men and women. Though it may not have been quite consistent with the naturalistic view, there was a new prizing of human freedom and a recognition of responsibility for human history. But Kant was wiser than most of his contemporaries in recognizing that we can easily form an exaggerated idea of human powers, and he insisted on what was at that time a very unpopular doctrine, namely that there is a streak of radical evil (original sin) in every human being.

It seems that whenever a new tendency appears in the history of human thought, no matter how strong it is, it calls forth a dialectical reaction. This has been the case with the naturalistic view of man. In the nineteenth and twentieth centuries, a variety of philosophical thinkers have made a deliberate and sustained attempt to restore a recognition of the uniqueness of human existence and to fight against the tendency to make the human being an object that can be exhaustively 'explained' by the empirical sciences. Indeed, some philosophers have gone too far in their protest, and have ended up with a form of dualism in which man and nature stand over against one another in a kind of onto-logical confrontation. An example of this is Sartre.

There are, I think, obvious points that favour the protest movement. When physics, chemistry, biology and the other natural sciences have said all that they can say about the human phenomenon, we seem to be left with an incomplete description. Presumably any scientific description is incomplete, but this seems to be specially the case with descriptions of the human being. For instance, the relation between mind and brain is still far from being understood. And even if some of the current gaps in knowledge came to be filled, the description would still be incomplete. This is because some human phenomena slip through the net, so to speak. They seem to be of a different order from the events which are objectifiable and accessible to scientific investigation. Even if one adds to the natural sciences such human sciences as sociology, the description still falls short. It could even be argued that the empirical sciences systematically miss what is most distinctively human in the human being.[6]

What distinguishes the human being from all other beings found on earth is the fact that this being not only *is* but knows that he is, and because of this knowledge has some responsibility for what he or she is and may become. In some often quoted words of Sartre, 'Man first of all exists, encounters himself, surges up in the world and defines himself afterwards. If man is not definable, it is because to begin with he is nothing. He will not be anything until later, and then he will be what he makes of himself.'[7] This claim is exaggerated, and this illustrates his tendency to dualism, mentioned earlier. But in a general way he is correct in distinguishing the human being as one who has to make his essence, while all manufactured and natural entities have their essences already given. Now, to the extent that this is correct (and in some cases it may be a matter of degree) we can never have full knowledge of a human being or even any knowledge of what is most distinctively human except by existing as a human being. But that means that we have to allow subjective experience to enter into our account, whereas the strength of the natural sciences has lain in their objectivity. How then can there be any reliable knowledge of the human phenomenon if we allow subjective or introspective contributions? I suppose an existentialist such as Sartre might reply that the techniques of phenomenology offer a way of safeguarding against distortion. But if we are to have access to what is distinctively human, I do not believe that the investigation can leave out of account the investigator's own experience of living as a human being.

Let me give a few examples of these distinctively human characteristics. Perhaps fundamental is the experience of freedom, which we know only in the exercise of freedom and which, as Kant maintained, all human beings assume in their relations with one another. Again, there is the sense of uniqueness or irreplaceability, for a human being is not just a member of a class or a specimen, to be subsumed under general abstract descriptions. There is also the negative phenomenon of outrage when either oneself or another has been treated in a way which we regard as 'inhuman', an evidence of how deeply the distinction between human and non-human is entrenched in our minds. Though one should not exaggerate it, mention must be made also of the sense of sin as an inner testimony to the distinctness of being human. In sin, I know that I have fallen short, that I have failed to be truly human, that I do not coincide with what I ought to be. No doubt there are some analogies to this in the non-human realm. There are good horses and bad horses, good apples and bad apples, good steel and bad steel. Good horses, good apples and good steel instantiate in their strongest form the essential properties of horsehood, applehood and steelhood. But when we talk about good men and bad men, good women and bad women, we are using the words 'good' and 'bad' in quite a different sense. One does not need to be a well-developed specimen of *homo sapiens*, an Olympic champion or a Miss World, let us say, to be a good man or woman, for in this case 'good' is an ethical term and on this planet human beings alone know the meaning of ethics and have the capacity for being moral or immoral.

But while the personalist or existentialist understanding of the human being has its rights and evidences as against reductionist forms of anthropology, it cannot and does not render such forms invalid or otiose. This becomes clear if we think again of the existentialist anthropology of Sartre and its dualism. He set over against one another the fragile human being, the *pour-soi*, who has understanding, will, transcendence, conscience, but is shot through with nothingness and lack of being, and solid, physical being, the *en-soi*, which certainly has massive but uncomprehending reality and is utterly alien to the *pour-soi*. The two are vividly contrasted in the novel, *La Nausee*, when Roquentin faces the chestnut-tree in the park. Sartre went wrong in his exaggeration of human freedom, his doctrine that a human being begins as nothing and then makes itself. No human being begins as nothing. Everyone, as a psychosomatic being, starts off in life with a quite substantial genetic inheritance which has already encroached on the freedom to become one type of person or another. It is already decided that this will be a human person, not a dog or an elephant, that this will be a man or a woman, and that his or her intelligence and temperament will lie within certain parameters.

So though we may accept that there is an important truth in the existentialist and personalist protests against reductionist anthropologies, on the ground that these seem to threaten what is distinctively human in the human being, the kind of existentialism that we find in Sartre does not offer a viable alternative. An adequate anthropology would have to take account both of empirical studies of man and of phenomenological studies coming from existentialist and similar sources. Reductionist views of the human being are to be rejected not because they are scientific or objectivizing or empirical, not even because they may impugn the dignity of human beings, but because they dismiss as mere subjectivism the self-questioning and self-understanding which give to humanity its distinctiveness. But equally the existentialist who holds that a human being begins from nothing and has a virtually unlimited freedom to make himself or herself into any chosen pattern has left out data that are essential to any adequate account. For, with all the distinctiveness that belongs to it, the human phenomenon is still something that belongs to this world, it has been born from the cosmos and in spite of its freedom is still subject to most of nature's laws. But to say this is surely to demand a reconception of the nature from which humanity has emerged. That nature must be more than the dense unthinking *en-soi* which Sartre represented it to be. A nature which has brought forth human nature with all its remarkable possibilities must itself be a nature in which remarkable possibilities are latent. Already in the early decades of this century, Whitehead was writing: 'It is a false dichotomy to think of nature *and* man. Mankind is that factor *in* nature which exhibits in its most intense form the plasticity of nature. Plasticity is the introduction of novel law.'[8]

At this point we may profitably turn to consider some of the traditional teaching concerning man that has come down to us in the Western tradition, both theological and philosophical. I begin with the biblical creation stories. As we noted in the earlier part of this lecture, these stories were discredited with the rise of modern sciences, such as astronomy, geology and biology. These stories were certainly discredited as literal accounts of how the world and the human race had their origin, but even as we have come to see their mythological character, we have also come to appreciate that their meaning is not to be sought in a literal reading, but in the truths about our own humanity which these stories express in mythological or poetic form. These stories still convey a view of the human being which avoids the errors both of naturalism and of gnosticizing theories. They see the human being as psychosomatic, made from the dust of the ground, that is to say, born out of the side of this material planet, yet at the same time a recipient of the breath or spirit of God, that is to say, animated by a reality that transcends nature. This is the picture given in the more primitive creation story found in Genesis 2, while the more sophisticated account in Genesis 1 claims that in man and woman, considered together in their community, the Creator God has included in the cosmos his own image and likeness, so far as it is possible to express this in the realm of finite entities. There has been much argument as to what this image is. It has often been equated with dominion, but this seems to reflect an inadequate idea of God as world-ruler. Another common interpretation is to say the image is rationality. This perhaps comes closer to the traditional teaching about the Word or Logos of God which has always been in the world, but the trouble is that rationality has often been understood in too narrow a way. It would have to include the notion of freedom, the limited creativity which belongs to the human being and dimly reflects the divine creativity. Above all, as we heard from Sartre, humanity has to create itself – not out of nothing, but at any rate out of some very plastic raw material.

This view of the human adventure had already been vividly expressed five hundred years before Sartre by the Renaissance scholar, Pico della Mirandola. In his parable, when God had created all the other things on earth, he made man and said to him: 'A limited nature in other creatures is confined within laws laid down by me. In accordance with your free judgment, to which I have entrusted you, you are confined by no bounds and you will fix the limits of your nature for yourself . . . You are the moulder and maker of yourself. You may sculpt yourself into whatsoever shape you prefer.'⁹ We note that Pico was nearer the truth than Sartre, for Pico is comparing the man to a sculptor confronting a block of marble, that is to say, the human task is not to make oneself out of nothing but out of a given material that may be shaped in many ways.

We must notice too that in the biblical account of the human creation, there is no hint of the dualism that we find in Sartre and in Gnosticism. Man is from the first a psycho-somatic being, constituted both by the dust of the ground and by the breath of God. But although there is no dualism, there is a dialectic. The human being lives in the tension between the givenness of the bodily nature, something to be accepted, and the openness, freedom or plasticity of the spirit, something to be chosen and moulded. It is nowhere suggested that the spirit is a mere epiphenomenon of the body, or that the body is an illusion, still less, a prison, as the Gnostics supposed. The dialectic of human existence could hardly be better expressed than it is in these ancient stories. The human being is part of the creation and therefore akin to animals, plants and the entire material universe; yet the human being has a distinctive place in all this, because touched by a spirit which imparts what Schleiermacher called 'the sense and taste of the infinite'.¹⁰

If there is something lacking in these biblical stories, it is perhaps the sense of movement – they could be understood in a static way as they were by Augustine and also by Michelangelo, in whose famous pictorial representation of the creation, Adam receives the touch of the divine life as one who is already adult, a ready-made human being, so to speak. But no human being can be ready-made, for he needs time and a history in which, through deeds and decisions, he makes himself. So it was an important development in Christian doctrine when in the second century Irenaeus and other fathers taught that Adam and Eve had been created not as adults but as children for whom the divine image was as yet only a potentiality, and that the goal of likeness to God could be achieved only through a life of responsible decision.

Irenaeus and those who thought like him did not hesitate to call this growth in likeness to God 'deification', though not in any pantheistic sense. But the biblical understanding of likeness to God seems to open up a virtually endless path for the human race. No termination is in sight. 'Now we are children; it does not yet appear what we shall be' (John 3.2). At a later time, Gregory of Nyssa claimed that 'the perfect life is the one whose progress into perfection is not limited by any boundary'[11] and for this teaching he gave the very good reason that since God is inexhaustible, there can be no end to the human quest for likeness to God.

This biblical anthropology and its subsequent theological development readily allied itself with some anthropological ideas derived from philosophical sources. We have already noted the term Word or Logos, a term common to theologians and philosophers, and applicable to both God and man. There was also the Platonic doctrine of *anamnesis*, or remembering. The human being is to search into his memory to discover his origin and true nature. To speak of memory in this connection is to speak in a way that is at least partly mythological, and Plato did in fact invoke the myth of the transmigration of souls to express his teaching. This is not a literal remembering, like the way in which I remember events of my personal past. In Christianity too it is claimed that the *anamnesis* of the eucharist is not a bare remembering of a past event, but a *repraesentatio*, to use the language of the Council of Trent, a making-present in its felt reality of a formative event in the life of the community. Among examples of this 'remembering' I would mention conscience, understood not just as a set of rules we have absorbed from the society in which we live but a deeper level of conscience, an almost inaudible voice that we may hear only once or twice in a long while and that comes out of the depth of our being, directing us in one way rather than another. Still another illustration of 'remembering' is mysticism, not a universal human experience but one that is widespread and that shows remarkable similarities across the wide spectrum of religious traditions. By going deeply into himself or herself, the mystic finds that the very *arche* or foundation of the self is united to the creative mystery that we call God, the mystic 'remembers' his or her origin. We find, for instance, in Catherine of Genoa: 'Then the soul was made to experience a spark of that pure love with which God had created it . . . The soul so passionately answered that love that her heart was brimming over, utterly absorbed in exchange, and came close to leaving the body, to leaving this earth, and transforming itself into God.'[12] Although I have been speaking mostly of Western thought, it may be permissible to mention an Eastern parallel which is close to the experiences just discussed. Some forms of Buddhism teach that every human being has an 'original face' which is deep within and of great beauty, even if it has been forgotten and covered over with sin. To dig down below the debris and to uncover the original face is to recover one's true nature, to remember who one truly is.[13]

I have been talking about Plato's idea of *anamnesis* or remembering, and relating it to the biblical teaching about the image of God in man. But are we perhaps overlooking a major difference between the philosophical and biblical ideas here? In theology, as interpreted from Irenaeus onwards, the image of God has been future-oriented and seen as a potential of the human being, to be fulfilled in some ultimate 'deification'. In Greek philosophy, and also in the Genesis story, the reference is to the past, to human origins. But what is common is the idea that the human being is between past and future, having an origin but still searching for a goal. This is clearly recognized in modern philosophical anthropologies, in which the term transcendence is commonly used of the human being. Philosophers who speak in this way think of human beings as moving towards boundaries which, as they advance towards them, turn out to be no longer boundaries, but open out on new vistas. These philosophers (some of them materialistic and Marxist) do not speak of 'deification' or of the 'image' of God, but the biblical ideas can be seen behind these modern formulations. Thus Heidegger quotes the words of Genesis, 'Let us make man in our image and likeness', and goes on to say: 'In modern times, the Christian definition of man has been deprived of its theological character. But the idea of "transcendence" – that man is something that reaches beyond himself – is rooted in Christian dogmatics.'[14] Existentialists of various kinds – Heidegger, Sartre, Marcel, for instance – all make use of the notion of transcendence in their expositions of the human persons. So do some neo-Marxists, such as Bloch and Marcuse, and though (so far as I can discover) Marx himself did not use the term, there is something resembling transcendence in his understanding of how man through his work makes both himself and his world. Recent Catholic philosophy has been given the name 'transcendental Thomism' because of the prominent place it has given to the idea of transcendence in its restatement of Thomist teaching. Karl Rahner relates transcendence to spirit, which he understands as the capacity in man to reach out beyond the immediate horizons. One danger in this modern fascination with transcendence is that it may easily degenerate into a facile dogma of progress. This is the point where 'remembering' becomes important, not least remembering that in the Genesis stories man's creation in the image of God was speedily followed by his fall into sin. We must always avoid one-sided views of the human phenomenon, both naturalistic views which look uncritically for the automatic evolution of the species, and idealist views which overlook the ties that bind the human being to the dust of the ground.

A corrective can be introduced if we recall still another contribution to anthropology. This one too came in part from Western philosophy and in part from the theological tradition. I mean, the teaching that man is a microcosm, a cosmos in miniature. The origins of this idea can be traced back to Greek philosophy, and through neo-Platonism it entered Christian theology and even reappears in some forms of modern philosophy. We find it among others in John

Scotus Eriugena, Nicholas of Cusa, Leibniz and Lotze. The human being has been called a microcosm because the whole cosmos, in all its levels of being, seems to be summed up in humanity. At one level, a man or woman can be seen as a physico-chemical process, so that what goes on in our bodies, including our brains, can be explained in terms of the same physics and chemistry that apply to the world around us. But at another level, the human being has to be seen as an 'organism', as are also plants and animals. It is not that any new 'substance' has been added, but that now we have to consider the whole, for the whole influences the working of the parts and the parts are what they are only in relation to the whole. So we have to bring in new biological categories of explanation, beyond physics and chemistry. But still we have not exhausted the complexity of the human person. Again, we need not suppose that some new 'substance' has been added, such as a substantial soul. But we do need new categories of explanation, going beyond not only physics and chemistry but even biology, for with personhood we strike on a way of being which, as existentialist and personalist philosophers have rightly claimed, is *sui generis* and not assimilable to lower levels.

But by some remarkable transmutation, the new levels seem to have arisen out of the earlier ones. This implies that the new levels that have emerged in the human race were already latent in the cosmos as potentialities. At this point in space and time, the cosmos itself has come to speech and self-questioning and self-understanding, the universal Logos is making itself heard in human language. In our *anamnesis* or remembering, the cosmos too is remembering its *arche*. In our transcendence, the cosmos is itself transcending towards an end that is still concealed.

We began by contrasting two inadequate anthropologies of the present time, the naturalistic view and the existentialist view. I think that if we go back into our Western heritage in both philosophy and theology, we find insights that can reconcile the 'two souls' that struggle together in the human breast, and that these insights can be updated and incorporated into a new human self-understanding that can guide us for the future.

The Ebb and Flow of Hope: Christian Theology at the End of the Second Millennium[15]

The earliest endeavours in Christian theology are found in the New Testament, and since then it has developed and diversified in innumerable ways, yet has consciously sought to maintain continuity with its origins. The world of the New Testament was, of course, conceived in ways very different from the world as we conceive it almost two thousand years later. Theology cannot and indeed has not stood still through that long period, but has responded to social and cultural changes and particularly to intellectual changes, in philosophy, the sciences, the understanding of history. When the New Testament was composed, people were still thinking in prescientific and even mythological terms. Theology in our time, therefore, cannot be merely a repetition of the New Testament themes. A very different conceptuality and language are needed. But in spite of all the changes and vicissitudes of twenty centuries, there are some constants of human nature that have remained recognizable through all the transitions. We can still recognize our affinity with the men and women of the New Testament, and acknowledge that many of their problems, hopes and values are close to our own. I do not say they are unchanged, for they may possibly have assumed new forms. But they are not just foreign to us, and indeed they can still attract and inspire some of the most influential people of modern times, such as Gandhi, Tolstoy, Mother Teresa and countless others. But even those who believe that there are great spiritual treasures enshrined in the New Testament acknowledge that much difficult and demanding work of interpretation needs to be done if these treasures are to be made available to generations whose cultural and intellectual environment is so different from that of the ancient world. This interpretative work is the task of theology, and it has to be done again and again as the centuries move on and new situations arise. Sometimes radical rethinking and reinterpretation are demanded, and this has been especially true in modern times; sometimes there are periods of relative stability, such as the Middle Ages in Europe; sometimes there is need for a return to the sources, an attempt to recapture the original creative vision, lest we become engulfed in a meaningless interpretation of interpretations of interpretations!

So what is the present state of the question? In order to understand where we are today, I think we must look also at the immediate past, as far back, let us say, as the beginning of the twentieth century. The story of theology which unfolds itself during these hundred years may, I think, be entitled 'The Ebb and Flow of Hope'.

The early years of the century were simply a continuation of the century that had gone before. The Western world was (on the surface at least) at peace and enjoying prosperity. The prevailing philosophies were, in the main, optimistic, science was steadily advancing, industry was expanding. Perhaps theology was too much concerned to adapt itself to this 'brave new world' and too little mindful of some of the sterner teachings of the New Testament, but it did reflect the general upbeat tone of secular society. The great historian and scholar, Adolf Harnack (1850–1930), represents the spirit of his time in his book *What Is Christianity?*[16] For the modern mind, he believed, Christianity must be reduced to its simple essence. This means cutting away all the dogmas and theological accretions that have grown up over the centuries. He believed that Christianity is primarily a practical affair, directed, like the preaching of Jesus himself, to the realization of the kingdom of God. The fatherhood of God, the infinite worth of the human soul, the ethical idea of the kingdom – these are the essentials, but they have been obscured by a mass of dubious doctrines. Other liberal optimistic theologies flourished at the beginning of the century, some of them drawing inspiration from the philosophy of Hegel who was still influential, especially in the English-speaking countries. Later, others drew on the philosophy of Whitehead, whose world-view was based on an interpretation of nature in the light of modern physics. Theologies based on evolutionary theory provide another version of the optimism of those days, and one such theology, that of Pierre Teilhard de Chardin (1881–1955) was still flourishing in mid century.

But most of these liberal progressive theologies were abandoned by about 1920. The reason for this is obvious, for the Great War (1914–18) had shattered the complacent belief in progress that had for so long held sway in the West. The war itself with all its horrors and tremendous slaughter, followed by bloody revolutions in some countries, by economic depression and mass unemployment in other countries, including the United States, induced a sombre mood that had not been known in the West for a long time. Now, when theologians turned to the New Testament, they became aware of other themes that had been ignored by the liberals: the presence of sin in human nature, the finitude of man amid the vastness of the cosmos, human powerlessness in the face of vast impersonal forces at work even in society itself. The most important theological figure to emerge in the post-war world was Karl Barth (1886–1968), one of the greatest Protestant theologians since the Reformation. Like the Reformers, Barth went back to the New Testament to seek the authentic vision of Christianity, as he believed. His first major writing was a commentary on Paul's Epistle to the Romans. For the people of that time (just after the end of the Great War) this was a new kind of commentary. The commentaries of the time had been mostly taken up with purely academic questions – questions of syntax and semantics, questions of textual criticism, questions of historical scholarship concerning date, authorship, the influences coming from Hellenistic society, and so forth. Barth did not ignore such questions, but his main interest was in the theological content of the text and what it might have to say to the Western nations in the post-war confusion. In fact, Barth did not hesitate to lay part of the blame for the war, and the suffering it had produced, on the theologians of Harnack's generation who, he believed, had paid no attention to some vital themes in the biblical message because they had been blinded by the brilliant achievements in material progress made by the nineteenth century. As Barth read the Bible, its teachings were in flat contradiction to the human values that had been so eagerly pursued in the previous century. The Bible does not contain a confirmation and endorsement of the type of human culture that collapsed in 1918, but is rather a judgment against it. The Bible contains a revelation of a humanity that is both finite and sinful, and of a God who is transcendent yet merciful.

The contrast between this new understanding of Christian theology and the one which Harnack had used may be illustrated from an exchange of letters between Harnack and Barth in 1923. Harnack maintained that 'the task of theology is one with the tasks of science in general'. By this he meant that theology has to treat Christianity as a historical phenomenon and to deal with the tasks mentioned earlier – problems of language, text, historical background and the like. Barth, in his reply, held that the task of theology 'is one with the task of preaching; it consists in taking up and passing on the word of Christ'.[17] Here Barth is introducing, shall we say, a more existential or personal note into the idea of theology, which he understands not as a disinterested or 'value-free' study of some objective phenomenon that we may call 'Christianity', but in trying to understand it as a word addressed to the human race in its actual life-situation.

Looking back to the Harnack-Barth debate from a much later date in the twentieth century, I think we might agree that both of these scholars were guilty of exaggeration. Harnack exaggerated the importance of the strictly scientific approach. This approach can indeed supply a great deal of information about Christianity. Even though there are great difficulties in the way of obtaining a detailed and accurate account of events that happened nearly two thousand years ago, the patient labours of many scholars have amassed a very considerable amount of trustworthy information concerning the life of Jesus, the beginnings of the church, the composition of the New Testament, and the spread of Christianity. This factual information does not, indeed, bring us to the heart of Christianity itself, yet it serves as a kind of control, filtering out the legends and mythology that invariably attach themselves to a religion, and enabling us to get a clear sight of the original phenomenon, so far as that is possible after so long a period of time. But however much material is accumulated and however carefully it is sifted, there remains a gap that cannot be bridged by more information. Something different is needed before the authentic message of Christianity can be heard. This was the point that Barth grasped, but unfortunately he too exaggerated the importance of his insight, and he tended, certainly in the earlier part of his career, to set aside the labours of critical scholarship as if they were of very secondary value. This kind of exaggeration, found in the early Barth, tends to discredit the whole theological enterprise as a serious study.

What then was of value in Barth's protest against the old liberal or scientific theology? Actually, the point at issue had been put very clearly by Kierkegaard in the middle of the nineteenth century. He argued that no amount of historical information would bring one nearer to understanding the meaning of Christianity, but only 'the consciousness of sin'.[18] But this is not an additional piece of information. It is indeed something that can be known, but such knowledge is of a different order from the knowledge of objective facts. It is awareness of the human condition, an awareness that arises through one's participation in that condition. Barth was misleading in saying that theology is closer to preaching than to science, for this could be misunderstood to suggest that theology is indistinguishable from mythology or from ideology. But given that Barth's choice of words was unfortunate, his essential point was correct. Theology cannot be value-free. It is doubtful if any study affecting the nature and destiny of human beings could be 'value-free', and certainly theology does touch very closely on these human questions. If theology is the intellectual interpretation of religion, then it must take into account the fact that the human person is not a purely intellectual being but encompasses also feeling and willing and whatever else is essential to a truly personal mode of existence. If religion is concerned with the enhancement of human life, what is traditionally called 'salvation', then it makes a lot of sense to say that theology, as the interpretation of religion, needs for its understanding not so much factual information about historical realities as rather that first-hand acquaintance with sin, for sin is the sense of falling short, and this in turn awakens the quest for that enhancement or fuller existence, promised by the religions. Of course, as I have already said, any developed theology will embrace both the kind of knowledge championed by Harnack and the existential awareness that seemed so important to Barth and to Kierkegaard before him.

In what I have just been saying, I have confined myself to the teaching of the early Barth and to only some aspects of that teaching. To fill this out, one would have to speak also of his doctrine of revelation, his distinction between revelation which comes from God and religion which (in his view) is the human quest for God and therefore the reverse of revelation. We cannot expand to take in all these other topics, but I think I have drawn attention to a decisive moment in the development of twentieth-century theology in highlighting the disagreement between Harnack and Barth as the moment when there is a turning away from liberal humanistic theology based on historical scholarship to a new style in which historical knowledge should not be despised but which stresses even more an intimate existential grasp on the part of the student of theology.

In the early part of the century, Barth was the leading light in a quite widespread revolt against the older liberal theology. Perhaps some of the theologians who belonged to this movement succeeded better than Barth had done in injecting the rediscovered existential dimension into theology without abandoning or, at least, putting in question the value of the academic historical approach. Among these theologians may be mentioned Rudolf Bultmann (1884–1976). He was, by common consent, the greatest New Testament scholar of the twentieth century, but, as one who had lived through World War II and had an excellent record resisting the attempts of Hitler to subjugate the German Church to the Nazi ideology, he was also keenly interested in the affairs of the contemporary world and spent most of his energies in an attempt to show how the message of the New Testament is still a message for men and women in the world today. Equally with Barth, he had turned against the liberal theology of Harnack and others like him, though he retained a great respect for Harnack's historical researches. Also, like Barth, Bultmann stressed the existential interpretation of the Christian message, but whereas Barth had been influenced by Kierkegaard, Bultmann's enthusiasm for existentialism was derived from Heidegger, who had been his colleague for several years after the Great War.

Bultmann's early work was directed mainly to the critical analysis of the New Testament. His work was reminiscent of that of Strauss almost a century earlier. Though they used different methods, both of these scholars raised serious questions about the reliability of the New Testament, especially the Gospel records of the career of Jesus. In particular, they both argued that the narrative had been strongly influenced by mythologies current in the first century. In Bultmann's view, men and women who have been educated in the twentieth century and have imbibed something of the scientific understanding of the world simply cannot accept the strange phenomena reported in the New Testament – miracles, voices from heaven, diseases caused by demons, and other ideas of the first century. But (and here we see some common ground with Barth) he believed that this mythological language is a kind of framework, the only one available in the Jewish-Hellenistic culture in which the New Testament was written, and within this framework may be discovered the essential message of the New Testament, if only we can find the key to interpret it. The first step towards a right interpretation is to ask the right question. The question is not, 'What happened?' but 'What does this mean for my existence?' That is because a religious document, such as the New Testament, is concerned, as we have said, with the enhancement of life, with setting before the reader a new possibility of existence. A religious document is not primarily a history book, though of course it may contain some history. This method of existential interpretation devised by Bultmann was called 'demythologizing', though perhaps this designation was too negative, for while the method eliminated the mythological strand in the New Testament narratives, it could also be applied in an affirmative way. For instance, ethical commands were understood existentially as demands made directly on the hearer or reader of the word, not just as general principles of conduct. The effect of Bultmann's hermeneutic was to stress that Christianity is in the first instance a way of life and only secondarily a doctrine. For instance, he taught that to believe in the cross of Christ is not primarily to believe that this event actually happened in the year 33 or thereabouts or to believe in a doctrine of atonement, but 'to make Christ's cross one's own'.[19]

Some critics claimed that Bultmann had subjectivized religion and abandoned any objective reference either to history or even to God. It is true that for him the narratives are primarily expressions of possibilities of human existence and that God is understood not as a 'substantial being' but as an event, when the human being is confronted with an ultimate demand. It is also true that in the aftermath of Barth and Bultmann, there was an attempt, especially in the United States, to devise a form of Christianity that would demythologize even the concept of God. Bultmann himself would not go to such lengths. He always opposed the objectification of religious beliefs, not because he denied that they referred to realities, but because such objectification obscures their more immediate significance as guides to human conduct.

In any case, the third part of the century, say from about 1965 onwards, brought in a new phase of theology. Whereas the liberalism of the Harnack years had been optimistic, while the existentialism of such men as Barth and Bultmann had been more conscious of the sin and finitude of human life, this third phase was ushered in with a reaction in which hope for the future and a new stress on the fundamental goodness of the human being began to assert themselves. The major event which led to this reorientation of theology was the Second Vatican Council, held at Rome in the years 1962–65. It is difficult to say why this Council took place when it did. It may have been due largely to the vision of one man, Pope John XXIII, for it is difficult to see how the public events of that time could have brought about a new wave of hope.

In any case, Pope John summoned his Council, and it brought a surge of new life not only to the Roman Catholic Church but to the Protestant churches of Europe and America as well. The philosophy which dominated the thinking of the Council was called 'transcendental Thomism'. For many centuries Thomism, the system of philosophy constructed by Thomas Aquinas in the Middle Ages, had been dominant in the Roman Catholic Church. Even at the beginning of this century, it was a philosophy of static entities, and much of its argumentation seemed to consist in ever finer definitions and distinctions. But in the present century, it has come alive again, perhaps demonstrating its claim to be the 'perennial philosophy'. This is due to the attempt by some Thomists to come to terms with modern European philosophy, especially the ideas of Kant, then later with evolutionary philosophies and with existentialism.

The Catholic theologian who had perhaps the greatest influence on the thinking of Vatican II was Karl Rahner

(1904–84). He had embraced some ideas from the new 'transcendental Thomism', and had also been a student of Heidegger. Fundamental to Rahner's thinking is his anthropology, or doctrine of man. Whereas the existentialists had stressed human finitude, Rahner saw the human being as a finite centre which reaches out toward the Infinite. The essence of man is spirit, and spirit is to be understood not as some thing or substance but as the capacity for going out. (In traditional Christian language, the Holy Spirit 'goes out' or 'proceeds' from God into the world.) A human being, therefore, is not a static entity with a fixed nature, but is a 'transcending' being, that is to say, is always passing across into new phases of existence.[20] This is not a doctrine of automatic progress, like the doctrine widely held in the nineteenth century and tragically proved wrong since then. It is not the doctrine of a brash optimism, that everything will come right in the end, but rather a doctrine of hope, and we must remember that hope is vulnerable. The end or goal of human transcendence is God. Since Rahner had a strongly mystical element in his make-up, he often speaks of God as the Nameless (which perhaps reminds us of the Tao of Chinese philosophy), but as a Christian theologian he also believed that the human spirit, with its capacity for transcendence towards the Infinite, is our best clue on the finite level to the meaning of God, and he believed also that the human spirit is seen at its most transcendent in the self-giving life and death of Jesus Christ.

Just about the same time as these developments were taking place in Roman Catholic thought, a parallel development had begun among Protestants. The leading figure in this was Jürgen Moltmann (b. 1926). His book *Theology of Hope* appeared in English in 1967.[21] He severely criticized the theologians of the previous generation. Barth, he claimed, was in error in making revelation rather than promise the basis for his theology; Bultmann was wrong in thinking that eschatology is merely a mythological framework for the Christian message whereas it belongs to the essence. He was particularly critical of Bultmann, and believed that resurrection is not a mythological idea but a reality, though some of the things he says in this connection make one wonder whether he is not guilty of a measure of remythologizing. Part of the philosophical conceptuality of Moltmann's theology is derived from the neo-Marxist philosopher, Ernst Bloch, whose book *Principle of Hope*[22] expounded a worldview in which not only the human race but even inanimate nature is claimed to be in a process of 'transcendence' towards an as yet unidentified goal. But no more than Rahner can Moltmann be blamed for teaching a bland optimism. He followed up his book on hope with a second called *The Crucified God*,[23] in which he makes it clear that hope is not fulfilled automatically but demands effort and suffering from human beings and even from God.

So much then for what I have called the 'ebb and flow' of hope as we find it expounded by some of the leading theologians of the century. The story opens with the inheritance from the nineteenth century of an unbounded optimism, though events were soon to show that this had no solid foundations. Then the pessimism of the years following World War I and extending beyond World War II brought a more chilling mood, culminating in the episode of the 'death of God' among some American theologians. The final third of the century has seen a revival of hope, but it is a chastened hope, quite different from the uncritical optimism of the early decades.

But to complete our survey, it will be useful now to look at some of the principal doctrines of Christian theology, and consider how they have changed, not only in the major theologians already discussed, but across the whole theological spectrum. The doctrines to be briefly examined are those of God, Christ, the church and the nature of the human being.

In Christian theology, although God has usually been regarded as both transcendent and immanent, that is to say, as both beyond the world and yet within it, the emphasis was usually placed on his transcendence. He was beyond or above

the world, a *deus ex machina* who might from time to time
intervene in the world's affairs. Since the time of the
Enlightenment, the world has been increasingly regarded as a
self-regulating mechanism, and it has also been thought that
the interventionist role assigned to God was, to say the least,
somewhat undignified. Already in the nineteenth century,
God was being more and more understood in terms of
immanence, sometimes coming near to a pantheism. The
reaction against the nineteenth century by Barth and his
collaborators included a new emphasis on the transcendence
of God. This was especially the case with Barth, who in his
early writings wrote of God's acting 'vertically from above'.[24]
In 1963 there was something of a crisis when an English
bishop, John Robinson (1919–83) published his short but
celebrated book *Honest to God*.[25] This called for a rethinking of the concept of God, and this rethinking has in fact
taken place in the later part of the century. It has moved, not
in the direction of pantheism, but towards a combination of
transcendence and immanence in a more complex concept.
This is sometimes called 'panentheism' – a word which means
literally 'everything in God', but is also understood as 'God
in everything', a kind of mutual indwelling. Some such idea
seems to be already implicit in the Christian idea of God as
Trinity – God over us (Father), God with us (Son), God in us
(Spirit). Some such understanding of God is to be found in
many contemporary theologians, such as Moltmann, discussed above.

On the question of the person of Jesus Christ, the traditional theology has again tried to hold a balance between
Christ's consubstantiality with God and his consubstantiality
with the human race. But although it has always been
deemed a heresy to deny the true humanity of Jesus Christ,
this has often been virtually ignored. But once more we can
see in this doctrine the same profile as in the doctrine of God.
The nineteenth century made much of the quest for the
'historical Jesus', that is to say, for the human Jesus of
Nazareth before he became swallowed up in the theological

construction of the God-man. So it is a very human Christ that we meet in Harnack. In Barth, on the other hand, we seem in some places to strike against what is virtually a monophysitism, that is to say, the doctrine that Christ had only one nature, a divine nature into which the human nature has been absorbed. But again in the more recent theology, the humanity of Jesus Christ is being uncompromisingly re-asserted. This is clearly the case with the Catholic theologian Rahner, and the same is true of a great many other theologians of our time.

There has likewise been a considerable modification in the conception of the church. Especially since Vatican II, what are called 'triumphalist' ideas of the church are increasingly disavowed. Though it is a mistake to associate the church too closely with the expansionist aims of European colonialism, there is little doubt that sometimes Christian missions were in fact contaminated by the imperial idea. However, this does not seem to be supported by the New Testament, where one of Christ's parables suggests that the kingdom of God (and so the church as a stage on the way) is like a little leaven which works in the whole lump of dough, leavening the lump but not itself claiming to be the lump. This has led to the idea of the church as a representative body, aiming indeed to make its contribution and to render its service to the whole, but not aiming to dominate the whole. Perhaps the most obvious symptom of this new attitude is to be found in the change that has taken place in the church's relations to other religions. Here again Vatican II has played a significant part through its 'Declaration on the Church's Relationship to Non-Christian Religions'. The Council declared that the church should recognize whatever is good and true in the non-Christian traditions, though once again the precedent for this goes back to the early days of theology, and can be found in such pioneering Christian writers as Justin and Origen. Protestants are moving in the same direction, and already a vigorous dialogue is in progress among the various world religions.

Finally, there is the question about human nature. Is man by nature good or bad, or perhaps a mixture? Following the Enlightenment and through the nineteenth century, especially after the influence of evolutionary theory made itself felt, belief in an inherent human goodness and an inevitable human progress gained ground, and was reflected in such a theology as Harnack's. But the wars and upheavals of the twentieth century put this optimistic belief in question. As we have seen, Barth and his colleagues in Europe spoke once more of man's limitations and of his sinfulness, while even in the burgeoning United States of America, Reinhold Niebuhr ventured to revive the doctrine of original sin. But once again, from about 1965 onwards, a different voice was heard. When Paul Ricoeur declared, 'However radical evil may be, it cannot be as primordial as goodness',[26] he was only reminding us of the teaching of the Bible, in the creation stories of Genesis. Certainly he was not returning to the naïve optimism of the Enlightenment and its aftermath, but trying to achieve that proper balance or dialectic which is truer to the authentic tradition. He goes on to say: 'Sin does not define what it is to be a man; beyond his being a sinner there is his being created. Sin may be older than sins, but innocence is still older.'[27] Karl Rahner has frankly acknowledged that in his theology, sin and evil have not been given a prominent place. It is because it has achieved this more nuanced understanding of the nature of the human being that modern theology can claim that it is in his very humanity that Christ manifests (so far as this is possible) the image of the invisible God.

Such then is one man's impression of the present state of Christian theology in the West, as it has emerged after a tumultuous and even chaotic century. I think it is still alive and well.

Dialogue among the World Religions[28]

One of the encouraging facts in the contemporary world is the dialogue going on among the great religious traditions, a dialogue that is becoming not only more widespread but more serious. In the past, these religions went their several ways with very little contact with one another, and where contact did take place, it was often marked by bitterness and rivalry. But as we are thrown more and more together in our shrinking world of instant communication and rapid transport, there has grown up among the religions a desire for friendship and mutual understanding. Indeed, this could be a major contribution towards peace among all peoples. A leading Catholic theologian of the present, Hans Küng, has given expression to these aspirations in a kind of slogan which he has caused to be printed at the beginning of most of his recent books:

> No peace among the nations without peace among the religions.
> No peace among the religions without dialogue among the religions.
> No dialogue among the religions without investigation of the foundations of the religions.[29]

Dialogue is the rational, civilized way of resolving conflict, as opposed to the methods of violence and coercion. Two conditions would seem to be necessary for a dialogue to take place. The participants must have some common ground, some respect for one another, otherwise the dialogue could not begin. Yet the participants must also be aware of differences between them, otherwise there would be no need for dialogue. I need hardly say that there must also be openness, a willingness to listen as well as to speak, to learn as well as to teach.

At what is the dialogue aiming? We must be very careful in trying to answer this question. The dialogue itself is fairly new, and we should be frank in acknowledging that we simply do not know where it will finally lead. Some enthusiasts, impressed with what the religions already have in common, have thought that there will be a steady convergence, and even that we may end up with a unified faith. I doubt very much if this is possible or even desirable, and in any case, it is a goal that would take a very long time to achieve. It is true that there is already much in common among the religions, both in belief and in ethics. But often what appears to be agreement turns out to conceal considerable differences when considered more closely. To say, for instance, that belief in God is common to many religions is a statement that soon needs to be qualified when we study the very different concepts of God that are all designated by this single term.

On the other hand, if there is much in common or that seems to be in common, there are many things that are different among the religions. But here we may notice that just as the common features may turn out to conceal difference, so the obvious differences may turn out to be less serious than we supposed, once we begin to discuss them. There is a certain dialectic in religion, so that opposites may actually require one another.

The dialogue must explore the whole situation, both what there is in common and what is different. In the course of such dialogue, understanding is built up, and this is itself a major gain, whether in the end (long after our time!) it leads to a unified faith, or settles for a pluralism-in-friendship, or reaches some entirely new kind of relationship which we are unable to envisage at present. And if there is hope in pursuing these ends, there is also danger. Too much stress on unity might lead to a barren homogeneity in which the diverse cultures and spiritualities of the several faiths would be impoverished, while a sheer pluralism (though this word has become very popular in recent years) could bring us to a fragmentation in which all the old rivalries and enmities among the faiths might reassert themselves. So while I advocate dialogue, I see the first result of this simply as increased understanding and friendship among the adherents of the various traditions, and am content to leave it to the future to decide how this is to be given best expression.

Let us begin by considering the already existing basis of agreement among the religions, the points at which there is (or appears to be) already a large measure of convergence.

The first such point is the universal religious conviction of the importance of the holy. I deliberately use this somewhat vague expression, 'the holy', rather than some more definite word, such as 'God' or 'the gods'. But even if it is vague, the word 'holy' is not devoid of content. I think that Langdon Gilkey offered a very helpful analysis when he took the notions of 'ultimacy' and 'sacrality' to be defining characteristics of the object of religion. The word 'ultimacy' points to the 'really real', that which cannot be derived from anything beyond itself and is therefore in a category of its own and other than the phenomena of the world. The word 'sacrality' points rather to our experience of the ultimate as striking us with a sense of awe and otherness.[30] I think I prefer myself something closer to the threefold analysis given by Rudolf Otto in his classic work, *The Idea of the Holy*.[31] He used the Latin formula, *mysterium tremendum et fascinans*. This could be rendered as saying that the holy includes at least the notions of mystery, affinity and transcendence. In ascribing mystery to the holy, what is meant is that in our experience of the world and also of our own existence, we encounter a depth and inexhaustibility that is not to be explained or explained away by the empirical sciences, for it always stretches beyond what has been reached at any given time. In mentioning transcendence, I mean that every horizon of knowledge, as we come towards it, opens out on a new horizon, opens towards that mystery which lies beyond both the natural and the human, though it is through the natural and the human that we become aware of it. Here I would mention the book of the American sociologist Peter Berger, *A Rumour of Angels*,[32] in which he argues that our empirical investigations reveal what he calls 'signals of transcendence'. But in speaking of the religious idea of the holy, one has to add a third characteristic, that of affinity. The transcendent is not *merely* other – in that case it might be demonic, inspiring terror rather than awe – a reality supernatural and super-human but not inviting worship or faith. We properly speak of the holy only when worship is called forth, and that happens only when the transcendent mystery is experienced as having some affinity with the human being and so as exer-cising on him an attraction or even, to use Otto's word, a 'fascination' that calls for the response of faith, trust and service. Some such idea of the holy is, I think, common to the major world religions of the present. I am not here concerned with religion in its primitive undeveloped forms, though even in them something of what I have described may be dis-cerned. It is the awareness and response to this realm of the holy, its claims and its promises, that makes the fundamental difference between religious and non-religious views of the world, and the practical attitudes that ensue upon them.

But when one claims that recognition of the holy is a common feature of the great religions, the statement has to be immediately qualified by adding that the holy is under-stood in a considerable variety of ways. Often, the holy reality is known as God, or the gods, but God too has been understood in many ways. In Christianity, God is understood to be both one and three, a single reality known in the three modes of Being, called Father, Son and Spirit. The idea of God as threefold is found in other religions or philosophies, including Hinduism and the philosophy of Plotinus. On the other hand, Islam rejects such ideas, and insists on the absolute unity and unicity of God. But however God is con-ceived, he unites in himself those qualities of mystery, tran-scendence and affinity which we have seen to characterize the holy. Thus, when we speak of God, we have in mind a kind of focus of the holy. Why then have I not said that belief in God rather than acknowledgment of the holy is the primary common ground that the religions have in common? The reason is that the word 'God', especially in the religions of the West, is usually understood as a personal being. But in other religions, especially in Asia, the holy is experienced in a more diffuse way, not concentrated in personal being but perhaps known diffusely as an impersonal or suprapersonal reality. Especially in mystical forms of religion, the holy or (to use Otto's word) the 'numinous' is so far beyond the objects of ordinary experience that it is nameless, such as the Dao of Taoism or the Dharmakaya of Buddhism or the Brahma of classical Hinduism. The mystery which these words denote is, in the mystic experience, the ultimate reality, but one can only say, 'It is not this, it is not that'. The mystic, however, is not usually content with the silence of the *via negativa*, and through symbol and analogy he or she tries to give expression in words to the experience of Holy Being.

A second point of convergence among the religions is their belief in the spiritual nature of man. It is in virtue of this spiritual nature that the human being can relate to and find affinity with that wider inclusive Being which may be called God or by some other name. This word 'spiritual' obviously calls for closer definition. In calling man 'spiritual', we are asserting that the human being, though a biological organism and therefore a part of nature, is not *merely* a part of nature. The appearance of the human race on this planet, or, to speak more accurately, the appearance of what is distinctively human in our race, has introduced a new dimension of being into the world. Man's freedom, creativity, quest for goodness, appreciation of beauty, desire for knowledge, capacity for love and sacrifice – these, and other qualities besides, constitute his spiritual being, and seem to have set him on a way of pilgrimage the end of which is unimaginable. To be spiritual, in this sense, is to stand in a fundamental openness, to embark on the way of transcendence, and this apparently unlimited potentiality for transcendence links up with the somewhat different notion of transcendence that we have seen to constitute part of the meaning of the holy. The goal of the human spirit according to the religions, is to attain to union or communion with the transcendent holy, or to participate in Holy Being. Of course, the nature of such union, communion or participation, has been differently envisaged in different religions, but the religions do converge in teaching that man as spirit is fundamentally oriented to the holy, to which his spirit makes him akin.

At this point the religions can be counted as standing together on a common ground which differentiates them from all purely secularist and materialist ways of conceiving humanity. In fact, the religious recognition of the distinctively spiritual nature of man is our greatest bulwark against all the modern onslaughts on human dignity and human worth, whether these come from totalitarian ideologies, from the greed of consumer societies, from behaviouristic psychologies, or any other similar source. 'Dehumanization' is a word we have often heard in recent decades, and it has been heard so frequently that it is in danger of being trivialized. But it does designate a real threat, for if the human being has potentialities for transcendence, he must likewise be in danger of regression. The world religions appear to me to be our front line of defence against the demeaning of humanity.

These remarks bring me to a third point of convergence, and this is in the field of ethics. Admittedly, when we survey the scene, differences in ethical practice may seem so great that we may at first think that this is an area in which relativism holds sway. But if we look more closely, we find that there are deep underlying agreements to be found beneath the surface. On such questions as abortion, monogamy, capital punishment, whether there can ever be a 'just war', opinions differ, not only among the religions but within the religions, where adherents of the same religion may take different views on some of these matters. But what is to be noted is that even these disagreements are argued on the basis of deeper norms on which there is a large measure of agreement – reverence for life, respect for the human person, basic justice, the prizing of love and compassion, surely one of the most constant features to be found across the broad spectrum of the religions. The already existing agreement among the religions on ethical questions affords ground for hope in a world where there is also much violence and rivalry. People in both East and West still look to the religions for leadership amid the moral perplexities of our time. The religious vision of peace, shared by all the major faiths and understood not just negatively as the absence of war but affirmatively as a solidarity and harmony on the spiritual level, has power to inspire men and women, and to draw our modern civilizations along paths that lead to fuller life rather than along those that lead to diminution and destruction.

So far, I have concentrated attention on three matters in which convergence among the religions is fairly obvious, though even in these we have found some differences as well. Still, we have seen enough to assure us that the religious experience and outlook is very widespread among the human race, and I believe that if we moderns took it more seriously, it could go far towards transforming for the better the ambiguous world in which we now live. But now I want to turn attention to areas where there are differences and even conflicts among the religions. It is important to face up to these, for they have often been destructive in the past. They call for honest dialogue, and I believe that such honest dialogue may lead us to see that at least some of these differences can be subsumed under more comprehensive truths, so that even in these cases a measure of convergence can be achieved and another step taken towards the peace and unity of mankind. It is not that the differences can be simply done away, but they can sometimes be seen as mutually corrective or as elements within a complex dialectic which, because of the very nature of the subject-matter, does not permit of simple one-sided or dogmatic views. Those dogmatic views are sometimes called by the name 'fundamentalism', and of course such fundamentalism may be anti-religious as well as religious. In both cases, a partial view has been wrongly elevated to normative status.

So, in turning to the differences, let me come back first to the question of the holy. I chose the somewhat indefinite expression, the 'holy', in preference to 'God' or 'the gods', because of the wide variety of ways in which the holy has been conceived or imaged. The most obvious conflict would seem to be between those who think of the holy in personal terms – and usually, though not always, those who speak of 'God' think in this way – and, on the other side, those who think of the holy in impersonal terms. Broadly speaking, the mainly Western religions (though it might be more accurate, in view of their place of origin, to call them the 'West Asian religions'), I mean Christianity, Islam and Judaism, think of God in personal terms, whereas the East Asian religions tend to have impersonal ideas of the holy, such as Brahman in Hindu thought, Dharmakaya or perhaps Nirvana in Buddhism, Tian in Confucianism, Dao in Taoism. It is very important to note that although I have used the word 'impersonal' for these conceptions, this word 'impersonal' can mean 'suprapersonal' just as easily as 'subpersonal', and perhaps it is enough to say in the present context that it leaves room for dimensions other than or beyond the personal in the mystery of the holy.

But what may surprise us is the fact that when we examine these different traditions of East and West more closely, we find an emerging dialectic which qualifies the difference, suggesting that it is not an absolute difference. For when we look more closely at the West Asian religions, we find various indications of an impersonal or suprapersonal understanding of the holy seeking to express itself, especially among believers of a mystical type; while in the East Asian religions, personal conceptions sometimes appear, even where the tradition has been overwhelmingly impersonal.

Let me give a few examples, first from the West. The early Christian thinker, Dionysius (Denys) the Areopagite who lived about 500 CE, was deeply influenced by the philosopher Plotinus, and initiated an influential stream of Christian mystical theology known as Christian neo-Platonism. Thus Denys often preferred to speak of the 'thearchy' rather than of 'God', and one of his most famous disciples, the German mystic Eckhart (thirteenth century CE) recognized a 'Godhead' beyond God, an ultimate reality or essence beyond the persons of the Trinity. He wrote: 'Intellect that presses on is not content with goodness or wisdom or the truth or even with God himself . . . it can never rest until it gets to the very core, crashing through to that which is beyond the idea of God and truth, until it reaches the *in principio*, the beginning of beginnings, the origin and source of all goodness and truth'.[33] Among theologians of recent times, Paul Tillich did not hesitate to speak of the transcending of theism, and claimed that 'the content of absolute faith is the God above God.'[34] Parallels can be found in various Western philosophers who, even if not practising Christians, were very much in the Christian tradition. F. H. Bradley argued that the very notion of personality is inseparable from finiteness, and so the Absolute cannot be personal. The Absolute, however, is not to be considered as *merely* impersonal, but as suprapersonal.[35] In a different philosophical tradition, Karl Jaspers held that the notion of a personal God is, in his terminology, a 'cipher' for the unthinkable Ultimate which he called simply 'Transcendence'. His argument was similar to Bradley's. He wrote: 'Only in man do we know personality. To be a person is possible only by limitation. Transcendence is the source of personality, therefore more than personality, not limited like personality.'[36] I have been quoting individual theologians and philosophers, and their views were not necessarily the teachings held officially by the church. But it could be argued that even ecclesiastical doctrine, the *magisterium* of the church, at least opens the way to speculation about the transpersonal character of the holy God. For Christian teaching declares that the triune God is three persons in one substance. Admittedly the language of that formula is obscure – the word 'person' is not used in quite its modern sense, and the notion of 'substance' has become elusive especially when applied to God. But it is significant that God is not said to be a person, but three persons, that is to say, more than a person. If we omit the nouns from the formula and say simply, three in one and one in three, what is this 'one'? The trinitarian formula does in fact suggest a God who has personal characteristics but who also transcends the limitations of a person.

The other side of this dialectic is to be seen in the emergence among some East Asian religions of the conception of a personal God, even though the dominant conception of the holy is impersonal. An obvious example is the *bhakti marga* of Hinduism, in which the way of devotion to a personal God appears as an alternative to the ways of works and knowledge. Krishna is held to be the manifestation or descent (*avatar*) in a human person of the high god Vishnu, though in fact Krishna tends to displace Vishnu.

What has just been said about the opposition of personal and impersonal (or suprapersonal) ways of understanding the holy, and about how these oppositions may eventually be reconciled, can be paralleled in other matters. We find, for instance, an opposition between the transcendence of deity and the immanence of deity. Again, Christianity, Judaism and Islam appear to be ranged on one side of the divide, the side of transcendence; while the religions of Eastern Asia, Hinduism, Buddhism and Taoism are on the other side, having a strong sense of the divine immanence. But sheer transcendence or sheer immanence would alike lead to something like a disappearance of the holy. Each requires to be qualified by the other, if it is to have significance.

In Christianity, the doctrine of divine transcendence, inherited from Judaism, is qualified above all by the doctrine of incarnation. That doctrine implies both the transcendence and the immanence of God, his transcendence over the world order and at the same time his deep involvement within it. Ideas resembling that of incarnation can be found in other religions. I have mentioned already the figure of Krishna in Indian religion, a historical personage who lived in the third century BCE, yet who came to be accepted as an *avatar* of Vishnu. Perhaps one could also bring into the comparison the notion of the *bodhisattva* in Mahayana Buddhism, the one who renounces his attainment of *nirvana* in order to live again in the human condition to work for the salvation of his suffering fellow men and women.

Another tension arises when we consider whether the divine is temporal or eternal. In the Judaeo-Christian tradition, God is a God of history, acting and manifesting himself in historical events, though not absorbed into history. Other traditions associate the divine with a timeless unchanging Absolute. But again, we have two ideas that are not mutually exclusive. In the course of dialogue, it may well transpire that each idea needs the other in order to give an adequate account of the divine. The Anglo-American philosopher, Alfred North Whitehead, in his book *Process and Reality* (1929), made a brilliant attempt through his concept of the dipolar God to reach a comprehensive view that would embrace both temporal and eternal aspects. In the end, it may not be possible to resolve these various oppositions completely and we have to remain content with a dialectical or even paradoxical account.

I have given some indication of the ways in which convergence among the religions may be encouraged, even in areas where there are very wide differences. But it may be the case that even after long and patient dialogue there will remain differences that are simply irreconcilable. The search for reconciliation must not be given up too quickly, but there may come a point when one is finally compelled to come down on one side or the other.

What do we say, for instance, about the status of the material world? Christianity, Judaism and Islam share the belief that the material world is created by a good God, and that therefore the world itself is good, at least in intention. Those who believe in this way think that we have a duty to study the world through the natural sciences and to make use for human purposes of its resources, though also, as we have been learning because of the environmental problems of recent years, to care for the world and to treat its intricate structures with respect. Here we meet another ambiguity. It has been claimed that it was the doctrine of creation that encouraged the rise of science in the West, though it would also have to be acknowledged that it is precisely the West which has been chiefly to blame for the reckless exploitation of the world's resources and for the pollution and other problems arising from the uncontrolled development of technology. By contrast, there have been in the past, and there still are, other religions which have regarded the material world as inherently evil, and have seen concern with material things as a threat to what is highest in our human nature. Especially now that the entire globe has entered into a scientific phase of culture, this deep difference may seem to be a very serious problem. As is often the case in human history, we find ourselves *already* in a situation where we can only go forward, making the best of it, and cannot go backward. We are already in the technological age, already in the atomic age, and whatever the dangers, this is the reality, and we have to learn to cope with it. It seems therefore that we cannot avoid agreeing with those religions which place an affirmative valuation on the material world. Does that mean, then, that we have simply to reject those religions which call for asceticism or which recommend a withdrawal from the world into a monastic way of life?

I don't think it is quite as simple as that. We cannot escape the destiny we have taken upon ourselves of continuing to develop the natural sciences and the technologies that arise out of them. We do, however, have to be far more aware of the moral responsibilities which such an orientation of human life lays upon us. Already in the West, and probably before long all over the globe, preoccupation with the material world is leading to a spirit of acquisitiveness, even of greed, and this can easily turn into a spirit of aggression. Such acquisitiveness and greed are never satisfied, for every partial satisfaction leads to greater demands and ever widening expectations. 'Market forces' become the measure of everything, and I know of no religion that would defend such an attitude. We cannot go back on our steps, but we must ask whether our present courses are sustainable over any considerable length of time. It is here that the voices of those who call for asceticism have to be heard. Theirs is a voice of contradiction. They are going against the stream, but their warnings must be heeded, even if they are in a minority.

They remind us that 'man does not live by bread alone'. But unfortunately the ascetic, world-renouncing forms of religion sometimes forget that man does not live without bread either. We have another question, closely related to the one about the status of the material world, when we ask about the meaning of salvation. Every religion promises to its adherents salvation in some form, and by salvation is meant usually a fullness of life, a life better and more worth living than what they have known previously. In the ascetic or otherworldly religions, salvation is itself conceived in an otherworldly way. It is not something that will be enjoyed in our earthly history, but is promised in some 'pure land' beyond. This has sometimes led these ascetic religions to have little regard for life as people have to live it in this world, so they have not been much concerned with the social and economic problems with which vast numbers of the human race have to contend. On the other hand, religions which set an affirmative value on the material world have in varying degrees sought to ameliorate the conditions of life in this world through pressing for greater social justice, better education, improvements in health and housing. They may indeed have believed that in an imperfect world, a total salvation is impossible, and could only be realized in a world beyond this one. But they have believed that such salvation must begin now, and that the enhancement of human life for all humanity in this world of space and time is an imperative for any religion worthy of the name. They have believed that a human being is not just a soul imprisoned in a body and longing to escape from it, still less have they believed that a human being is no more than a complex biological entity. They have accepted that man is psychosomatic, a unity of body and soul, and that the fullness of life which we call 'salvation' must take account of all dimensions of the human being, physical as well as spiritual. I think that virtually all the major religions of the world would nowadays accept this. Even Hinduism, in which 'leaving the world' was long regarded as the highest life and the way to salvation, has nowadays adopted a more this-worldly stance. This happened partly through the pressures exerted in India by the West Asian religions, first Islam and then Christianity, and reached a remarkable fulfilment in the person of Gandhi, a man of the deepest spirituality who was at the same time concerned in the highest degree with human beings in their daily lives and struggles.

This is only the merest glimpse into the current dialogue among the religions, surely one of the most exciting and promising developments in our time. The road towards greater understanding and friendship among these faiths is going to be a long one. There can be no shortcuts, and the road must be followed with honesty, respect and understanding. But the journey along this road is vital for the future of humanity if it is to profit from the ancient wisdoms and achieve that level of peace and well-being which men and women all over the globe so deeply desire. Nevertheless, we have a firm starting-point in the convergence already existing, and there is reason to hope that differences, even those which seem quite fundamental, can be reconciled as the dialogue proceeds.

6

An Ecumenical Encounter: A Dialogue with Eamonn Conway

As I indicated at the end of chapter 5, this final chapter is not a continuation of the story (though it does in fact focus on an occasion in 1998) but gathers up a problem that has emerged from time to time in earlier chapters, namely, the ecumenical problem: how can the Christian churches attain to a greater and more visible unity than they presently exhibit? I did express dissatisfaction with what may be called the old-fashioned ecumenism. 1. It was pan-Protestant, and it really is absurd to talk of ecumenism if the largest of all the Christian communions is left out. Any 'united church' achieved by such a process could be no more than another Protestant denomination. 2. The view was too narrow, for the aim was a united church in each country or region. But the only kind of unity worth aiming at is a unity that extends across national and racial boundaries, transcending and not reduplicating the political boundaries that have proved so destructive. 3. The form of unity was some kind of uniform organization – the word 'merger' was often used, borrowed from the business world. The unity needed must be conceived in terms that will allow the greatest possible diversity of expression within one great communion. I think we have indeed made some progress in the directions I have indicated, but it has been slow and hesitant, and there is a very long way to go.

The change of direction has, of course, come about as a result of Vatican II. The Roman Catholic Church ceased at that time to stand aloof from the other communions and confessions which claim to be parts of the Christian church, and became, as indeed was its right, the leader of the moves towards greater Christian unity. When I was teaching in Glasgow, there was virtually no contact of a theological kind between the Roman Catholic Church and other Christian bodies. I think the only event of that kind which I experienced was when the Roman Catholic chaplain of the university came to see me in order to talk about German theology. On the other hand, my friend and colleague, Ian Henderson, was a relentless critic of the ecumenical movement, which he saw chiefly as an attempt to extend control and limit freedom of thought. His book, *Power without Glory*,[1] was and remains a strong dissuader from certain kinds of ecumenism.

The change of direction came about mainly as a result of Vatican II, which was going on during my early years at Union. One of the first signs of the new spirit was the enrolment in 1963 of two Roman Catholic priests in Union's summer school. This was an unprecedented event. It so happened that I was teaching in the summer school that year, and I became very good friends with one of these priests in particular, John Sheets, a Jesuit who taught theology at Marquette University in Milwaukee. He invited me there in the following year to hold a week-long seminar on religious language, a subject which had not thitherto been in the curriculum. I had many later contacts with John Sheets, who eventually became a bishop. Another significant invitation came from Monsignor Myles Bourke, who was at that time Rector of Corpus Christi parish in New York City, and a noted New Testament scholar. He asked me to preach at the main mass on the feast of Corpus Christi! About the same time, Union Seminary made an arrangement with Fordham University (a Jesuit foundation in the Bronx) whereby each year a professor from the one institution would offer a seminar in the other. So for a full semester I travelled once a week to the Bronx. Although official circles in Rome have been disappointingly slow in following up the ecumenical initiatives of Vatican II, many individual Catholics, both clerical and lay, have shown themselves more enthusiastic about ecumenism than Protestants, who seem now to be suffering from ecumenical fatigue.

Yet Protestants too were responding to the feelers being put out by Rome. In the United States at that time there was being floated a plan for a Protestant superchurch, to be designated COCU, an acronym for Church of Christ United. In spite of Union's long history of support for ecumenism, many of the faculty were unhappy at the thought of such a superchurch, and I edited a booklet in criticism of the idea, *Realistic Reflections on Church Union*. One of the contributors was John Knox, and some of his words are worth quoting:

> The major split in the Christianity of the West is obviously the separation between Rome and the other denominations, and the ultimate healing of the division in the Western church involves, above all other separations, this primary and basic rift. This rift can be overcome, it seems to me, only through what one can hardly avoid calling a 'return' – not, I hasten to add, that the whole responsibility for Christian reunion in the West rests with the Anglicans and Protestants. Rome, too, must make a return to the more ancient standards of church life represented by scripture and the earliest traditions, reaching a ground not only for possible union in the West, but for reunion with Eastern Orthodoxy as well. The return we are contemplating is not so much the return of one body to another as a turning by all of us together to the apostolic and early catholic sources and norms of the church's life as a historic community . . . Anglicans and Protestants cannot make the return by by-passing the Roman Catholic Church. There is no possible detour or shortcut. The Roman Church lies squarely and massively in the way we must travel. We can make the return only as the Roman Church makes it too, so that we make it together . . . This new openness on the

part of Rome is the major, the miraculous, the incomparably significant ecumenical fact of our time.[2]

Knox showed courage in writing these words back in 1967, but I think they have come to be increasingly accepted in the decades that have passed since then. I have said already that the Roman follow-up to Rome's own initiatives in Vatican II has been disappointing, but it has become increasingly clear that for Anglicans and Protestants, *rapprochement* with Rome takes precedence over anything else in the area of ecumenism.

This does not mean that the way will be easy. An estrangement that has lasted for more than four centuries cannot be ended without a great deal of repentance, rethinking and humility on both sides. I think that the 'agreed statements' produced by ARCIC gave an excellent example of what is needed. But even these statements seemed to come to an impasse when the subject of authority was reached. Here one has to consider the papacy. Is this institution compatible with that loose form of unity which was mentioned above as desirable? Or is it perhaps even more threatening to reasonable freedom and diversity than the uniform 'schemes' devised by old-fashioned ecumenists? In my *Principles of Christian Theology*, I wrote that 'there is at least the possibility of developments that could make the papacy a centre of unity for all Christians', and it would be hard to think of a more powerful symbol of Christian unity than the coming together of all Christians in communion with the see of Rome. Indeed, when any of my Anglican colleagues decide to go over to Rome, I often say to such a person that the only thing I shall envy in their new situation is that they are in communion with the primary see of Christendom. I expressed my views and hopes more fully in a chapter on the papacy in my book *Christian Unity and Christian Diversity*, and then, in the light of exchanges with Bishop Butler and others, I revised this chapter in a lecture entitled 'The Papacy in a Unified Church'. The lecture was given in Australia and published in an Australian journal,[3] but it is reproduced here together with a reply by Dr Eamonn Conway. So let us now turn to the theme of

The Papacy in a Unified Church

In ecumenical discussion, the papacy is almost bound to present itself as something of a paradox. On the one hand, as an already existing and, indeed, very ancient centre of Christian unity or even uniformity, it seems one of the obvious structures around which a growing unity among the divided communities of Christendom may be built up, comparable, let us say, to the creeds, the sacraments and the apostolic ministry. Thus, Frederick C. Grant, one of the Anglican observers at Vatican II, wrote that

> the Papacy is one of the most priceless elements in the Christian heritage. Reformed and restored to a pristine state in which, among the Church's leaders, it should once more be first among equals, *primus inter pares*, rather than a monarchical sovereignty, the Papacy might well become the acknowledged leader, guide and chief of the whole Christian Church, and the greatest influence for good in the whole world.[4]

This is an enthusiastic statement, though it is already beginning to say what the papacy must be and what it must not be if it is to fulfill the writer's vision. On the other hand, it could be argued that the papacy is the greatest single obstacle to the churches' coming together in a new unity. Whether we are thinking of the great Orthodox Churches of the East or the Reformed Churches of the West, we have to recognize that among them there remains, even today, considerable suspicion of the papacy and even hostility towards any such institution. To some people at least, it might seem that the abolition of the papacy would be the best way to open the door to a drawing together of the churches. It is generally agreed nowadays that the kind of unity at which the separated Christian communions and denominations should be aiming is a 'unity without absorption', that is to say, a form of unity which would allow for a good deal of diversity and pluralism. But can such an ideal be entertained if one is prepared to accept the claims made on behalf of the See of Rome?

I suppose the answer to this question depends on precisely what claims are made for the See of Rome. Sometimes these claims have been stated in such strong terms that even loyal Roman Catholics would find unacceptable. For instance, in 1302, Pope Boniface VIII in his Bull, *Unam Sanctam*, after comparing the Church to the Ark which had a single captain and helmsman, namely Noah, and outside of which all human beings perished, claimed that outside of the Roman communion there is no salvation. He concluded: 'We declare, state, define and pronounce that it is altogether necessary to salvation for every human creature to be subject to the Roman Pontiff.' It can hardly be denied that Boniface understood the papacy as a power structure, and it is hard to imagine that either the Orthodox or the Reformed Churches of the West would ever accept the papacy in such a form – or equally that most Roman Catholics would want to impose it in such a form. But I do not think either that those non-Roman Catholic Christians who are willing to entertain the idea of a papacy in some unified church of the future would want to see it stripped of all authority and reduced to a mere 'primacy of honour', as some have advocated. If the Pope were turned into a mere figurehead, he would cut no ice in the world. He certainly could not be that great influence for good which Frederick Grant envisaged. There is a wide spectrum of possibilities between that absolute monarchical papacy of *Unam Sanctam* and the colourless notion of a 'primacy of honour'. In any case, I think we have got to recognize that at the present day the papacy, though it has been stripped of many of the temporal powers which it once possessed, is more influential than it has ever been in its history, not only among Catholics and other Christians, but among secularists and adherents of other faiths. Whether or not we approve of everything he says, the present Holy Father, John Paul II, by his numerous visits to countries all over the world and by his evident concern for the well-being of all peoples, has given to the papacy a prestige which has made it very much a power in the world. This prestige has been growing strongly since the time of John XXIII. We have recently had a remarkable evidence of this in Oxford. Oxford University Press published last year *The Oxford Dictionary of the Popes*, the work of the well-known historian of Christian doctrine, John Kelly. Who would have guessed that this book would turn out to be a best-seller? But that is what has happened. The papacy is not just an institution of the past, but has a very lively interest for people today. Millions who have never heard of the controversies over infallibility and the like instinctively take the Pope to be the representative of the Christian mind on a whole range of topics. So in spite of all the problems the papacy has caused for the church and all the quarrels it has aroused, I do not think we can do without it or imagine a church in which the Papacy has been either abolished or else reduced to such a condition of impotence that it does not matter any more.

The case for the papacy, it seems to me, rests on a variety of considerations which spring from different sources. There are considerations that arise out of the scriptures themselves; there are considerations which come from the later tradition as it has developed in the church after the canon of scripture had been closed; and there are considerations of a more philosophical, or perhaps sociological, nature – considerations about what constitutes a church, and what kind of offices and organs of authority and government would properly belong to it.

Let us begin with scripture. Certainly I do not think that from the scriptures alone one could derive the concept of the papacy as it has existed throughout most of the church's history. So if there are still in the world today any group of Christians who hold, like some of the Reformers, to the principle *sola scriptura*, that is to say the principle that only what is explicitly commanded or sanctioned in scripture, in questions of doctrine and practice, is to be received in the church, then such groups of Christians would not be able to accept the papacy in any form recognizably continuous with the institution as we have known it in the past or in the present day. But, in fact, I think that both at the Reformation and today, the principle of *sola scriptura* cannot be rigidly observed. Inevitably elements of interpretation enter in, and we find that the scriptures always come to us already carrying certain interpretations that have arisen in the church. Scripture and tradition are not usually rivals but, as Vatican II expressed it, they are two streams flowing from a single well-spring, each enriching the other. So when we enquire of the scriptures we do not find, nor should we expect to find, a fully-fledged doctrine of the papacy. We can only ask whether we detect features in earliest Christianity which point in the direction of the papacy, or whether, on the contrary, we find in scripture teachings that would rule out the papacy as false development and misleading tradition. The most important evidences on the question are those supplied by the Petrine texts, those passages of scripture which tell us something about Peter and his place among the Apostles. The testimony that Peter held a unique position of leadership is very strong indeed. This may have been the case even during the ministry of Jesus. Nowadays, scholars generally make much of the differences among the four gospels, but on the question of Peter's leadership there is unanimity among the evangelists. Peter is credited with being the first to recognize Jesus as the Christ, he is named first among the Twelve, he is described as the rock on which the church would be built, he was the first among the Apostles to be granted an encounter with the risen Christ, and it was he who rallied the disciples after the crucifixion and resurrection. In the early chapters of Acts, we see Peter acting as spokesman for the church, and he is the first to open the church to the Gentiles. Nor is there anything in the rest of the New Testament that would contradict this impression that to Peter there belonged some kind of primacy. Even Paul, who claimed that he had derived his apostolate directly from Christ and who also ventured on at least one occasion to oppose Peter, nevertheless makes it clear that he regarded Peter as occupying a special place in the church.

But while the scriptures undoubtedly recognize that Peter had a leadership role, it is equally clear that he was one of the Twelve, and his apostolic office was one that he shared with the others. So when there was a crisis in the church over the question of how far Gentile converts to Christianity should conform to Jewish law, it was not Peter who decided this on his own, but a council in which Peter was associated with the other leaders of the church. In the beginning, then, the primacy of Peter was set quite definitely within a context of collegiality and conciliarity and, as we have seen in the case of Paul, that Peter might be opposed on one issue or another. To sum up, the scriptural record seems to visualize the leadership of Peter, but it is not a monarchical leadership, but one exercised in consultation with colleagues.

When we go from scripture to tradition and seek to form a clearer view of the papacy, it is important again to remember that this appeal to tradition is not something unusual and that much which has its roots in scripture only gets its developed form in the later tradition. This would be true, for instance, of something as basic as the doctrine of the Trinity. It is true also of the threefold ministry of bishops, priests and deacons. The presence of such a ministry is often held to be the mark of apostolicity in a church, and apostolicity is one of the four essential notes of the church mentioned in the Nicene Creed. We believe in 'one, holy, catholic and apostolic Church'. This apostolic ministry is like the papacy in this respect that its precise structure cannot be derived from scripture alone, but when it develops in post-scriptural history it is claimed to be a legitimate, perhaps providential or even necessary unfolding of the scriptural legacy. Yet, in another important respect, the papacy and the apostolic ministry are different. Apostolicity is counted a note of the church, one of the essential characteristics which make the church truly the church. But would one say the same about the papacy? The question is briefly discussed by Avery Dulles in his book, *The Catholicity of the Church*. He points out that the texts of Vatican I include the expression 'The (one) holy, catholic, apostolic and Roman Church'. He goes on: 'This title raised in some minds the question whether *romanitas* or "Romanness" might not be a fifth mark of the true church in addition to the four traditional ones of unity, holiness, catholicity and apostolicity.'[5] Obviously, to make an addition of this kind to the ecumenical creed would drive a new wedge not only between Rome and the Reformed Churches but between Rome and Orthodoxy. One remembers how bitterly the Orthodox have resented the Western addition of *filioque* to the Nicene Creed, but the addition of *romanitas* would be even more inflammatory, since it would amount to a virtual unchurching of all the Orthodox Churches of the East. Dulles acknowledges that some zealous Roman apologists of the nineteenth century were willing to go all the way back to Boniface VIII and to make submission to the authority of the Roman See a criterion of belonging to the true church. But the teaching of Vatican II has taken a different line. While it is still maintained that the Catholic Church of Christ 'subsists' (and this is surely an ambiguous term!) in that church which preserves communion with the successor of Peter, the Bishop of Rome, nothing is said that would simply unchurch those who are outside this communion. It is indeed said that to be outside is to lack some of the means of grace bequeathed by Christ to his church (and I do not think that those who desire reunion with Rome would quarrel with this), but it is also said that the separated churches possess elements of the church of Christ and that some of these churches (the Orthodox and Anglican Churches are specifically noted) retain authentic Catholic traditions and institutions. But the document stops short of calling the Orthodox and Anglican communions 'Catholic Churches' or 'parts of the Catholic Church'. The point I want to make, however, is that if the papacy is to be commended to non-Roman Christians, it must be seen as having its place within the total apostolic ministry rather than as an isolated institution. This would accord with the place of Peter in the New Testament, as both leader of the Apostles, yet at the same time one of the Twelve, and also with the fact that throughout the church's history, even at times when the papacy has been most exalted, the Pope has never ceased to be also a bishop, namely Bishop of Rome. Thus, whatever the special prerogatives of the Pope may be, the papacy is not a new or higher order of ministry, but is located within the universal episcopate of the church, so that the holder of this office is at the same time in a collegial relation to his fellow bishops and may not usurp their functions.

But we must concentrate our attention more closely on the development of the papacy in tradition. The first important point here is the tradition that Peter went to Rome and became bishop or leader of the church in the imperial city. This marks the transition from the Petrine office of the New Testament to the papal office associated with the See of Rome. In saying this, of course, we are using terminology which did not come into use until very much later. It was not until the time of Pope Stephen I (254–7) that the claim was made that the Lord's charge to the Apostle Peter formed the basis for the Roman primacy.[6] We should note, however, that this claim does not necessarily depend on the historical truth of the tradition that Peter eventually went to Rome and presided over the church there. Actually, the tradition that he did so and that he died in the Neronian persecution is so ancient and firm that it is very highly probable. But even if historical research ever came to cast doubt on it, the real point at issue is whether the primacy which the New Testament certainly ascribes to Peter was something that was meant to be passed on as a permanent feature of the church.

I think it was, and we shall see reasons for this judgment later. Now, if it were to be passed on to the next generation of the successors of the Apostles, was it not inevitable that it should be held by the Bishop of Rome? For in those days Rome was the centre of the world, and the natural choice for the centre of the church. It was not long before early Christian apologists were claiming that Rome and its empire were part of God's providential preparation for the gospel, for the system of communication which radiated from Rome was ideally suited for the propagation of a world mission. The church in Rome was, apart from any other considerations, bound to be from early times influential and respected, just because of historical, geographical and political reasons. Yet I suppose we must say that the papacy is not absolutely bound to the city of Rome or perhaps we should say the 'Rome' in this connection is defined not by its location but by its relation to the church. After all, for most of the fourteenth century, the papacy functioned at Avignon in France. Even in our own days, it has sometimes been envisaged that if Italy were to be overrun by some hostile, anti-Christian power, the Pope could continue to exercise his pontificate in a new location, perhaps in North or South America, just as at one point the New York Stock Exchange contemplated moving to Texas. It would still have been the New York Stock Exchange, with all its prestige, for considerations of geographical location, which were once important, have nowadays become much less so. In an age of instant communication, there is no centre of the world. Nevertheless, we may suppose that for reasons of tradition and sentiment, Rome will continue to be the seat of the papacy.

The important contribution made by tradition to the concept of the papacy is, therefore, the belief that the primacy exercised by Peter is transmissible through a line of duly elected successors. The analogy is obviously with the apostolic ministry, which was likewise passed on from the Twelve to their successors, the bishops. Both of these practices are justified by the tradition; they have in fact happened in the history of the church, and have established themselves as integral structures of the church. But although there is an analogy there is also a difference. We can see clearly enough the necessity for a continuing ministry in the church. But it is not so obvious that the primacy belonging to Peter must also have continued. It is here I think that we have to seek a justification which takes us beyond scripture and tradition, and appeals to a broader ground, which might be termed philosophical or even sociological. It is this kind of justification which I promised earlier, when I simply asserted that the transmission of the Petrine office was justified. I think, too, this is the kind of justification which is fundamental to the Anglican-Roman Catholic agreed statement on authority. That document points out that local churches or dioceses have to be kept aware of other local churches and dioceses if the unity of the church is to be maintained. So at an early stage in the history of the church we find the emergence of patriarchs and archbishops, that is to say bishops of prominent sees who had the additional responsibility of ensuring the unity of the church over a whole region, comprising several dioceses. The Bishop of Rome emerged as having a primacy and responsibility for the whole church. In spite of possible abuses, whether by popes or by regional primates, the exercise of such primacy makes a vital contribution to the well-being of the church. In the words of this ARCIC statement, the primacy, rightly understood, implies that the primate exercises his oversight in order to guard and promote the faithfulness of all the churches to Christ and to one another. Communion with the primate is intended as a safeguard of the catholicity of each local church, and as a sign of the communion of all the churches.[7] The document recommends the idea of a universal primate who will, on the one hand and in the closest association with his fellow bishops and the whole company of the faithful, maintain the unity and catholicity of the church, and, on the other, be a spokesman for the church to the world. In the one world in which we now live, the arguments for such an office are very strong. Indeed, if we did not already have such a universal primate in the Bishop of Rome, we should probably have to invent some such office.

Up till now I have been defending the institution of the papacy or universal primacy, and claiming that it must have its place in any vision of a unified or more nearly unified church of the future. But I did warn that in the case of any primacy, and especially a universal primacy, there is the danger of abuse. It can become a concentration of power which is then used oppressively, or it can become a centre of authority which is then exercised without that charity and understanding which ought always to characterize authority in the church of Christ, or it can go wrong in many other ways. Who can deny that from time to time it has in fact gone wrong in the history of the church? I cannot deny, either, that although I have stated a broadly affirmative attitude to the papacy, there are many Anglicans who would take a different stance, and who have in fact been unreceptive toward the ARCIC statement on authority, and there would be still more dissidents among the Orthodox and the Protestants. Even those who might agree that there is a case for the development of the Petrine office into a universal primacy in the church, might say that in the course of that development some objectionable features have emerged and that these cannot be regarded as legitimate developments from the New Testament sources. There are two such features that constitute a serious obstacle to the wider accept-ance of the papacy. One is the dogma of papal infallibility, and the other is the papal claim to jurisdiction over the whole church. Let me say something on these points.

In 1975 I wrote in very negative terms about infallibility, saying that 'I could not see any way in which this doctrine could ever become acceptable to Anglicans and Protestants.'[8] I made this judgment though I clearly understood that very carefully specified conditions have to be fulfilled before any papal pronouncement can be regarded as infallible, because I thought that infallibility is not attainable so long as the church is *in via*. I have, however, come to change my mind of the subject of infallibility, chiefly as the result of an exchange with the late Bishop B. C. Butler. The Bishop made two important points. The first is that any verbal formula is involved in the fallibilities of language, so that it may be 'inadequate, misleading, and even trailing clouds of (culturally derived) error'. Bishop Butler asks us to look rather at what he calls the 'governing intention' behind the formula. His other point is that the word 'infallibility' is unfortunate, 'because it seems to stress the negative notion of inerrancy, whereas what is really at stake is guaranteed truth – a positive notion'.[9]

It does seem to me that these two points made by Bishop Butler allow us to see the question of infallibility in a new light, and take away some of the difficulties which I had earlier expressed. Infallibility, he says, is a negative term but really expresses an affirmative idea. I would have difficulty with his expression 'guaranteed truth', but I think I could put the matter as follows. The church has been given the promise that the Holy Spirit will lead it into all truth. It may in fact at one time or another go astray, but it is constantly being brought back to truth to the extent that it is open to the prompting of the Spirit. I find the analogy of a magnetic needle helpful to illustrate this. The needle may be diverted from the true direction by the distracting influences of metal objects in its immediate neighbourhood, but when these distractions are eliminated, it swings back to north under the prevailing influence of earth's magnetism. So if the Christian church can turn away from distracting influences and be open to the Holy Spirit, it too will turn again to the truth and resume its true direction. I have been speaking here of infallibility as belonging to the church, but of course this is quite compatible with referring it in a special way to the one who leads the church, but recognizing, also, that he does not lead it as an isolated individual, for to link infallibility with openness to the Spirit is to link it with the community of the

Spirit, and so to set it in a corporate or collegial context. Bishop Butler's other point, about the imperfections of language, is also important. Even the most hallowed formulae of the church come to a point where they are no longer saying clearly what they were intended to say. They call for restatement. Yet such restatement must (in the Bishop's phrase) be true to the 'governing intention'. We are never able, of course, to catch that governing intention in its essence – it will always have clothed itself in some new language. But what we must ensure is that the new language says all that the old language intended to say. For example, we may think that the Chalcedonian way of speaking of the person of Christ as one person in whom there concur two natures presents severe problems for our contemporary understanding. We may, therefore, feel impelled to construct a new christology. But we should ensure that the new christology says as much as the Chalcedonian fathers. Along some such lines as indicated here, I believe, the dogma of papal infallibility can make sense, and be acceptable to Christians who are at present not in communion with Rome.

The second difficulty I mentioned is jurisdiction. In the terminology of Vatican I, the Pope has universal, ordinary and immediate jurisdiction within the church. This certainly sounds like an enormous concentration of power in an individual, and the mere quoting of such language arouses anxieties in the minds of those who, while seeking closer ties with Rome, are also desirous of maintaining what they believe to be a reasonable measure of freedom within the church. The very word 'jurisdiction' is unfortunate. It is a legal term and has connotations of authoritarian rule more appropriate to the secular state than to the Christian church. The adjectives 'universal', 'ordinary' and 'immediate' are technical terms, and an attempt is made to explain these in ways which might allay possible anxieties in the second of the two ARCIC statements on authority. To quote:

Difficulties have arisen from the attribution of universal, ordinary and immediate jurisdiction to the Bishop of Rome, and misunderstanding of these technical terms has aggravated the difficulties. . . The attribution of such jurisdiction is a source of anxiety to Anglicans who fear, for example, that he could usurp the rights of a metropolitan in his province, or of a bishop in his diocese; that a centralised authority might not always understand local conditions or respect legitimate cultural diversity; that rightful freedom of conscience, thought and action could be imperilled.[10]

In response to such anxieties, the Commission declared that 'the universal primate should exercise, and be seen to exercise, his ministry not in isolation but in collegial association with his brother bishops' and claimed also that there are moral limits to the exercise of jurisdiction which cannot be defined precisely by canon.[11]

But these views might be just the expression of a pious hope unless they were spelt out more concretely. In a contribution to the small volume of essays, entitled *Their Lord and Ours*,[12] published at the time of the present Pope's visit to Britain, I ventured to make a suggestion which, I think, might help to resolve some of the difficulties in accepting the notion of a universal papal jurisdiction. The presupposition behind this suggestion was that papal jurisdiction might be exercised in different ways in different parts of the church, according to local circumstances. Thus, within the diocese of Rome, it is obvious that the jurisdiction of the Pope would be immediate and direct. Within the church in Italy, it would be somewhat less direct, because the Pope would be in collegial relationship with the Italian primates, such as the Patriarch of Venice. In the case of the church in France, let us say, or Germany or the United States, the mode of jurisdiction would be modified further. When we come to an entity like the Church of England or the whole world-wide Anglican communion, my suggestion was that papal jurisdiction should be exercised through the existing primates, namely the Archbishops of Canterbury, York and the other primatial sees. I do not mean that papal jurisdiction would be only nominal. I visualize, rather, a constant interchange and consultation between the Pope and the primates concerned. To some extent there would indeed be a delegation of authority, but this does not mean any diminution of the responsibility of the universal primate, nor of his right and duty to be sometimes spokesman for the whole church. But I think that it would go far to ensure that the specific ethos of Anglicanism would not be simply submerged in the new relation with Rome. It would in fact ensure the point made in 1970 at the beginning of these consultations by Pope Paul VI who said, 'There will be no seeking to lessen the legitimate prestige and the worthy patrimony of piety and usage proper to the Anglican Church.' I have mentioned these proposals with special reference to the Anglican communion, to which I belong, but clearly, *mutatis mutandis*, parallel arrangements might be possible with Orthodox churches, Lutheran churches, and others.

Clearly, there are many difficulties still to be solved on the long way that leads toward a unified church, and the working out of details may take many years. Nevertheless, the vision of a new relationship of solidarity within the Body of Christ is one that we shall not let go, now that we have glimpsed it. And within that vision, an important place belongs to the papacy as a great unifying force, the modern equivalent and successor of the special apostolate of Peter, to whom our Lord gave the command, 'Feed my sheep.'

The Papacy in a Pilgrim Church

A Response to Professor Macquarrie by Eamonn Conway

I am honoured to have been invited to respond to Professor Macquarrie's article 'The Papacy in a Unified Church'. His views on the future of the papacy are both balanced and challenging and merit serious reflection.

Macquarrie is anxious to avoid two extremes: on the one hand, an absolute monarchical papacy; on the other, reducing the papacy to a mere primacy of honour. He then sets out to find a middle course between those extremes and around which most Christians, he believes, could find agreement. Macquarrie is guided by both scripture and tradition which, he believes, together provide ample evidence for the primacy exercised by Peter and the transmission of same through a line of duly elected successors. He is also guided by practical considerations: the church, spread as it is throughout the world, needs such an office if it is to safeguard its catholicity; the church, if it is to fulfil its mission to the world, needs a spokesman who can speak to the whole world on its behalf.

There is no doubt that, as Macquarrie notes, the papacy today is more influential in the secular realm than ever before. One has only to think of the crumbling of the Berlin wall, or of the recent papal visit to Cuba. With the loss of temporal power, and particularly in the person of John Paul II, the Pope's relationship to the world has been re-defined, and very successfully so from the church's point of view. World-wide, perhaps especially among non-Christians, the Pope is acknowledged as a very effective bridge-builder. In contrast, however, much less progress in the development of the papal office has been made in the intra-ecclesial realm. Professor Macquarrie has highlighted the two most serious obstacles in this regard: papal infallibility and papal jurisdiction. Here I would like to comment briefly on his observations concerning both of these.

To take the first of these: the doctrine of papal infallibility. Following a conversation with the late Bishop Butler, Macquarrie now sees less difficulty with this from the Anglican point of view then he did when he wrote *Christian Unity and Christian Diversity* in 1975. He now understands infallibility as a guarantee that, although the church may 'at one time or another go astray . . . it is constantly brought back to truth to the extent that it is open to the prompting of the Holy Spirit'. He provides the analogy of a magnetic needle which always eventually swings back to North under the prevailing influence of the earth's magnetism. 'So', Macquarrie notes, 'if the Christian church can turn away from distracting influences and be open to the Holy Spirit, it too will turn again to the truth and resume its true direction.'

If I have understood Professor Macquarrie correctly, he sees the doctrine of papal infallibility as a guarantee that, though the church may err on its pilgrim journey, it will not remain in error but will always eventually find its true direction. In my view the Roman Catholic understanding of the doctrine goes further than this. The Roman Catholic understanding of papal infallibility claims that as the church makes its pilgrim journey, a certain number of its teachings are taught with a guarantee of truth and freedom from error. To express this in terms of Macquarrie's analogy, the doctrine of papal infallibility claims that, at *particular* decisive moments on its journey the Christian community can be assured that the compass needle is not under any distracting influences and is, in fact, pointing north.

It is important to stress here that the exercise of papal infallibility, as well as that of the ordinary and universal magisterium, is carefully circumscribed. In particular, papal infallibility is a guarantee of truth which pertains to certain doctrines, not a quality pertaining to the church as such. Very often opposition to the doctrine of papal infallibility arises from a lack of attention both to the conditions for its exercise and the ecclesiology upon which it is based.

In his article Professor Macquarrie makes one other point which he believes might make the doctrine of papal infallibility more acceptable to non-Roman Catholic Christians. He believes it is important to distinguish between the 'governing intention' behind a particular doctrine which might be taught infallibly, and the particular formulation of this doctrine which may well be culturally determined or reflect the imperfections and limitations to which all language is subject. This is true. All human truth is formulated and expressed in concrete and therefore limited historical contexts. And this is why, it seems to me, one can go a step further and say that, objectively speaking, even a defined doctrine is open to development not just in terms of its formulation but also in terms of its content. This is true of all defined doctrine and is therefore also true of the doctrine of infallibility itself, an observation which, one would hope, might contribute to the doctrine's wider acceptability among Christians.

Professor Macquarrie also comments on the teaching of Vatican I that the Pope has universal, ordinary and immediate jurisdiction within the church. He notes that this legal, technical language is off-putting, and the apparent concentration of such power in an individual is unacceptable to many Christian churches. He goes on to point out, however, that papal jurisdiction can act as a useful counter-balance to abuses of power among individual bishops and to suggest that, in the world church, papal jurisdiction might be exercised in different ways. So, for example, with regard to the Anglican communion papal jurisdiction could be exercised through the Archbishop of Canterbury.

The Second Vatican Council dealt with the issue of jurisdiction in its Constitution, *Lumen Gentium*. It is interesting to note that it uses the term 'jurisdiction' sparingly, and then only with reference to the office of bishop. The term is not used at all with regard to the papal office. Instead, the Pope, according to *Lumen Gentium*, as pastor of the entire church, is understood to have full, supreme and universal *power* over the whole church, a power which he can always exercise unhindered (§ 22). But it also says that the order of bishops, in communion with the Pope, has supreme and full *authority* over the universal church. There is room for much theological reflection on the relationship and distinction between jurisdiction, power and authority. Whatever the outcome of such reflection it is clear that at Vatican II the office of bishop very much came in to its own. The power of bishops, we are told, which they exercise personally in the name of

Christ, is 'proper, ordinary and immediate' (§ 26). Although the exercise of this power is controlled by the supreme authority of the church, it does not derive from this authority. It derives from Christ. This is a key point, the significance of which has yet to be grasped by many bishops, judging by the way they seem to exercise their office.

Two further observations by way of conclusion. First, we must remember that the papacy is a *charisma*, i.e. both a gift to and a service within the church. If we are agreed on that then we are obliged both to receive this gift graciously and to continually discover ways in which this gift can bear fruit both for the church and the world.

Second, it seems to me that the structure of the conciliar constitution *Lumen Gentium* suggests the context within which the role of the papacy in a unified church is best discussed. The constitution begins by highlighting the mystery of the church. It then speaks of the Church as the whole people of God. Only subsequently does *Lumen Gentium* consider the hierarchical nature of the church. Even then, a lengthy consideration of episcopal collegiality precedes consideration of the papal office, which is presented as a *pastoral* ministry at the service of unity and fidelity. Above all *Lumen Gentium* stresses that Christ is the Supreme Pastor.

Finally, we can all take heart from the penultimate chapter of *Lumen Gentium*. Here we are reminded that 'the pilgrim church, in its sacraments and institutions, which belong to this present age, carries the mark of this world which will pass, and she herself takes her place among the creatures which groan and travail yet and await the revelation of the sons of God (§ 48, cf. Rom. 8. 19–22). The papacy guides the pilgrim church along its way; nevertheless it is itself one of the institutions which belong to this present age and which bear the mark of this world which will pass.

Outlines of Major Works

Georgina Morley

An Existentialist Theology (1955, 1972³) explores the way in which Rudolph Bultmann uses the existentialist philosophy of Martin Heidegger to re-present St Paul's theology to a twentieth-century audience. As well as introducing the work of Bultmann and Heidegger, the book assesses whether such an approach to theology is viable and offers some specific clues as to its weaknesses.

The introductory section of the book examines the general issue of the use of philosophy by theology. It affirms that it has an apologetic function in so far as it makes use of current ideas to commend Christian faith to the modern mind. But, more importantly, it admits that a philosophical under-standing is always presupposed in theology, and insists that this must be scrutinized to ensure that it is appropriate for the genuine interpretation of theological texts and concepts. It agrees that an existentialist philosophy is indeed appropriate to theology because it raises the question of what kind of being the human existence to whom God relates is, and insists on our responsibility when faced with the summons to decision.

The main argument of *An Existentialist Theology* is divided into two parts, which correspond to Heidegger's two-fold division of human existence as inauthentic or authentic. Inevitably, the book becomes increasingly technical at this point, but a full glossary and careful explanations are pro-vided. The first part of the main argument deals with 'exist-ence as inauthentic and fallen', and introduces Heidegger's analysis of human existence as always 'in a world', and of the ways in which we become aware of the character of our existence. The negative possibilities of inauthentic existence in relation to the world and to others are explored, as is Heidegger's notion of death as the ultimate possibility by which inauthentic existence can be re-evaluated. In the course of this exploration, Bultmann's interpretation of Paul's anthropology is traced out, to show how Heidegger's categories can restore the meaning of Paul's use of terms such as the body and the flesh, the natural body and the spiritual body, the creation and the world, and sin.

The second part of the main argument examines 'the Christian life as authentic existence'. It begins with an exploration of the extent to which Heidegger's notion of authenticity corresponds with the Christian understanding of true life or life in the Spirit, and how the transition or 'conversion' to authentic existence takes place. It traces the character of the life of faith in relation to existentialist categories, and pinpoints where the characteristics of Christian life have a unique content because they arise as the gift of God's act of grace in Jesus Christ – rather than from human existence itself.

For the most part, *An Existentialist Theology* makes a positive assessment of Bultmann's use of Heidegger in interpreting Paul's theology. However, three areas of concern emerge. The first is that Bultmann's theology is too focussed on the individual, who is considered apart from the contexts of church, human race or cosmos. The second is that, in concentrating on the existential significance of Christ's person and acts, Bultmann underestimates the importance of understanding them also as objective historical events. The final concern is that by presenting faith as a new self-understanding for which we decide, Bultmann follows Heidegger too far in ascribing this transition to human resources and does not give a full enough account of the act of grace. These concerns, however, are genuine concerns rather than overt criticisms, and in his foreword to the book Bultmann himself agrees that they should be areas for continuing discussion.

The Scope of Demythologizing (1960) examines the debate which arose over Bultmann's 'demythologizing' of the New Testament, and assesses the objections of two camps of critics – conservative and radical. To the extent to which Bultmann sought to translate the teaching of the New Testament into statements concerning human existence, his work was subject to a variety of criticisms of conservative scholars who were anxious to safeguard the unique act of God in Christ. But to the extent to which Bultmann himself sought to safeguard this act and hold open human existence to the summons of God, his work was criticized by radical scholars for failing to pursue his project into a complete rendering of the New Testament into a philosophy of existence.

On the conservative side of the debate, three groups of objections are considered. Firstly, the question of whether demythologizing is adequate or appropriate to the task of exegesis is assessed, in conversation with the criticisms of Thielicke and Barth that it reduces or even negates the extent to which the Bible addresses the hearer. Secondly, the question of whether an existentialist interpretation of the New Testament is adequate to the historical character of the incarnation, atonement and resurrection is assessed in conversation with historians such as Cullmann, Troeltsch and Toynbee. Thirdly, the question of whether an emphasis on the existential significance of New Testament teaching is appropriate to the traditional understanding of dogma as expressing objective, eternal truths is assessed in relation to modernizing tendencies in the Roman Catholic Church and their critics.

A further three sets of objections are introduced on the radical side of the debate. Firstly Buri's objection is considered, that to retain the specific act of God in opening the way to authentic existence is mistaken and arrogant, and not only limits dialogue between philosophers and theologians but also displaces grace from its true place in human existence itself. Secondly, Jaspers objection is considered, that

Bultmann relies too heavily on a specific revelation in Christ and gives insufficient account of a more universal revelation within human existence Thirdly, the challenges of philosophers of religious language are considered, that Bultmann's definition of myth is confusing and that, in any case, it does not help to establish the fundamental question of the validity of Christian faith in the modern world.

In making an assessment of the debate, *The Scope of Demythologizing* largely defends Bultmann against the charges of his critics in terms of the content of their argument. However, it does also suggest that the criticisms arise because of a misleading aspect to Bultmann's work which obscures the way in which statements about human existence and statements about the act of God do hold together. The misleading dimension is the failure to distinguish between the modern world-view as the context in which Christian faith must be communicated, and the modern self-understanding of human being as ultimate which the Christian faith must contradict. *The Scope of Demythologizing* argues that whilst Bultmann's approach to the first of these is wholly appropriate, it is his ambivalence over the validity of the second which raises both the fears of the conservatives and the expectations of the radicals.

Twentieth-Century Religious Thought (1963, 1988[4]) provides a survey of the enormous range of contemporary religious thought in the West. It covers not only theology and philosophy of religion, but also the criticisms of religion by those who take a negative stance towards it, and gives special attention to those thinkers on the boundary between theology and philosophy. As well as offering a succinct exposition and assessment of the work of key thinkers, it draws them together according to schools of thought, so that common characteristics can be identified, and influences traced. In addition, despite the impossibility of offering a strictly chronological development, the century is divided into four distinct yet overlapping phases, in order to indicate the shifting moods and intentions of religious thought throughout the period, especially in relation to cultural changes. Each of these phases is introduced in a brief chapter which forms an 'interlude' between the galleries of significant thinkers.

The first phase is characterized by the continuation of ideas from the nineteenth century, and lasts approximately to the First World War. It is typified by a buoyancy of spirit and the assumption of an inevitable progress in human affairs, and the possibility of achieving a single comprehensive understanding of reality.

The second phase is a transitional period characterized by the collapse of optimism and its replacement with sober realism, prompted by the events of the second decade of the century. Facts rather than ideals become the focus of attention and the intellectual task becomes more modest and limited in scope, directed, for example, to the philosophy of history or the sociological interpretation of religion. As human being experiences itself less as scientific master and more as stranger and pilgrim, God also becomes a suffering or even an evolving (that is, inexperienced!) God.

The mid-century period, up to the mid 1960s, is the phase in which distinctive twentieth-century ideas crystallize. The key dividing line is between those who remain confident in the capacity of human reason to understand ultimate reality (for example, neo-Thomists), and those who reject this confidence (both sceptical logical positivists, and Barth-inspired theologians of the Word).

The final (and current) phase is less clearly definable without some degree of historical perspective. It appears to be characterized by a returning (if ambivalent) confidence in science, and an awareness of the connectedness of the world. Theological strands intermingle more than previously, and are influenced as much by neo-Marxism as by philosophy, and by the religious watershed provided by Vatican II. The emphasis is on the social, rather than the individual, the practical rather than the theoretical, and the future rather than the past.

A brief final chapter points to some general insights which can be drawn from the bewildering array of religious thought which has been presented. Firstly, that a degree of relativism is appropriate, between the exaggerated confidence that an absolute understanding of religious truth is attainable and the absolute scepticism that nothing can be known. Secondly, that religious questions arise in a specific cultural context and are influenced by the mood of that context. And thirdly, that since religion is not a theoretical matter but engages the whole person in their cultural context, some attitude must be taken towards it (even if it is that it is illusory) which is reasonable and contemporary, even if provisional.

Studies in Christian Existentialism (1965) is a volume of collected essays and lectures from 1955–1963, including the Inaugural lecture for Union Theological Seminary, 'How is Theology Possible?', gathered from a period in which the grip of secularity was keenly felt.

In the course of the five parts of the book, the existentialist approach to theology is introduced and defended. Its fundamental philosophical concepts (human existence, feeling as understanding, death, temporality, being and nothing) are explored, and their relevance to the interpretation of New Testament language is defended. Three other approaches to re-expressing Christian faith in the context of the modern world are assessed: Braithwaite's 'demythologizing' of religious language into statements of human intention, Teilhard de Chardin's evolutionary approach to natural theology, and Rahner's dynamic re-working of Thomist theology. In the course of this assessment, what becomes explicit is the commitment of existentialist theology to maintain a balance between the significance of theological themes for the human person and their grounding in some objective 'ontological' reality. What also emerges is an understanding of transcendence as the sense in which God is ahead of (rather than above) his creation, relating to it in self-giving love.

Finally, the existentialist approach to Christian theology

which the book has commended is applied to three specific doctrines. Its applicability to a 'classic' or 'dramatic' view of the atonement (such as that of Gustav Aulén in *Christus Victor*) is demonstrated, and its role in restoring this view of the atonement to wider use is welcomed. It is offered as a means of clarifying the apparently opposing views that death is the penalty for sin and that death can be an affirmation of true life. Lastly, it is explored in relation to the issue of how the Holy Spirit can be said to work on the human person and yet without violating his or her integrity and responsibility; the 'seven gifts of the Holy Ghost' are used as illustrations.

Principles of Christian Theology (1966, 1977²) is a one-volume systematic theology which gives a careful account of how the various parts of Christian theology constitute a unity, and how they relate to other attitudes and under-standings in the modern world. The existentialist approach to theology continues to be predominant, but there is an increased emphasis on the way in which language about human existence points beyond itself to a more ultimate reality in Being itself. This style of doing theology is given the technical description 'existential-ontological'.

A substantial introductory chapter surveys sources and method in theology, and establishes both its relationship to neighbouring disciplines and the relationship of the various disciplines within theology to one another. The main explor-ations of *Principles of Christian Theology* are divided into three parts.

Part One deals with 'Philosophical Theology', and develops a new style of natural theology, derived from the existentialist analysis of the human situation (rather than from the natural realm). This shows how the quest for God emerges from our human condition, and indicates what this means for under-standing God as Being which is gracious to the contradictions and desires of human being. This section also includes a dis-cussion of the character of revelation in relation to other kinds of human knowing, the nature of religious language, and the function of religion itself, each interpreted according to the form of natural theology being advocated.

Part Two explores 'Symbolic Theology', or doctrinal theology. It explicates particular concrete elements in the teaching of the Christian faith – the triune God, creation, evil, the person and work of Jesus Christ, the Holy Spirit, the Last Things – and interprets them in the language of existence and being for a modern readership, and in a way which is consistent with their traditional meaning and intention. The dramatic, narrative form of Christian faith is emphasized, and justifies the dynamic understanding of God as giving himself, bringing into being and gathering into unity which is offered, and which infuses all the concrete symbols considered.

The final part of *Principles of Christian Theology* concerns 'Applied Theology', and investigates the practical outworking of the previous sections in the church and the world, in liturgical and sacramental practice and church order, in prayer and in ethics. The consistent emphasis in this section is that since human life is always lived in particular historical and cultural embodiments, and since God as Being is always disclosed there, a faith which arises from human existence will find these embodiments not only prone to the distortion of sin but also vehicles for grace.

God-Talk (1967) investigates the nature and validity of religious language, especially in the shadow of the hostilities of philosophical positivism. The book places this narrow strand of positivism in a broader and more sympathetic school of empiricism, and also addresses language issues raised by the *Honest to God* debate and the so-called 'death of God' theologies. The key thrust of *God-Talk* is to demonstrate that religious language is as defensible in its logic and coherence as language which refers to 'things in the world'.

After introducing the general problem of religious language, and pointing to the weaknesses of some contemporary approaches, the book traces out the logical structure common to all discourse, and shows how religious language shares in this structure. In any 'discourse-situation', language is expressive of the person who speaks, communicates to the person who is spoken to, and refers to that which is spoken of. This threefold structure establishes the key tasks for a defence of religious language.

Firstly, a defence of religious language must give an account of the way in which it is expressive of the person who uses it. To this end the existentialist understanding of religious language is re-introduced, to show that language which speaks of God also always speaks of our human condition, and reveals the speaker's attitudes and commitments.

Secondly, such a defence must show that religious language does in fact communicate to its audience. Here the issues of demythologizing and of re-interpreting traditional images are explored, to establish that religious language can indeed be 'translated' into a contemporary shared world. This in turn raises the issue of which images are appropriate and how a 'likeness' between an image and what it refers to can be understood and established, especially if God is the referend.

Finally, a defence of religious language must justify its claim to refer to a reality beyond the subjective realm of the speaker. This is the point most vulnerable to the attacks of positivism, and it is here that *God-Talk* draws on a broader range of empirical thought to show that whilst faith is not proved by sense data in the world it can be supported by reference to, for example, observable facts in the natural world, historical assertions and the empirical results of faith in human experience. In addition to this, *God-Talk* shows how Heidegger's thought establishes that language about human existence does also refer to a reality beyond the confines both of that existence and of what empirical language can say, by showing both the cognitive content of feelings (and thus of those associated with religious experience) and also the way in which thinking receives reality, and does not merely analyse or shape it, and can thus receive the fundamentally religious truth of the wholeness of reality. In this way, *God-Talk* shows not only how religious language shares the structure of all human language, but also that it has a distinctive logic which embraces and transcends existentialism and empiricism, and is fundamental to its interpretation.

God and Secularity (1968) addresses the exaltation of secularity by contemporary theology, and the trend to reduce and humanize Christian faith. It argues that there can be no theology 'without God' (so that, for example, theology cannot be reduced simply to a practical human ethic) but that, since theology must now be done in a secularized world, the task at hand is to do it so that it communicates with its particular context but without losing hold of its own distinctive character and insight.

The early chapters of *God and Secularity* assess various projects to secularize theology in America, Britain and continental Europe, and trace the roots of the process in the thought of Tillich, Bultmann, Bonhoeffer and Barth. The nature of secular culture under discussion is then clarified by identifying a cluster of characteristic preoccupations. These consist of a concern with this temporal world rather than an eternal realm, with everyday activities rather than particular 'religious' practices, with the kind of knowledge gained by human endeavour rather than by special sources of knowledge, and with human autonomy rather than the 'heteronomy' of divine rule.

Subsequent chapters address the stereotyping and false polarities which emerge in such a presentation of secular versus sacred, and present an understanding of Christian faith which overcomes this dichotomy whilst remaining clear what it is that theology cannot give up: an account of the ultimate reality which lies behind human experience, an account of the reciprocal relationship between God and the world, and an account of the person of Christ which expresses the transcendent (and not merely psychological) character of grace.

Finally, a 'theology of the secular' is sketched out with the aid of five significant doctrines, which together provide a vision of the world which allows theology to do justice to the secular without diminishing the centrality of God in the Christian faith.

Martin Heidegger (1968) is one of the slim volumes in the 'Makers of Contemporary Theology' series. It offers a straightforward introduction to the philosophy of Martin Heidegger, and shows how his thought provides the kind of conceptual system which is helpful for explaining Christian faith in the modern world.

The book starts with a brief biographical sketch, and then gives an exposition of the main themes of Heidegger's work. Attention is given principally (though not exclusively) to his earlier writings, especially *Being and Time* (1927), so themes under consideration include phenomenological method and existential analysis, the nature of truth, temporality and history, and typical Heideggarian notions such as 'Being-in-the-world' and 'authentic existence'. As well as offering the clearest possible explanation in the text, a glossary is provided for over twenty technical terms. Finally, an assessment is made of the very considerable significance of Heidegger's philosophy for contemporary theology. His influence on the doctrines of human being and of God is commended in the context of a less hospitable Western tradition; his work on language and hermeneutics is shown to have facilitated a more positive interpretation of myth in the Bible than was previously possible for the modern period; his account of the variety of forms of thinking has offered an alternative to a dominant Western positivism which has given no credence to mysticism and revelation.

The much more recent *Heidegger and Christianity* (1994) furthers this introductory work. It is the text of the Hensley Henson lectures in Oxford, 1993–94, and is of necessity more technical. So, for example, it offers no glossary, but provides a multi-lingual bibliography and it explores the problem of Heidegger's use of word-play and (sometimes unconvincing) etymology in relation to the task of translation.

The biographical sketch is somewhat extended, and the supposed scandal of Heidegger's interest in National Socialism is carefully dealt with – and firmly debunked. In this later work, the focus is on the progression of Heidegger's thought concerning various key themes, and developments are teased out to show differences and continuities between the early *Being and Time* period, the later post-war period, and the brief post-retirement period. Distinctions are drawn between Sartre's pessimistic humanism and Heidegger's more measured account of human ultimacy in the face of the self-giving of Being. Attention is given to the issue of whether Heidegger can be deemed a theist; affinities are noted between his later thought and both Western and Eastern mysticism, and the meaning of 'theism' is scrutinized to see under what conditions Heidegger can, and should not, be deemed to be so defined – especially in the light of Heidegger's own disregard of such defining categories!

Three Issues in Ethics (1970) explores three fundamental questions in the relation between theology and ethics in the contemporary world: the relation of Christian morals to non-Christian morals, the shape of a theological ethic appropriate to our time, and the place of faith in the moral life. These questions are addressed in relation to changing understandings of human nature, a re-thinking of natural law, the meaning of conscience, sin and grace, and the role of hope in the moral life.

Before dealing with these questions, *Three Issues in Ethics* offers an introduction and critique of the so-called 'new-morality' emerging principally in Protestant circles. Agreeing that there is a need for a new reflection on morality, and especially one which balances hardened principles with attention to persons, love and the context, *Three Issues in Ethics* is unconvinced by a radical revolt against all forms of rule, and provides a sharp critique of situational ethics. The approach favoured here aims at a more comprehensive position which holds together this Protestant emphasis on liberty with the traditional Catholic stress on the stability of moral law and virtue.

The first task towards such an ethic is to update traditional notions of human nature as fixed and occurring in a static, hierarchical universe. Accordingly, a chapter traces out new developments in our self-understanding, which differ from the traditional Western understanding of human nature, but which all have a place in the biblical understanding. These characteristics establish that a contemporary ethic must be dynamic, social and fundamentally embodied and related to the world. *Three Issues in Ethics* then investigates the concept of natural law to show that an ethic of these qualities can indeed emerge from a recognition of 'how things are' – because human being and the cosmos itself exhibit a directedness, a tendency towards a goal in which the human capacity for moral striving participates.

The role of conscience in the moral life is explored, and 'sin' and 'grace' are explained in terms of factors which 'disable' or 'enable' an appropriate response to the conscience's summons to the moral life. A careful use of theological terms, together with the revised understanding of natural law, is shown to offer a way of grounding the call to a moral life in an objective reality beyond the conscience of the individual agent and the standards of the historical community.

The cumulative approach of *Three Issues in Ethics* is to emphasize the continuity and common goals of Christian ethics and general moral ideals and endeavours, without the need to dilute Christianity to conform to acceptable secular standards or, conversely, to attempt to 'annex' non-Christians to the Christian cause as anonymous or crypto-Christians.

Paths in Spirituality (1972, 1992²) argues that the practice of religion – prayer, worship, spirituality – still has a place in the modern world, and offers new ways of thinking about traditional practices that take into account theological developments in understanding the nature of God and human being.

An introductory chapter notes that within the trend for 'religionless' Christianity energies have been channelled into personal and social relationships, and prayer, worship and spirituality have been under-emphasized. Indeed, it has even been claimed that this specifically religious dimension is the barrier that prevents people in our secular culture from committing themselves to a practical Christian lifestyle. *Paths in Spirituality* argues that, on the contrary, the capacity for religion belongs to us all, and that it is only by developing this capacity that we can become fully human.

The book offers four guidelines for a renewed spirituality that will take account of contemporary critiques of religion. Firstly, spirituality must safeguard human dignity and show that it opens up the fulfilment of human being. Secondly, spirituality must show that it does not simply locate the believer in patterns inherited from the past, but is forward-looking and brings that which lies in the future into the present. Thirdly, spirituality must engage with the world in which it is set, neither escaping from it nor absorbed by it. Finally, spirituality must be true to the corporate character of human life, and not simply aim at individual wholeness.

Paths in Spirituality addresses the particular meanings of worship, prayer and spirituality under these guidelines so that their sources in the Christian heritage are valued but they are re-expressed for the particular context in which they are to be practised today. This involves a discussion of the contemporary dangers of subjectivism and anti-intellectualism in the spiritual life, as well as the converse danger of the prevailing demand that human knowledge be 'objective' and value neutral.

A final cluster of chapters explores a variety of traditional devotional practices (eucharist, benediction, offices, stations of the cross) and advocates a strongly eucharistic approach to contemporary spirituality, in which word and sacrament are held together to interpret and inform one another. The sacramental nature of the world is emphasized, although it is not general knowledge but the gift of revelation that allows us to 'see in depth' the signs of God's presence in everyday realities. And it is participation – in God's presence in the world and in the habits of Christian discipline – which is shown to be the way to a renewed spirituality that can defend its validity in the secular world.

The Faith of the People of God: A Lay Theology (1972) advocates the doing of theology as a joint enterprise between (mostly clerical) professional theologians and lay people – a 'co-theologizing' to rank alongside concelebration in its broadest sense of shared worship and collegiality in the field of church government. As such, a lay theology is not a watered-down simplistic version of academic theology, but a distinct theological genre which expresses the life of the whole people of God engaged in the world. As well as contributing to a theological self-understanding of the people of God, a lay theology pays special attention to expressing Christian beliefs in ways which show that they are reasonable and can find support in the common experience of being human. This means that although a lay theology reflects on the distinctiveness of the community of faith, it also insists on the solidarity of the people of God with the whole of humanity.

As a contribution to lay theology, *The Faith of the People of God* provides a systematic introduction to the key doctrines of the Christian faith (God, human nature, creation and providence, sin and evil, Christ, the Holy Spirit, the 'last things') and its key practices (prayer, sacraments, ministry and mission). These are all viewed in their particular form most relevant to the explicit theme of the people of God: that is to say, in the way that sheds most light on the corporate life of the community of faith and on the full humanity to which we are all called.

During the course of this systematic exploration, a number of other topics emerge for discussion: the developing self-understanding of the people of God in the Old Testament from the call of Abraham to Israel's time in exile, the nature of language about God, the quest for the 'historical Jesus', the character of the contemporary world. These, too, are dealt with in the double focus of the self-understanding of the people of God and of the fact that this faith community is embodied in the concrete material and historical world and must make sense here also.

The Faith of the People of God provides an extensive guide to further reading which, far more than a simple bibliographical listing, offers comment and advice on the recommended texts in their contexts.

Existentialism (1972, 1973²) is a comprehensive introduction, guide and evaluation of the broad field of existentialist thought. Unlike the majority of surveys on this subject, it does not arrange its material by author but deals with it thematically, giving extensive illustration from the writings of major thinkers in the field.

Two preliminary chapters introduce existentialism as a way of doing philosophy rather than a clearly defined body of content, and trace an existentialist tendency throughout the history of philosophy from its earliest roots in prereflective myth to its full variety of form in nineteenth- and twentieth-century philosophy.

The largest segment of *Existentialism* offers a comprehensive examination of a selection of recurring themes which, whilst not to be regarded as the defining content of existentialism, do in practice tend to identify a distinctively existentialist approach to philosophy. These are arranged in the order of the existentialist analysis itself, so they begin with the basic understanding of the term 'existence' and how this occurs 'in the world' and 'with others'. They include the distinctive approach to truth, understanding, thinking and feeling; and the nature of the existent as agent, as well as the things which frustrate responsible action and which enable the achievement of authentic selfhood.

All of these themes tend to be concerned primarily with the individual, but two subsequent chapters deal with more corporate dimensions of existentialist thought. History is investigated as a fundamentally human concern not with what is past but with what the possibilities of human existence are in practice because they have already been demonstrated; and the role of existentialist philosophy in society and politics is explored in terms of its critical function with regard to what restricts human freedom and diminishes human dignity. The capacity of existentialist thought to offer insight on the whole 'encompassing reality' is discussed in a chapter on existentialist metaphysics.

Two final chapters offer an assessment of existentialism. The first of these notes the influence of existentialist thought in the arts (literature and visual), psychology and psychiatry, educational methods, ethics, and theology. The second assesses the validity of a number of criticisms typically levelled against existentialism: for example, that it is anti-reason, amoral, pessimistic, anthropocentric and individualistic. Whilst recognizing that there is such a variety of thought within the field that no criticism will be universally applicable, the criticisms are generally deemed to be accidental distortions rather than integral weaknesses *per se*; where such distortion has occurred, a call is made for modification and a broadening of understanding for the sake of balance. The overall assessment, however, is that the merits of existentialist thought outweigh the objections because it has been able consistently to offer a protection and enhancement of humanity in a time when humanity has been under significant threat.

The Concept of Peace (1973) is a slim volume of presentations given for the Firth Lectures at Nottingham in 1972. It is neither an emotional treatment nor a merely speculative exploration, but investigates the *concept* of peace, and offers a guide to an intelligent and practical pursuit of peace.

In seeking a corporate or, indeed, global ethic, *The*

Concept of Peace distinguishes between a lesser and a greater vision of peace. The lesser vision is the absence of strife and conflict. This essentially negative understanding of peace is typified in the Greek *eirene* and Latin *pax* which both indicate a state of peace achieved in the midst of conflict by truce or agreement. It is also represented philosophically in, for example, the Hobbesian tradition in which the primary state of human nature is struggle, and peace a secondary and temporary achievement. The greater vision of peace is demonstrated in the biblical notion of *shalom* (as well as the Russian *mir* and Sanskrit *santi*), which points to a positive condition of wholeness and completion. This is both a primordial condition and an eschatological one, and understands peace as the primary state of affairs, the 'natural law', from which conflict is an aberration.

The radical difference between these two concepts of peace is seen in the fact that the first seeks to restrain all conflict, even that which strives towards a more justly peaceable world long-term, whereas the second concedes that there may be some conflict along the 'growing edge' in the movement towards wholeness. In commending the second, greater, vision of peace, *The Concept of Peace* tackles the fraught question of whether violence can ever be harnessed in the pursuit of peace. It offers stringent guidelines as a test to the legitimacy of violence, on the model of 'just war', and admits that there may indeed be very rare occasions when circumstances more degrading than violence require violence for their cessation. Such are the moral ambiguities of this world, and such were the conditions that Dietrich Bonhoeffer faced, explored here in a small case-study.

Peace is given a 'metaphysical' grounding in the Christian understanding of grace, atonement and resurrection – each taken in their most ultimate sense as truths about the total reality within which we strive towards peace. These motifs are given practical application in very concrete suggestions about how we can be instruments of peace: all are admitted to be obvious and small scale, but earth the argument of the book in precisely that place where it sees that its effect may be secured, in the commitment of individuals to re-humanize the 'military-industrial complex' of modern culture.

Christian Unity and Christian Diversity (1975) is written in the context of the ecumenical movement, and argues that diversity is just as essential as unity to the well-being and vitality of the church. As well as the need for diversity if the church is to address a pluralistic culture, the book points to the theological justification for diversity in the multiplicity of creation, and suggests that the true goal of ecumenical unity lies beyond the churches in the final, eschatological union of all humanity.

Within the ecumenical process, the theological task is deemed to be twofold: firstly, the churches' shared work of articulating Christian truth for our time, and, secondly, the conversation between the churches about agreements and differences in belief and practice. This second type of theology centres on the differences which arise from a primarily Catholic concern with the received tradition and a primarily Protestant preference for a return to earliest sources.

The structural setting within which this theology can be done is envisaged as being sufficiently open to respect the integrity and autonomy of particular traditions and yet able to provide a genuine point of unity. *Christian Unity and Christian Diversity* rejects the models of organic and organizational unity, which both tend to encourage a single, monolithic structure, and advocates the motif of the people of God as an image which moves towards a uniate form of communion in which a significant degree of autonomy is retained. Rome is seen to have an important role in this relationship.

Christian Unity and Christian Diversity explores a number of the specific questions around which Catholic and Protestant differences tend to polarize (for example, the criteria for apostolicity in ministry, the real presence in the eucharist, divorce and remarriage, the place of Mary in Christian faith), and offers solutions which attempt to retain the mutually corrective truths from both perspectives. Finally, it places the whole ecumenical debate in the wider conversation required in a multi-faith culture, which demands both open dialogue and the genuine commitment which characterizes all religious faith.

Thinking about God (1975), collects together a number of lectures, essays and articles from the late 1960s and early 1970s, including the inaugural lecture, 'Creation and Environment' given at Oxford in 1970.

The first part of the book contains seven chapters on concept and method in theology. The nature of theological language is discussed in relation to the character of language as a whole, and a number of creative tensions particular to theological language are traced out. The issue of truth in theology is explored in various ways: criteria are offered for the evaluation of the truth of theological assertions, and the need for mystery as well as intellectual clarity within the category of truth is affirmed. Theological and practical cautions are raised to an exaggerated hunting out of heresy, and it is argued that bad theology is better countered by good theology than by ecclesiastical administration. The character of 'gospel' is assessed, and ways of determining the adequacy of reformulations are offered to take account of both the constancy and the multi-dimensional inexhaustibility of the content of the gospel. Liberal and radical approaches to the gospel are compared, and their historical developments are traced.

The second part of *Thinking about God* deals more specifically with belief in God, and how this can be successfully articulated in the contemporary context – especially in relation to the peculiarly modern exhilaration of humanistic atheism. Several partially successful attempts to reformulate a doctrine of God are discussed, and the idea of God as Being is commended for the situation. In this section of the book, particular attention is given to the issue of God's relation to the world: to monarchical versus organic models in Christian theology, to the recovering doctrine of the Holy Spirit, to the question of whether the world itself has such a character to suggest the reality of God, and to the doctrine of God's relation to the world as it might be conceived for a technological and ecological context.

Thinking about God concludes with seven chapters which explain and assess a number of – generally helpful – modern approaches to theology, by exploring the work of particular representative thinkers. So, for example, Schleiermacher's work on inward experience in religion is reconsidered, and a more careful reading of his work is offered to correct a subjective and individualistic (mis)interpretation. The doctrine of God in Bultmann's existentialist theology and Williams' process theology is discussed, and relative strengths and weaknesses are assessed, as are those of various theologies of hope. The broad contribution to the theological scene made by Ian Henderson is applauded, as is John McLeod Campbell's work on the atonement, written (and vilified) in the nineteenth century but highly relevant to twentieth-century developments.

The Humility of God (1978) brings together a number of meditations, mostly given at Christ Church, Oxford, which emphasize the humility of God, his down-to-earthness, his involvement in the life of his creatures. The 'almost universal tendency' to make power rather than love the defining characteristic of God is counteracted chapter by chapter, as the drama of God's humble concern for his creation is explored. Starting with creation and culminating in the ultimate perfection of all things, *The Humility of God* places the humility of the incarnation within a consistent pattern of God's self-giving to his creatures.

The first chapter, evocatively titled 'The Sharing', explores the way in which existence itself is a gift, and one which is not simply external to God as giver but deeply participative in his own being. Despite the ambiguities of original sin and original righteousness, we share the shaping of the world with God as he opens up new possibilities and we bring them to realization, responding to the elusive voice of God where it encounters us.

The remaining chapters deal with the revolution – indeed, the paradigm shift (as Kuhn himself intended the phrase) – of the coming of Jesus Christ and his teaching, passion and resurrection. *The Humility of God* insists that now all our thinking about what it means to be human, and all our thinking about God, must be conformed to what is unveiled in the incarnation. It is Jesus Christ who 'makes unhidden' what we have in us to become, and Jesus Christ who makes known in his person and in his teaching and passion God's self-giving love and availability. Even in the cross, there is no sense that there is 'another' God at one remove untouched by suffering; Christ's passion is explored in Trinitarian form, and shown to be consistent even with the unknowable depths of the Father, the source of all being.

The perfecting of God's self-giving continues with the resurrection and ascension and the life in the Spirit, by which Christ continues to be a living person, present but no longer bounded by the particularities of human existence in time and space. Believers share in the paradox of Christ's life, that only in going out from the self in self-giving love and living for the other do we become truly ourselves and fully human. It is the experience of this constancy of God's self-giving that gives hope for a final perfection for the whole of creation: a total hope that God will fulfil creation in his purpose of love.

Christian Hope (1978) examines the variety of Christian thought concerning the 'last things'. It places the specifically Christian understanding of hope in the context of the universal phenomenon of hope in human life, and, against a certain weight of tradition, insists that Christian hope does address human life in this world and is not an other-worldly escape mechanism.

The breadth of meaning of 'hope' intended in the book is

explored in the first chapter. Hope is to be understood as a disposition of the whole person – emotional, volitional, intellectual – and carries with it a particular understanding of the world as an environment open to change by human action. This dynamic quality of hope, tempered with a vulnerability to the world's evils, sufferings and lacks, is of key importance in distinguishing genuine hope from 'that counterfeit', mere optimism. Its realism in the face of an ambiguous world suggests that there may be an ultimate religious underpinning to hope: the fact that hope has appeared in the universe at all is at least a ground for 'hoping that hope is at home in the universe'.

Having set out the general phenomenon of hope, *Christian Hope* traces the history of hope in Israel from the call of Abraham. Explaining the shift from cyclical fertility cults to the forward-focussed religion of the Israelites, it shows how messianic expectations and an interest in individual destiny developed. It also shows how a religion which is orientated to the future must maintain its identity by repeating in its worship key moments of its corporate past, so that it lives in the light of both past and future.

In the face of the debate about how the fulfilment of God's promises can be assessed when there is always a gap between promise and understanding, a chapter entitled 'Christ Our Hope' explores the way in which Jesus Christ was seen to fulfil the hopes of Israel, and yet to revolutionize the understanding of what God's promises had been. The hope of his coming again with glory adds yet another dimension to a pattern in which each hope leads to a new one, and each is more comprehensive than the one that went before.

After this mainly biblical exploration, *Christian Hope* notes some highlights in the history of Christian thought on hope from the Church Fathers to the twentieth century. In particular comparisons are made between emphases on hope as this-worldly vs. other-worldly, individual vs. social, and evolutionary vs. revolutionary. Although relative strengths are assessed, the various views are commended as fragments of an inclusive vision which confront and correct each other, rather than as ultimately rival theories.

Finally, a contemporary statement is offered which brings together all the aspects under discussion – the individual and social/cosmic, the future and the present, the evolutionary in which we co-operate and the revolutionary which transforms beyond our imagination. Although it is recognized that Christian hope ultimately depends on Christian faith, it is shown that it is not incompatible with contemporary thought; evolutionary theory and relativity theory are introduced to provide analogies by which the content of Christian hope might be understood in the current context of human life and thought.

In Search of Humanity (1982) is a collection of short essays which explore an understanding of the human condition drawn from experience of self and others, the Christian tradition, and various philosophies concerned with human nature and destiny.

The book starts with the question, 'what is a human being?', and with the suggestion that we are better described as 'human *becoming*' since our nature is not entirely fixed, but is dynamic, open to development and always to an extent self-created. This theme is developed under various motifs such as freedom, transcendence and egoity; and it is placed in its material and social context by a consideration of embodiment, language and having, and by an understanding of cognition as a creative activity characterized by participation in what is known and openness to it.

Various ethical themes concerned with our formation as persons are explored, namely alienation, conscience, commitment, belief and love. Playful dimensions of human life are included in a discussion on art; and suffering and death are charted in their role as not merely limiting but re-valuing and transforming human existence, and moving us into the realm of an inclusive and universal hope.

The final chapter of *In Search of Humanity* reveals that

this has not been simply a collecting together of sundry aspects of our human condition. Arguing from the tradition that the human person is not only a microcosm of the universe but also of the ultimate spiritual reality which brings all things into being, the book concludes with 'an anthropological argument for the existence of God'. This argument relates the clusters of concepts previously explored to the ways in which God may be glimpsed in our human experience of existence – as the source, support and goal of the possibilities of existence and of its fundamentally social character, as the contradiction of finitude, and as the unifying factor not only of our human polarities but also of the whole of reality. The understanding of God which emerges from this argument is not oppressive to our human condition, but deeply supportive and encouraging of us at our most human.

In Search of Deity (1984) was the Gifford Lectures at St Andrews for 1983–84, and argues that natural theology is essential to the religious task if faith is to be seen as a viable *human* activity. It commends an alternative tradition to that of classical (Thomistic) natural theology as a worthwhile basis for a modern approach.

The first part of the argument considers traditional natural theology in its context of classical theism, and identifies two weaknesses that must be overcome in a contemporary re-working. The first is the question of the kind of knowledge proper to the enquiry. Natural theology has typically fallen into the error of attempting (or claiming) to know God in the same way that it is possible to know facts and objects of nature – thus 'natural' theology; a new-style natural theology must offer a different model of knowledge, which is participative and open to the self-revealing initiative of what is known and yet which is still clearly a natural human resource, common to all. The second weakness to be overcome concerns the concept of God. Traditional natural theology can result in an image of an autocratic, distant and impassive monarch; a new-style natural theology must give an account of God which is both religiously satisfying and also intellectually credible in a scientific age concerned with the organic integrity of the cosmos and with questions of human scope and autonomy.

In Search of Deity poses the question, 'what must God be if he is to be both the focus of human worship and aspiration, and at the same time to be seen as the source, sustainer and goal of all that is?' To develop an answer which both lies within the Christian tradition and speaks freshly to the modern time, the book traces the creative use of neo-Platonism from Plotinus through Dionysius, Eriugena, Cusanus, Leibniz and Hegel to Whitehead and Heidegger in the twentieth century. Central to the theological resources provided by this alternative form of theism is a natural theology of the triunity of God, with its account of how God is both unimaginably prior to and other than creation, and yet also intimately connected to it in affinity and reciprocity. This tradition also provides the understanding of human being developed in *In Search of Humanity*, that we are both a microcosm of the universe and a revelation of God.

The cumulative argument of *In Search of Deity* provides the clue as to why this is the 'companion volume' to *In Search of Humanity*. In being both microcosm and revelation, human being raises the universe to a new – personal – level in which it questions and points beyond itself to an ultimate reality which is its source and goal. This pointing beyond a network of mutual dependence to an ultimate source is the heart of the old cosmological argument for the existence of God, but it is now re-presented to speak to modern pre-occupations by showing how it is our own experience of human existence in the cosmos which points us to the reality of God.

Theology, Church and Ministry (1986) is a collection of essays from the period 1975–84. Published in the year of the author's retirement, it includes an autobiographical reflection on some fifty years of theological engagement, entitled 'Pilgrimage in Theology'.

Theology, Church and Ministry addresses a spectrum of inter-related topics, all concerned in some form or another with the engagement of Christian faith in its contemporary context. The first group of essays considers the nature, task and sources of Christian theology in the current intellectual situation. The relationship within the discipline of systematic theology and biblical studies is discussed, and a lecture entitled 'The Anthropological Approach to Theology' given in honour of Karl Rahner is included, together with Rahner's own response and questions. This section concludes with an exposition of 'The Anglican Theological Tradition', which forms something of a bridge with the next section on the church.

Five essays on the church commend both a reasonable pride in the church, to the extent that God is truly manifested and exalted there, and a genuine openness to those who are not part of the church. The idea of 'the people of God' is advocated as an inclusive model which points to the ultimate vision of the whole human race as the people of God. The need for both commitment and openness in a multi-faith world is explored with regard to the role of religion in a technological culture, and in its philosophical presuppositions and practical implications.

Theology, Church and Ministry concludes with a section of essays on Christian ministry. In the context of clerical uncertainty, the constancy of priestly function and character is affirmed, and the question of women priests in the Anglican Communion plainly addressed. The shared task of 'co-theologizing' in the church is encouraged, whereby theologians, bishops and laity each bring an expertise (academic, pastoral, worldly), and politics is commended as a proper form of lay ministry.

Jesus Christ in Modern Thought (1990) gives an account of the person of Jesus Christ which fully recognizes his true

humanity, whilst acknowledging that the initiative in incarnation is wholly God's. The book explores the primary sources
for the classical doctrine of Christ, and the critique of both
doctrine and sources in the eighteenth and nineteenth
centuries, as well as more recent attempts to reconstruct the
doctrine. It offers a fresh account which is faithful to the
intention of the earliest church writings but accessible to
modern understandings.

The first part of *Jesus Christ in Modern Thought* scruti-
nizes the development of the church's understanding of Jesus
from its 'prehistory' in contemporary expectations, through
the writings of the New Testament, to the formal credal
expressions at Nicaea and Chalcedon. This section of the
book establishes that in this early period there was a shift
from regarding Jesus as a man who by his resurrection was
made Lord and Christ by God (adoptionism) to the belief
that in Jesus the pre-existent divine Son took a truly human
life (incarnationism). It argues that this shift was not a once-
for-all development so that adoptionism has been superseded
by incarnationism, but a constantly repeating process in
which the two understandings mutually inform and correct
each other. Incarnationism teaches the initiative of God and
guards against seeing Jesus as a natural or arbitrary evolution; adoptionism insists on Christ's genuine humanity and
the need for his co-operation with God.

The second part of the book traces how the church's traditional teaching about Christ has been challenged in the
modern period, by confidence in human reason and autonomy and by developments in biblical and historical criticism, and indicates the attempts in the mid-nineteenth and
early twentieth centuries to return to a more orthodox
approach. The contributions of new theologies in the latter
part of the twentieth century are noted, especially the significance of the renewal of Roman Catholic theology post-
Vatican II.

The final part of *Jesus Christ in Modern Thought* takes up
Bonhoeffer's question, 'who really is Jesus Christ for us

today?', to restate an understanding of Jesus Christ which is true to the aim of the earliest sources and yet also appropriate to the modern situation. This takes account of current approaches to history and metaphysics, as well as the questions of the uniqueness of Christ and his relationship to the whole human race. The restatement insists that in the modern period we start with Jesus' humanity, and in themes familiar from *In Search of Humanity* shows how it is possible to think of human being transcending its limitations and distortions so that, precisely by being fully human, God's own being is revealed. This movement from human being to God is met by a reciprocal movement from God, which has already been explored in *In Search of Deity* and consists in God's continual self-giving to create and to make himself known. It is in the person of Jesus Christ that these two personal movements, both at their most open, meet, and for this reason Jesus is understood as the divine humanity, or the God-man.

Mary for All Christians (1991) offers to a wider audience material initially prepared for the Ecumenical Society of the Blessed Virgin Mary, in the hope that the churches might find in Mary resources for reconciliation rather than conflict. In doing this, it is suggesting that although Marian doctrine is not strictly central to the Christian faith, it is at least a meeting point – like a significant railway junction – where lines meet and connections are made. In this case, the doctrine is the meeting place for the doctrines of human nature, of the person and work of Christ, and of the church. As well as providing biblical and historical surveys and doctrinal explanation, *Mary for All Christians* proceeds by means of autobiographical anecdote and reflection, which gives the book a devotional significance in addition to its technical argument. This significance is enhanced by the inclusion of the Society's Ecumenical Office of Mary the Mother of Jesus, for individual or group use.

The theological discussion about Mary is placed, first of

all, in a consideration of the changes in society of the role and status of women. The fact that the impetus for these developments towards greater dignity and equality has not come from the Church itself suggests that the Church might need to rethink aspects of its teaching, and rediscover the elements of its own tradition which speak explicitly of the worth of women. Correctly understood, the theology of Mary can be one such corrective tendency.

Having surveyed the appearances of Mary throughout the New Testament, and noted the theological significance of these particular accounts of Mary's person and presence, *Mary for All Christians* examines three key Marian doctrines: the Immaculate Conception, the Glorious Assumption, and Mary as Corredemptrix. In each case, a key issue for discussion is whether these rather elaborate doctrinal developments can be justified from the more meagre biblical sources. The method which is adopted is not whether they themselves have explicit scriptural reference (a method deemed appropriate to more central doctrines), but whether they are fitting and consonant with the overall truth of Christian teaching and whether they shed fresh light which strengthens the coherence and unity of the whole. This means that these Marian doctrines, which might otherwise be read narrowly as of personal reference to Mary alone, take on a broader significance, pointing to the much more primary theological contexts in which they arise: questions concerning the origin and formation of personal being, the nature of sin and righteousness, the fulfilment of personal being in union with God, and the degree to which human beings may co-operate with God's redemptive work. In agreement with the Second Vatican Council, Mary becomes a model and exemplar for the church and, indeed, for the human race.

A further issue under consideration in *Mary for All Christians* is the place of Marian devotion in the modern world. This is dealt with explicitly in the final chapter, 'Mary and Modernity', but is a persistent theme throughout the book in the explicit interpretation of doctrines in personal

mode. So, for example, sin is understood in terms of alienation or a lack of right relationship, rather than as some kind
of stain which is hereditary via the event of procreation. This
makes it possible for the church's traditional teaching about
Mary to be commended in a way which is specifically
familiar and appropriate to the concerns of contemporary
human living.

Invitation to Faith (1995, previously published as *Starting
from Scratch*, 1994) is a slim volume consisting of four
chapters originally delivered as Lent lectures, together with
some of the discussion they provoked.

Beginning with the decline of religion and the rise of secu-
larism, the book asks 'Why believe? Why bother with faith?'
It points to the irrepressibly questioning nature of human
beings, and the ultimate questions (Who am I? What is the
meaning of life, of the world?) which demand an answer that
lies beyond our knowledge. Even though no definitive answer
can be given, the questions cannot be evaded because they
have a practical bearing on how we live. It is within the
ambivalence of the answers (that I am limited yet full of
possibility, that the world is ordered yet full of waste) that
Christian faith offers a clue: that in Jesus Christ we glimpse
the deepest reality. In Christ we learn what human life and
the world are about, and we glimpse the glory of God.

Invitation to Faith then considers the revolution that must
take place in the understanding of God with the Christian
teaching that God was incarnate in Jesus Christ. Far from
being supposed to be a supreme and distant monarch exer-
cising a tyrannous rule, God can only be understood to be at
the heart of reality, indwelling the world and sharing its
suffering. Intellectual, emotional and moral forms of atheism
are questioned against this new revelation of an involved
God.

But how is it possible to make sense of this claim – that, in
Jesus, God has become incarnate? How is it possible that
divinity and humanity are united in this person? *Invitation to*

Faith traces the development of this belief in the New Testament, and in the earliest church, and places the current belief in the context of two key teachings. Firstly, human being is made in the image of God and grows into the true likeness of this image; perhaps, then, one man might grow wholly into God's likeness so that he becomes the bearer and manifestation of divine life. But secondly, God constantly gives himself, expresses himself, in creation; so perhaps he might express himself most fully in a human being who bears his true image.

The self-giving of the incarnate Jesus Christ is continued in the self-giving of his followers, and in the life of the church where it is revivified by the Spirit of God. The challenge this presents is considered in the final chapter in relation to the four distinguishing marks of the church – one, holy, catholic, apostolic – and their embodiment in the actual life of the church.

The Mediators: Nine Stars in the Human Sky (1995) is written as a contribution to inter-faith dialogue, in the recognition that learning from other traditions purifies and enriches our own tradition. It accepts that there are genuine revelations of God outside the Judeao-Christian tradition, and advocates an openness to what is true and holy in other faiths whilst retaining a commitment to the particular tradition in which God has become known to us.

An introductory chapter gives a brief overview of the history of inter-faith dialogue, from Justin Martyr's *Dialogue with Trypho a Jew* in the second century, to the Parliament of Religions in Chicago (1893), the early twentieth-century backlash in Barthian theology of revelation, and the recovery of dialogue in the second half of the century, due not least to the conciliatory position of Vatican II. *The Mediators* acknowledges that dialogue is a difficult task in a vastly complex field, but one which is made urgent by the proximity in which people of different faiths now live to one another. *The Mediators* makes its contribution to mutual understanding by offering studies of some of the outstanding spiritual geniuses from various religions, whose visions of God in relation to our human situation have been most influential in human culture.

The bulk of the book consists in these studies: Moses, Zoroaster, Lao-zu, Buddha, Confucius, Socrates, Krishna, Jesus, Muhammad. They are deemed 'mediators' as the most inclusive term which best characterizes their role as a human figure who has brought to the people a new or renewed sense of God or the highest reality. The studies trace a number of family resemblances amongst these mediators, in their genuine humanity and the later accretion of mythological material from their followers; in the concern of their teaching with God (or the highest reality), human being and the status of the material world; in their own example and their instruction in prayer and worship, and in their ethical concern with reverence, compassion and righteousness. Amongst these family resemblances, however, differences are not masked, and the value is emphasized of a dialectic between transcendence and immanence, and between personal, impersonal and supra-personal models of God.

The end of dialogue to which *The Mediators* seeks to contribute is neither an exaggerated pluralism which is tantamount to individualism, nor to a syncretistic merging of religions into a shallow and sentimental unity. Rather, the vision is of a plurality of traditions characterized by commitment and respect, within which the claims of unity and diversity can be equally met.

A Guide to the Sacraments (1997) commends the seven traditional sacraments of the church for practical Christian living today, and presents them in such a way that their genuine mystery is retained but magical and superstitious interpretation is removed.

Initially, *A Guide to the Sacraments* shows that we live in the kind of world in which sacraments are possible, because the universe itself is sacramental. That is to say, things are never 'mere' things, but are bearers of meaning and value; when they are seen in depth they become 'transparent' and reveal the presence of God. This is sacramental rather than pantheistic because the initiative is always God's, and because some things are more effective sacraments than others in so far as they participate in the life of God. Human being, then, is the most adequate sacrament, and Christ himself is the supreme sacrament – the visible, embodied human being within the material and historical world who, on God's initiative, most fully manifests the very presence of God. Whatever may be said about Christ's institution of the sacraments in his earthly ministry, he is more profoundly their founder because it is his own mediation of God in the world which they participate in and extend.

Having shown this wider context in which the traditional sacraments of the church take their place, *A Guide to the Sacraments* explores each sacrament in turn: baptism, confirmation, penance, the eucharist, unction, ordination and marriage. In each exposition, the outward aspects (matter and form) and inward reality are explained, and the roots in scripture and the early church are traced. A critical assessment is made of the historical development, and the contemporary meaning and value are explained and commended, not only in relation to the traditional understanding but also with regard to 'plain common sense' about human living in the world. The eucharist receives a central place as the 'jewel in the crown' of the seven sacraments.

A key intention of the book is to foster ecumenical unity, grounded in the sacramental life of the church. A middle way is advocated between a typically Protestant emphasis on Word and a typically Catholic emphasis on Sacrament, and between subjective and objective accounts of the efficacy of sacramental grace. Considerable reference is made to the ARCIC process as well as to specifically denominational texts, and traditional areas of dispute (the doctrine of real presence, the papacy) are dealt with in a way that encourages a move towards unity without blurring genuine difficulties.

Christology Revisited (1998) does indeed revisit some of the topics of the earlier *Jesus Christ in Modern Thought* with renewed insight. Principally the text of the Albert Cardinal Meyer Memorial Lectures, Chicago, *Christology Revisited* examines the 'absolute paradox' of Jesus Christ the God-man in the light of traditional accounts of his humanity and divinity, and the need to retain but re-express both aspects of the paradox for contemporary culture.

Christology Revisited insists on the full humanity of Jesus Christ, not only as a practical apologetic for a secular world concerned with our own self-understanding, but also as a theological necessity: if Christ is not wholly identified with our human situation, he cannot be our Redeemer. However, the book also insists on the need to recognize the 'something more' in Jesus (which is that 'God was in Christ . . .') which emerges in the later New Testament writings, and without which Christ would himself be too immersed in the human condition to save. The traditional ways of expressing these two aspects of Christ's person – and his fundamental unity – are explored, and what is admitted to be a 'conceptual jungle' of technical terms is explained and subjected to critical scrutiny. Although weaknesses and distortions are ruthlessly identified, the 'governing intention' of these earlier formulations are pin-pointed and preserved, and the whole process is valued as part of the endless task of bringing to expression the unsearchable riches of Christ. Ways are suggested by which both Christ's humanity and his divinity can be expressed for the present time, and the work of a range of theologians is drawn into the discussion to show how the claim that Christ is the centre of reality (of human existence, of history, and of the relation between God and human being) can make sense in secular culture.

Christology Revisited also addresses the question of how we know Jesus Christ. It advocates a much broader range of knowing than the narrowly objective rationality which the modern period has principally valued, and which tends to focus on the question of how much historically reliable information can be known about Jesus. The knowledge of Jesus which accompanies faith owes more to the kind of knowing that goes with intra-personal relations, where there is some kinship and mutual participation, and to the kind of self-understanding which arises from the total experience of human existence in the world (the awareness of finitude, for example). Our knowledge of Jesus must also be understood in a much broader way than a purely one-to-one encounter, as one which occurs within – and is mediated by – the complex web of relationships which constitute the Christ-event which includes with Jesus Christ his ongoing community of followers.

Bibliography of Published Writings and Translations

'Feeling and Understanding.' *Theology* 58, 419, May 1955.

An Existentialist Theology: A Comparison of Heidegger and Bultmann. SCM Press, London and Macmillan, New York 1955. Second Edition, with foreword by Rudolf Bultmann. SCM Press, London and Harper and Row, New York 1965. Third Edition. Penguin Books, London 1972.

Helmut Thielicke, 'Reflections on Bultmann's Hermeneutic.' Translated by John Macquarrie. *The Expository Times* 67, February – March 1956.

'Demonology and the Classic Idea of Atonement.' *The Expository Times* 68, October – November 1956.

'A New Kind of Demythologizing?' *Theology* 59, 473, November 1956.

'Bultmann's Existential Approach to Theology.' *Union Seminary Quarterly Review*, 1957.

'Changing Attitudes to Religion in Contemporary English Philosophy.' *The Expository Times* 68, July 1957.

'The Service of Theology.' *The Reformed & Presbyterian World* 25, 1958.

'Demythologizing and the Gospel.' *The Chaplain* 16, 1959.

'Modern Issues in Biblical Studies: Christian Existentialism.' *The Expository Times* 71, March 1960.

The Scope of Demythologizing: Bultmann and His Critics. SCM Press, London and Harper and Row, New York 1960.

'The Natural Theology of Teilhard de Chardin.' *The Expository Times* 72, August 1961.

'Existentialism and the Christian Vocabulary.' *The London Quarterly and Holborn Review* 186, 1961.

'History and the Christ of Faith.' *The Listener* 67, 12 April 1962.

Martin Heidegger, *Being and Time.* Translated by John Macquarrie and Edward Robinson. SCM Press, London and Harper and Row, New York 1962. Second Edition. Basil Blackwell, Oxford 1973.

'How is Theology Possible?' *Union Seminary Quarterly Review* 18, 1963.

'Theologians of our Time: Karl Rahner, S. J.' *The Expository Times* 74, April 1963.

'True Life in Death.' *The Journal of Bible and Religion* 21, 1963.

'Beelzebub' and other entries. In *Hastings' Dictionary of the Bible* ed. F. C. Grant and H. H. Rowley. Second Edition. T. & T. Clark, Edinburgh 1963.

Twentieth-Century Religious Thought: The Frontiers of Philosophy and Theology, 1900-1960. SCM Press, London and Harper and Row, New York 1963. Second Edition, with additional chapter 1960–70. SCM Press, London 1971. Third Edition with Postscript, 1960–1980. SCM Press, London and Charles Scribner's Sons, New York 1981. Fourth Edition with additional chapter, 'The Fourth Phase'. SCM Press, London and Trinity Press International, Philadelphia 1988.

Twentieth-Century Religious Thought, Spanish Edition (*El Pensamiento Religioso en el Siglo XX: Las Fronteras de la Filosofía y la Teologia 1900–1970*). Translated by Juan Estruch from the Second English Edition. Editorial Merder, Barcelona 1975.

Twentieth-Century Religious Thought, Chinese Edition (*Er Shi Shi Ji Zong Jiao Si Xiang*). Translated by He Guanghu and Gao Shining. Shanghai People's Publishing House, Shanghai 1989. Revised by Zeng Quingbao from the Third English Edition, Laureate Books Company Ltd, Taipei 1992. Translated by Portia Ho from the Fourth English Edition, Chinese Christian Literature Council, Hong Kong 1997.

'Second Thoughts: The Philosophical School of Logical Analysis.' *The Expository Times* 75, November 1963.

'Christianity and Other Faiths.' *Union Seminary Quarterly Review* 10, 1964.

'The Problem of Natural Theology.' *Pittsburgh Perspective* 5, 1964.

'Christianity and Other Faiths' [A Rejoinder]. *Union Seminary Quarterly Review* 10, 1965.

'Rudolf Bultmann.' In *A Handbook of Christian Theologians* ed. M. E. Marty and D. G. Peerman. World Publishing, Cleveland 1965.

'A Dilemma in Christology.' *The Expository Times* 76, April 1965.

'How Can We Think of God?' *Theology Today* 22, 1965.

'Benediction of the Blessed Sacrament.' *Ave* 34, 1965.

Studies in Christian Existentialism: Lectures and Essays. McGill University Press, Montreal 1965. SCM Press, London and Westminster Press, Philadelphia 1966.

'Philosophy and Theology in Bultmann's Thought.' In *The Theology of*

Rudolf Bultmann ed. C. W. Kegley. SCM Press, London and Harper and Row, New York 1966.

'God and Secularity.' *Holy Cross Magazine* 77, 1966.

'Mother of the Church' [a poem]. *Holy Cross Magazine* 77, 1966.

'The Pre-existence of Jesus Christ.' *The Expository Times* 77, April 1966.

'The Tri-Unity of God'. A reply to P. H. Lehmann. *Union Seminary Quarterly Review* 21, 1966.

Principles of Christian Theology. SCM Press, London and Charles Scribner's Sons, New York 1966. Second Edition, revised and enlarged. SCM Press, London and Charles Scribner's Sons, New York 1977.

Principles of Christian Theology, Dutch Edition (*De Beginselen van de christelijke Theologie*). 3 vols. Translated by Jos Mertens from the First English Edition. J. J. Romen & Zonen, Roermond 1968.

Principles of Christian Theology, Chinese Edition (*Ji Du Jiao Shon Xue Yuan Li*). Translated by He Guanghu. Institute of Sino-Christian Studies, Hong Kong 1998.

'Some Thoughts on Heresy.' *Christianity and Crisis* 26, 1966.

'Heidegger's Earlier and Later Work Compared.' *Anglican Theological Review* 49, 1967.

'Stations of the Cross.' *Ave* 36, 1967.

'Subjectivity and Objectivity in Theology and Worship.' *Worship* 41, 1967.

'Maurice Blondel' and other entries. In *The Encyclopedia of Philosophy* ed. Paul Edwards, 8 vols. Macmillan and Free Press, New York 1967.

God-Talk: An Examination of the Language and Logic of Theology. SCM Press, London and Harper and Row, New York, 1967.

God-Talk, Italian Edition (*Ha Senso Parlare di Dio?*). Translated by Giancarlo Rocca. Borla, Turin 1969.

God-Talk, German Edition (*Gott-Rede: Eine Untersuchung der Sprache und Logik der Theologie*). Translated by Annemarie Pieper. Echter Verlag, Wurzburg 1974.

God-Talk, Spanish Edition (*God-Talk: el analisis del lenguaje y la logica de la teologia*). Translated by M. B. Garrido. Ediciones Sigueme, Salamanca 1976.

God-Talk, Chinese Edition (*Tan Lun Shang Di*). Translated by An Qingguo, revised by Gao Shining. Sichuan People's Publishing House, Chengdu 1992.

'Faith, Worship, Life.' *Holy Cross Magazine* 78, 1967.

'I Recommend You To Read: Some Recent Books on Theology.' *The Expository Times* 78, July 1967.

Editor and contributor. *Realistic Reflections on Church Union*. Argus-

Greenwood, Albany 1967.

'New Ways in Moral Theology.' *The Nashotah Quarterly Review* 7, 1967.

'Divine Omnipotence.' *Proceedings of the Seventh Inter-American Congress of Philosophy*. Laval University Press, Quebec 1967.

'The New Man and the Christian Ethic.' *St Luke's Journal* 11, 1967.

A Look at the New Theology (pamphlet). Forward Movement Publications, Cincinnati 1967.

Editor and contributor. *A Dictionary of Christian Ethics*. SCM Press, London and Westminster Press, Philadelphia 1967.

'Will and Existence.' In *The Concept of Willing* ed. J. N. Lapsley. Abingdon Press, Nashville 1967.

God and Secularity. Lutterworth Press, London and Westminster Press, Philadelphia 1968.

God and Secularity. Spanish Edition (*Dios y la Secularidad*). Translated by C. R. Garrido.Centro de Publicaciones Cristianas, San Jose 1969.

God and Secularity. Japanese Edition (*Kami to konoyo*). Translated by Hiroki Funamoto. Shinkyo Shuppansha Publishing, Tokyo 1971.

'Existentialism and Christian Thought.' In *Philosophical Resources for Christian Thought* ed. P. LeFevre. Abingdon Press, Nashville 1968.

Editor and contributor. *Contemporary Religious Thinkers: From Idealist Metaphysicians to Existential Theologians*. SCM Press, London and Harper and Row, New York 1968.

Martin Heidegger. Lutterworth Press, London and John Knox Press, Richmond 1968.

'The Holy Spirit and the Church.' *Holy Cross Magazine* 79, 1968.

'Bultmann's Understanding of God.' *The Expository Times* 79, September 1968.

'The Doctrine of Creation and Human Responsibility.' In *Knowledge and the Future of Man* ed. W. J. Ong, S. J. Holt, Rinehart and Winston, New York 1968.

'Karl Barth' and other entries. *A Dictionary of Christian Theology* ed. Alan Richardson. SCM Press, London and Westminster Press, Philadelphia 1969.

'Some Comments on the Trial Liturgy.' *American Church Quarterly* 6, 1969.

'Priesthood and the Trial Liturgy.' In *Towards a Living Liturgy* ed. D. L. Garfield. Church of St Mary the Virgin, New York 1969.

'What's Next in Theology?' *The Tower*, Union Seminary Alumni Magazine, Spring 1969.

'The Nature of Theological Language.' In *Lambeth Essays on Faith* ed. A. M. Ramsey. SPCK, London 1969.

'Prayer Is Thinking.' *Eucharist* 8, 1969.

'Schleiermacher Reconsidered.' *The Expository Times* 80, April 1969.

'Religious Language and Recent Analytical Philosophy.' *Concilium*, June 1969.

'Secular Ecumenism.' *The American Ecclesiastical Review* 161, 1969.

'Self-Transcending Man.' *Commonweal* 91, 1969.

'The Ministry and the Proposed New Anglican-Methodist Ordinal.' *The Anglican* 25, 1969.

'What Still Separates Us from the Catholic Church? An Anglican Reply', *Concilium*, April 1970.

Three Issues in Ethics. SCM Press, London and Harper and Row, New York 1970.

Three Issues in Ethics, Japanese Edition (*Gendai rinri no soten*). Translated by Yasuo Furuya. Jordan Publishing Company, Tokyo 1973.

'Eschatology and Time.' In *The Future of Hope* ed. Frederick Herzog. Herder and Herder, New York 1970.

'What is the Gospel?' *The Expository Times* 81, July, 1970.

'On Gods and Gardeners.' In *Perspectives in Education, Religion and the Arts* ed. H. E. Kiefer and M. K. Munitz. State University of New York Press, Albany 1970.

'Eucharistic Presence.' In *Worship in Spirit and Truth* ed. D. L. Garfield. Church of St Mary the Virgin, New York 1970.

'Word and Idea.' *International Journal for the Philosophy of Religion* 1, 1970.

'Is Organic Union Desirable?' *Theology* 73, 604, October 1970.

'Theologies of Hope: A Critical Examination.' *The Expository Times* 82, January 1971.

'A Modern Scottish Theologian: Ian Henderson, 1910–69.' *The Expository Times* 82, April 1971.

'The Humanity of Christ.' *Theology* 74, 612, June 1971.

Martin Heidegger, 'From the Last Marburg Lecture Course.' Translated by John Macquarrie. In *The Future of our Religious Past* ed. James Robinson, SCM Press, London 1971.

'Martin Heidegger.' In *Twelve Makers of Protestant Thought* ed. G. L. Hunt. Association Press, New York 1971.

'Creation and Environment.' *The Expository Times* 83, October 1971.

'Pluralism in Religion.' *Veritas* 3, 1972.

Paths in Spirituality. SCM Press, London and Harper and Row, New York 1972. Second (Enlarged) Edition. SCM Press, London and Morehouse Publishing, Harrisburg 1992.

Paths in Spirituality. Japanese Edition (*Reihai to inori no honshitsu*). Translated by Osumi Keizo. Jordan Publishing Company, Tokyo 1976.

The Problem of God Today (pamphlet). Christian Evidence Society, London 1972.

'Anglican-Methodist Dialogue on the Unification of Ministries.' *Concilium*, April 1972.

Existentialism. Hutchinson, London and Westminster Press, Philadelphia 1972. Second Edition. Penguin Books, London and Baltimore 1973.

'John McLeod Campbell, 1800–72.' *The Expository Times* 83, June 1972.

'Anglicanism and Ecumenism.' In *Anglicanism and Principles of Christian Unity* ed. F. T. Kingston. Canterbury College, Windsor, Ontario 1972.

'Liberal and Radical Theologians: An Historical Comparison'. *The Modern Churchman* 15, 1972.

'God and the World: Two Realities or One? *Theology* 75, 526, August 1972.

'The Faith of the People of God: A Lay Theology. SCM Press, London and Charles Scribner's Sons, New York 1972.

'The Real God and Real Prayer.' In *The British Churches Turn to the Future* ed. D. L. Edwards. SCM Press, London 1972.

'What Place Has Individual Conscience in Christianity?' In *Asking Them Questions*, New Series, Part 1. Oxford University Press, Oxford 1973.

'A Theology of Alienation.' In *Alienation: Concepts, Terms and Meanings* ed. Frank Johnson. Seminar Press, New York 1973.

'The Struggle of Conscience for Authentic Selfhood.' In *Conscience; Theological and Psychological Perspectives* ed. C. E. Nelson, Newman Press, New York 1973.

The Concept of Peace. SCM Press, London and Harper and Row, New York 1973. Reissued SCM Press, London, and Trinity Press International, Philadelphia, 1990.

'Women and Ordination: A Mediating View.' In *Sexuality, Theology, Priesthood* ed. H. K. Lutge. Concerned Fellow Episcopalians, San Gabriel, CA 1973.

Mystery and Truth (pamphlet), Marquette University, Milwaukee 1973.

'Theology.' In *Encyclopaedia Americana*, New York 1973.

'Kenoticism Reconsidered.' *Theology* 77, March 1974.

'What Kind of Unity?' *Faith and Unity* 18, 1974.

'Ethical Standards in World Religions: Christianity.' *The Expository Times* 85, August 1974.

'Some Reflections on Freedom.' In *The University Forum*. University of North Carolina, Charlotte 1974.

'The Hundredth Archbishop of Canterbury.' *New Divinity* 4, 1974.

'Whither Theology?' In *Great Christian Centuries to Come* ed. C. Martin. Mowbray, Oxford 1974.

'What a Theologian Expects from the Philosopher.' In *The Impact of Belief* ed. George F. McLean. Concorde Publishing Company, Lancaster 1974.

'Some Problems of Modern Christology.' *The Indian Journal of Theology* 23, 1974.

'Burns: Poet, Prophet, Philosopher.' *The Expository Times* 86, January 1975.

Thinking About God. SCM Press, London and Harper and Row, New York 1975.

'The Nature of the Marriage Bond.' *Theology*, 78, May 1975.

Christian Unity and Christian Diversity. SCM Press, London and Westminster Press, Philadelphia 1975.

'God and the Feminine.' *The Way*, Supplement 25, 1975.

'The Uses of Diversity.' *The Tablet*, 19 July 1975.

'The Meeting of Religions in the Modern World: Opportunities and Dangers.' *The Journal of Dharma* 1, 1975.

'The Idea of a Theology of Nature.' *Union Seminary Quarterly Review* 30, 1975.

'The Importance of Belief.' *New Fire* 3, 1975.

'New Thoughts on Benediction.' *Ave* 44, 1975.

'On the Idea of Transcendence.' *Encounter and Exchange*, Bulletin 14, 1975.

'The Church and Ministry.' *The Expository Times* 87, January 1976.

'Priestly Character.' In *To Be A Priest* ed. R. E. Terwilliger and U. T. Holmes. Seabury Press, New York 1975.

'Authority in Anglicanism.' *Agnus Dei* 2, 1976.

'Recent Thinking on Christian Beliefs: Christology.' *The Expository Times* 88, November 1976.

'Unity.' In *The Upper Room Disciplines, 1977* ed. Ruth Coffman et al. The Upper Room, Nashville 1976.

'Rest and Restlessness in Christian Spirituality.' In *Spirit and Light* ed. W. B. Green and Madeleine L'Engle. Seabury Press, New York 1976.

'Why Believe.' *Hillingdon Papers* 1, 1976.

'A Magnificent Achievement of the Christian Intellect.' *Religious Media Today* 1, 1976.

'Philosophy and Religion in the Nineteenth and Twentieth Centuries: Continuities and Discontinuities.' *The Monist* 60, 1977.

'Christianity Without Incarnation? Some Critical Comments.' In *The Truth of God Incarnate* ed. Michael Green. Hodder and Stoughton, London 1977.

'Pride in the Church.' *Communio* 4, 1977.

'Death and Eternal Life.' *The Expository Times* 89, November 1977.

'The Bishop and Theologians.' In *Today's Church and Today's World* ed. John Howe. CIO Publishing, London 1977.

The Humility of God: Christian Meditations. SCM Press, London and Westminster Press, Philadelphia 1978.

The Humility of God. Italian Edition (*L'Umiltà de Dio: Meditazione sul mistero della salvezza cristiana*). Translated by Bruno Pistocchi. Jaca Book, Milan 1979.

The Significance of Jesus Christ Today (pamphlet). Anglican Book Centre, Toronto 1978.

'Christian Reflections on Death.' *St Francis Burial Society Quarterly* 2, 1978.

'Faith in Jesus Christ.' *Christian World* 1, 1978.

'Religious Experience.' *Humanities* 12, 1978.

'The One and the Many: Complementarity of Religions.' In *Meeting of Religions* ed. Thomas Aykara. Dharmaram Publications, Bangalore 1978.

'The Recognition of Ministries.' *Christian World* 1, 1978.

Christian Hope. Mowbray, Oxford and Seabury Press, New York 1978.

'The Purposes of Reservation.' *The Server* 11, 1978.

'On the Ordination of Women to the Priesthood.' In *Report of the Lambeth Conference*, 1978 ed. Michael Perry. CIO Publishing, London 1978.

Immaculate Conception (pamphlet). Ecumenical Society of the Blessed Virgin Mary, London 1979.

'Existentialism and Theological Method.' *Communio* 6, 1979.

'The Aims of Christianity.' *USA Today* 108, 1979.

'The Humility of God.' In *The Myth/Truth of God Incarnate* ed. D. R. McDonald. Morehouse-Barlow, Wilton, CT 1979.

'Foundation Documents of the Faith: The Chalcedonian Definition.' *The Expository Times* 91, December 1979.

'Commitment and Openness: Christianity's Relation to Other Faiths.' *Theology Digest* 27, 1979.

'Transcendent Belief.' In *Science, Faith and Revelation* ed. R. E. Patterson. Broadman Press, Nashville, 1979.

'Pilgrimage in Theology.' *Epworth Review* 7, 1980.

'Tradition, Truth and Christology.' *The Heythrop Journal* 21, 1980.

'Today's Word for Today; Jürgen Moltmann.' *The Expository Times* 92, October 1980.

'God in Experience and Argument.' In *Experience, Reason and God* ed. Eugene T. Long. Catholic University of America Press, Washington, 1980.

'Religion' and other entries. In *Academic American Encyclopedia*. Arete Publishing Company, Princeton 1980.

'Why Theology?' In *Religious Studies and Public Examinations* ed. E. Hulmes and B. Watson. Farmington Institute, Oxford 1980.

'Systematic Theology and Biblical Studies.' *Kairos* 2, 1980.

'Truth in Christology.' In *God Incarnate: Story and Belief* ed. A. E. Harvey. SPCK, London 1981.

'The Concept of a Christ-Event.' In *God Incarnate: Story and Belief* ed. A. E. Harvey. SPCK, London 1981.

Glorious Assumption (pamphlet). Walsingham Parish Church, 1981.

'A Generation of Demythologizing.' In *Theolinguistics* ed. J. van Noppen. Free University, Brussels 1981.

'Existentialist Christology.' In *Christological Perspectives* ed. R. E. Berkey and S. A. Edwards. Pilgrim Press, New York 1982.

'The End of Empiricism?' *Union Seminary Quarterly Review* 37, 1982.

'Being and Giving.' In *God: The Contemporary Discussion* ed. F. Sontag and M. D. Bryant. Rose of Sharon Press, New York 1982.

'Aspects of the Human Being.' *The Virginia Seminary Journal* 34, 1982.

'Structures for Unity.' In *Their Lord and Ours* ed. M. Santer. SPCK, London 1982.

In Search of Humanity. SCM Press, London 1982 and Crossroad, New York 1983.

'The Need for a Lay Ministry.' *The Times Higher Education Supplement* 529, 1982.

'The Future of Anglo-Catholicism.' *Church Times*, 20 May 1983.

'William Temple: Philosopher, Theologian, Churchman.' In *The Experiment of Life* ed. F. K. Hare. Toronto University Press, 1983.

'God' and other entries. In *Funk & Wagnall's New Encyclopedia*. Funk & Wagnall, New York 1983.

'Celtic Spirituality' and other entries. In *A Dictionary of Christian Spirituality* ed. Gordon Wakefield. SCM Press, London and Westminster Press, Philadelphia 1983.

'Being' and other entries. *A New Dictionary of Christian Theology* ed. Alan Richardson and John Bowden. SCM Press, London and Westminster Press, Philadelphia 1983.

In Search of Deity. An Essay in Dialectical Theism. The Gifford Lectures delivered at the University of Saint Andrews in session 1983–84. SCM Press, London and Crossroad, New York 1984.

'Theological Implications of the Oxford Movement.' In *Lift High the Cross* ed. J. Robert Wright, Oxford Movement Sesquicentennial Committee, New York 1984.

'Wycliff on Dominium.' *Insight* 17, Wycliff College, Toronto 1984.

'The Anthropological Approach to Theology' (lecture given in honour of Karl Rahner's eightieth birthday, followed by a discussion with Fr Rahner). *Heythrop Journal* 25, 1984.

'Prayer and Theological Reflection.' In *The Study of Spirituality* ed. Cheslyn Jones et al. SPCK, London 1986.

'The Idea of a People of God.' In *Renewing the Jewish-Christian Wellsprings* ed. Val McInnes, Crossroad, New York 1987.

Theology, Church and Ministry. SCM Press, London and Crossroad, New York 1986.

Co-editor (with James Childress) and contributor, *A New Dictionary of Christian Ethics*. SCM Press, London and Westminster Press, Philadelphia 1986.

'Individual and Social Values: Love and Peace.' In *Peace Studies: The Hard Questions* ed. Elaine Kaye. Rex Collings 1987.

'W. P. Dubose and Modern Thought.' *St Luke's Journal of Theology* 31, Sewanee 1987.

'A Theology of Personal Being.' In *Persons and Personality* ed. A. R. Peacocke. Blackwell, Oxford 1987.

'Baptism, Confirmation, Eucharist.' In *Signs of Faith, Hope and Love* ed. E. Russell and J. Greenhalgh. St Mary's Bourne Street, London 1987.

The Reconciliation of a Penitent (pamphlet). Church Information Office, London 1987.

'Convergence of Religious Traditions on One Experience.' *Scottish Journal of Religious Studies* 10, 1989.

'The Papacy in a Unified Church.' *Pacifica* 2, 1989.

'Believing in God Today.' *Colloquium* 21, 1989.

'The Anglican Communion Today.' *The Episcopalian* 155, 1990.

Jesus Christ in Modern Thought. SCM Press, London and Trinity Press International, Philadelphia 1990.

Arthur Michael Ramsey: Life and Times (pamphlet), All Saints Church, New York, 1990.

Mary for All Christians. Collins, London and Eerdmans, Grand Rapids 1991.

'Antropologie filosofiche e teologiche.' In *Filosofia e teologia nel futuro dell' Europa* ed. G. Ferretti. Maretti, Genoa 1992.

'Heidegger's Philosophy of Religion.' In *New Visions* ed. Val McInnes, Crossroad, New York 1993.

'Development of doctrine: Searching for Criteria.' In *The Making and Remaking of Christian Doctrine* (essays in honour of Maurice Wiles) ed. S. Coakley and D. Pailin, Oxford University Press, Oxford 1993.

'Incarnation,' 'Natural Theology.' In *The Blackwell Encyclopedia of Modern Christian Thought* ed. A. E. McGrath, Blackwell, Oxford 1993.

'If it's metaphor, handle it with care.' *Church Times*, 29 October 1993.

'The Annunciation.' *The Marian Library Newsletter*, 28, 1994.

Heidegger and Christianity. SCM Press, London and Continuum, New York 1994.

Invitation to Faith. SCM Press, London and Morehouse Publishing, Harrisburg 1995.

Thinghood and Sacramentality (pamphlet). Centre for the Study of Theology in the University of Essex, Colchester 1995.

The Mediators (US title: *Mediators between Human and Divine*). SCM Press, London and Continuum, New York 1995.

'The Figure of Jesus Christ in Contemporary Christianity.' In *Companion Encyclopedia of Theology* ed. P. Byrne and L. Houlden. Routledge, London and New York 1995.

'Incarnation as the Root of the Sacramental Principle.' In *Christ: The Sacramental Word* ed. David Brown and Ann Loades, SPCK, London 1996.

'Peace.' In *Dictionary of Ethics, Theology and Society* ed. P. B. Clarke and A. Linzey, Routledge, London and New York 1996.

'I Saw Signs of Growth in Chinese Church.' *Church of England Newspaper*, 4 April 1996.

'This Bread and this Cup.' *Church Times*, 4 April 1996.

'The Legacy of Bultmann.' In *Heythrop Journal* 37 (essays for Bruno Brinkman on his eightieth birthday), July 1996.

'Ebb and Flow of Hope: Christian Theology at the End of the Second Millennium.' Lecture given at the University of Beijing. *The Expository Times* 107, April 1996.

'Dialogue among the World Religions.' Lecture given at the Chinese Academy of Social Sciences. *The Expository Times* 108, March 1997.

A Guide to the Sacraments. SCM Press, London and Continuum, New York 1997.

'And it Came to Pass in Those Days.' *Church Times*, 19 December 1997.

Christology Revisited. SCM Press, London and Continuum, New York 1998.

'Mascall, E. L.' In *Handbook of Anglican Theologians* ed. A. E. McGrath, SPCK 1998.

'Mascall and Thomism.' *Tufton Review* 2, May 1998.

'Train Them, then Allow them to Think.' *Church Times*, 23 October 1998.

On Being a Theologian ed John H. Morgan et al. SCM Press, London 1999.

Notes

1 My Scottish Background

1. For a historical account of these saints, see Alan Macquarrie, *The Saints of Scotland*, John Donald, Edinburgh 1997.
2. The Gaelic poems are taken from Alexander Carmichael's collection, *Carmina Gadelica*, translated by him and originally published in 1900. A reissue appeared in 1972 from the Scottish Academic Press.

3 The American Years

1. The best and most comprehensive history of Union is by Robert T. Handy: *A History of Union Theological Seminary in New York*, Columbia University Press 1987.
2. John A. T. Robinson, *Honest to God*, SCM Press 1963.
3. Thomas J. J. Altizer, *The Gospel of Christian Atheism*, Westminster Press, Philadelphia 1966

Appendix to Chapter 3: Lecture in New York

1. The title of John Macquarrie's inaugural lecture given in October 1962 at Union Theological Seminary on the occasion of his assuming the position of Professor of Systematic Theology. As might be expected of a lecture given in 1962, it takes little account of inclusive language. It is reprinted in *Studies in Christian Existentialism*, 1965.
2. John Calvin, *Institutes of the Christian Religion*, Vol. I, James Clarke 1953, p.37.
3. Henry P. Van Dusen, *Spirit, Son and Father*, A.& C. Black 1960, p.3.
4. Hans Zehrer, *Man in this World*, Hodder 1952, p.13.
5. Jean-Paul Sartre, *L'Etre et le néant*, Gallimard, Paris 1943, pp.708, 721.

6. Ibid., p.515.
7. Rudolf Bultmann, *Jesus Christ and Mythology*, Scribner, New York 1958 and SCM Press, London 1960, p.63.
8. Oliver Quick, *Doctrines of the Creed*, James Nisbet 1938, p.18.
9. Ps.139.1.
10. Paul Tillich, *Systematic Theology*, Vol.I, University of Chicago Press 1951 and James Nisbet 1953; reissued SCM Press 1978, p.124.
11. Martin Heidegger, *Was ist Metaphysik?* 7th edn, V. Klostermann, Frankfurt 1955, p.13.

4 Life at Christ Church

1. See C. H. Cooper, *The Lady Margaret*, CUP 1874.
2. See David L. Edwards, *The British Churches Turn to the Future*, SCM Press 1973.
3. A. C. Headlam, *Christian Theology*, OUP 1934.
4. Hugh Montefiore, *Can Man Survive?*, Collins 1970.
5. John Hick (ed), *The Myth of God Incarnate*, SCM Press, London and Westminster Press, Philadelphia 1977.

Appendix to Chapter 4: Lectures in the UK

1. The title of John Macquarrie's inaugural lecture as Lady Margaret Professor of Divinity, given in Oxford on 23 February 1971. At this time, inclusive language was still not a major issue. The lecture is reprinted in *Thinking about God*, 1975.
2. Harvey E. Cox, *The Secular City*, Macmillan, New York and SCM Press, London, 1965, pp.22–23.
3. Johannes Metz, *Theology of the World*, Herder & Herder 1969, pp.65–66.
4. Lynn White, 'The Historical Roots of Our Ecological Crisis' in G. de Bell (ed), *The Environmental Handbook*, Ballantine 1979, pp.20–23.
5. Herbert Marcuse, 'Marxism and the New Humanity' in J. C. Raines and T. Dean (eds), *Marxism and Radical Religion*, Temple University Press 1970, p.7.
6. W. O. E. Oesterley, *The Psalms*, Vol.1, SPCK 1939, p.168.
7. Richard Rubenstein, *After Auschwitz*, Bobbs-Merrill 1966, p.124.
8. Paul Tillich, *Biblical Religion and the Search for Ultimate Reality*, Chicago University Press 1955, pp.5ff.
9. Michael Foster, 'The Christian Doctrine of Creation and the Rise of Modern Natural Science', *Mind*, Vol. xliii, 1934; reprinted in

D. O'Connor and F. Oakley (eds), *Creation. The Impact of an Idea*, Scribner 1969, pp.29ff.

10. Ibid., p.52.
11. Ludwig Feuerbach, *The Essence of Christianity*, Harper & Row 1957, p.110.
12. Reinhold Niebuhr, *The Nature and Destiny of Man*, Vol. I, James Nisbet 1941, p.21.
13. Aristophanes, *The Clouds*, ll. 167–68.
14. Hugh Montefiore, *Can Man Survive?*, Collins 1970, p.53.
15. A. J. Heschel, *Who Is Man?*, Stanford University Press 1965, p.82.
16. A lecture delivered in honour of Dr Karl Rahner's eightieth birthday at Heythrop College, London, on 17 February 1984, in the presence of the *honorandus*. It was first published in *The Heythrop Journal*, Vol. XXV, 1984, and subsequently reprinted in *Theology, Church and Ministry*, 1986, with the addition of a transcription of a question and answer session between Dr Rahner and Professor Macquarrie, and the text of a letter from Cardinal Basil Hume.
17. John Calvin, *Institutes of the Christian Religion*, Vol. I, James Clarke 1953, p.37.
18. F. D. E. Schleiermacher, *The Christian Faith*, T. & T. Clark 1928, p.366.
19. Bernard Lonergan, *Method in Theology*, Darton, Longman & Todd 1971, p.341.
20. Martin Buber, *I and Thou*, T. & T. Clark 1958, p.75.
21. J. H. Newman, *Sermons Bearing on Subjects of the Day*, 1869, p.353.
22. R. C. Selby, *The Principle of Reserve*, OUP 1975, p.22.
23. Peter Berger, *A Rumour of Angels*, Doubleday 1969 and Allen Lane 1970, p.66.
24. Immanuel Kant, *Critique of Practical Reason*, Macmillan 1929, p.200.
25. Denys (Dionysius), *The Divine Names*, iv, 13.
26. G. Leibniz, *Monadology*, OUP 1898, p.266.
27. Karl Rahner, *Theological Investigations*, Vol. I, Darton, Longman & Todd 1961, p.184.
28. See above, n.18.

5 Retirement

1. Friedrich Hölderlin, *Selected Verse*, Penguin Books 1961, pp.79f.
2. Although the name of the Chinese capital is now transliterated as Beijing, the university, founded in 1893, is still called Peking University.

Appendix to Chapter 5: Lectures in Moscow and China

1. Paper given at a conference on 'Religion and Culture' at the Soviet Academy of Social Sciences in Moscow in 1989.
2. Goethe, *Faust*, ll. 1112–13.
3. Charles Sherrington, *Man on his Nature*, CUP 1940, p.82.
4. Jacques Monod, *Chance and Necessity*, Collins 1972, p.137.
5. Immanuel Kant, *Werke*, Vol.4, Leopold Voss, Leipzig 1867, p.159.
6. G. Ryle, *Dilemmas*, CUP 1954, passim.
7. J.-P. Sartre, from an essay entitled 'Existentialism is a Humanism', included in Kaufmann's collection *Existentialism from Dostoyevsky to Sartre*, World Publishing, Cleveland 1956, p.290.
8. A. N. Whitehead, *Adventure of Ideas*, Penguin Books 1942, p.98.
9. Pico della Mirandola, *Oration on the Dignity of Man*, Regnery, Chicago 1956.
10. Friedrich Schleiermacher, *On Religion*, Harper Torchbooks 1958, p.39.
11. Gregory of Nyssa, *Life of Moses*, Sources Chrétienne, Cerf, Paris 1968, p.315.
12. Catherine of Genoa, *The Spiritual Dialogue*, SPCK 1979, p.140.
13. William Johnston, *The Mirror Mind*, Harper and Row 1981, p.37.
14. Martin Heidegger, *Being and Time*, SCM Press 1962, p.74.
15. Lecture given at the University of Peking in October 1995.
16. Adolf Harnack, *What is Christianity?*, Williams and Norgate 1961.
17. Karl Barth, *Theologische Fragen und Antworten*, Evangelischer Verlag 1957, pp.10ff.
18. Søren Kierkegaard, *Training in Christianity*, Princeton University Press 1944, p.71.
19. Rudolf Bultmann, *Kerygma and Myth*, Vol. I, SPCK 1953, p.42.
20. Karl Rahner, *Spirit in the World*, Sheed and Ward 1957, p.220.
21. Jürgen Moltmann, *Theology of Hope*, SCM Press and Harper and Row 1967
22. Ernst Bloch, *Principle of Hope*, Blackwell 1986.
23. Jürgen Moltmann, *The Crucified God*, SCM Press and Harper and Row 1974.
24. Karl Barth, *The Epistle to the Romans*, OUP 1933, p.102.
25. John A. T. Robinson, *Honest to God*, SCM Press and Westminster Press 1963.
26. Paul Ricoeur, *The Symbolism of Evil*, Harper and Row 1967, p.156.
27. Ibid., p.251.
28. Lecture given at the Chinese Academy of Social Science in Beijing, October 1995.

29. See, e.g., Hans Küng, *Judaism*, SCM Press and Crossroad 1992 and *Christianity*, SCM Press and Continuum 1995, the first two titles in his trilogy 'The Religious Situation of our Time'.
30. See Langdon Gilkey, *Naming the Whirlwind*, Bobbs-Merrill 1969.
31. Rudolf Otto, *The Idea of the Holy*, OUP 1924.
32. Peter Berger, *A Rumour of Angels*, Doubleday 1969 and Allen Lane 1970.
33. Meister Eckhart, *Sermons*, Harper & Row 1967, p.169.
34. Paul Tillich, *The Courage to Be*, Collins 1962, p.176.
35. F. H. Bradley, *Appearance and Reality*, OUP 1893, pp.470ff.
36. Karl Jaspers, *Philosophical Truth and Revelation*, Harper & Row 1957.

6 *An Ecumenical Encounter*

1. Ian Henderson, *Power without Glory*, Hutchinson 1967.
2. John Knox, 'A Plea for Wider Ecumenism' in John Macquarrie (ed), *Realistic Reflections on Church Union*, Argus Greenwood, Albany, NY 1967, pp.27f.
3. *Pacifica*, 2, 1989, pp.123–34.
4. F. C. Grant, *Rome and Reunion*, OUP, New York 1965, p.144.
5. A. Dulles, *The Catholicity of the Church*, Clarendon Press 1985, pp.131–21.
6. J. N. D. Kelly, *The Oxford Dictionary of the Popes*, OUP 1987, p.21.
7. ARCIC, *The Final Report*, SPCK/CTS 1982, p.58.
8. John Macquarrie, *Christian Unity and Christian Diversity*, SCM Press and Westminster Press 1975, pp.99–100.
9. See *The Tablet*, 5 July 1975, pp.621–24.
10. ARCIC, The Final Report, p.89.
11. Ibid.
12. John Macquarrie, 'Structures for Unity' in Mark Santer (ed), *Their Lord and Ours*, SPCK 1982.

Editor and Collaborators

John H. Morgan, who did his doctoral studies at Hartford Seminary, is the John Henry Cardinal Newman Fellow in Theology and President of the Graduate Theological Foundation in the United States. Currently teaching in the University of Oxford Summer Programme in Theology, he has held postdoctoral appointments to Harvard, Yale, and Princeton, and has been a Postdoctoral Associate in the History and Philosophy of Science and a National Science Foundation Science Faculty Fellow at the University of Notre Dame.

Georgina Morley, a Reader in the Church of England, did her doctoral studies at the University of Nottingham with a dissertation on the theology of John Macquarrie. She is a member of the teaching faculty of the Graduate Theological Foundation in the United States.

Eamonn Conway, who did his doctoral studies at the University of Tübingen, is a Catholic priest and the Associate Director of the Western Theological Institute in Galway, Republic of Ireland. He is a member of the teaching faculty of the Graduate Theological Foundation in the United States.

Index of Names